CW01338572

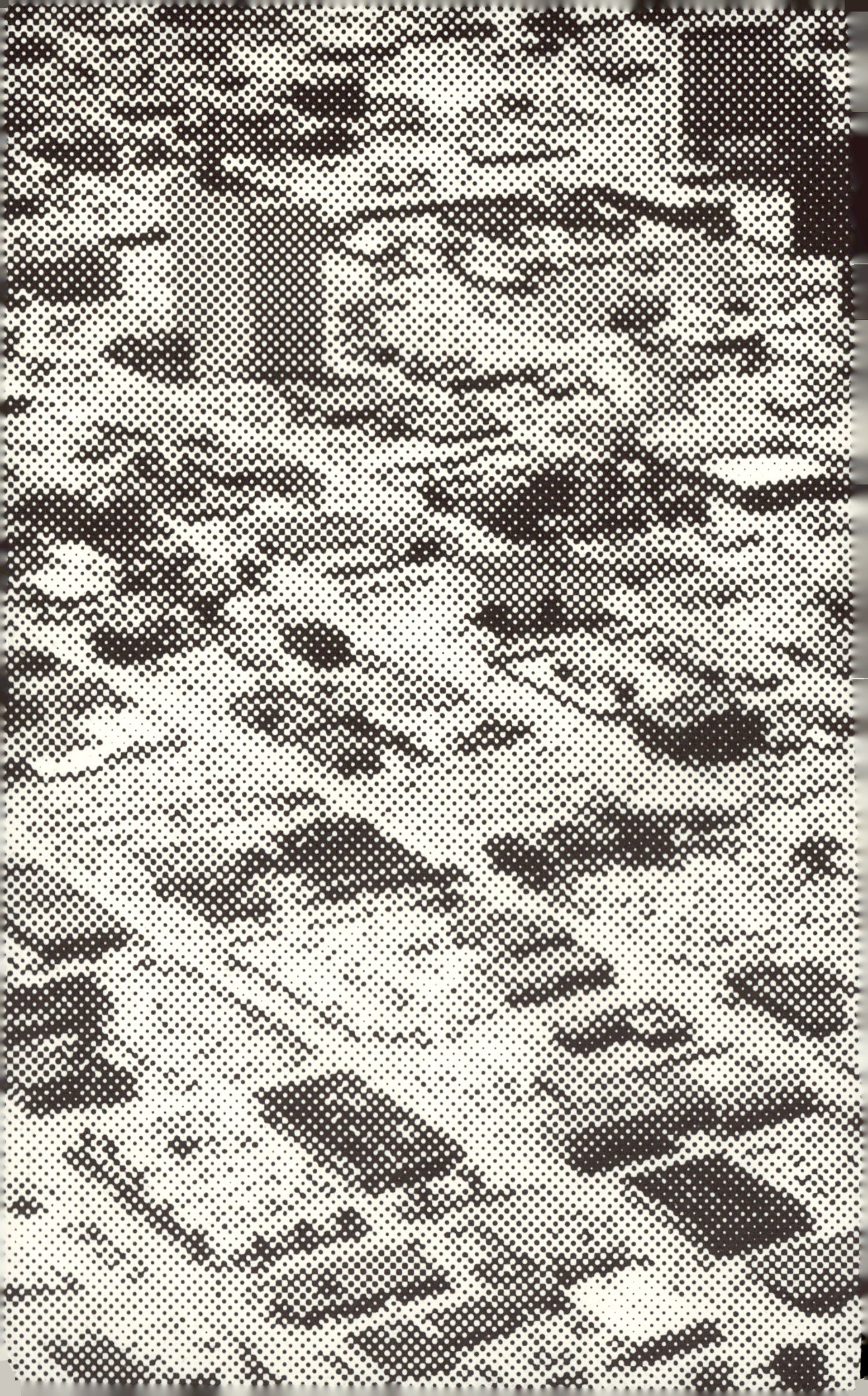

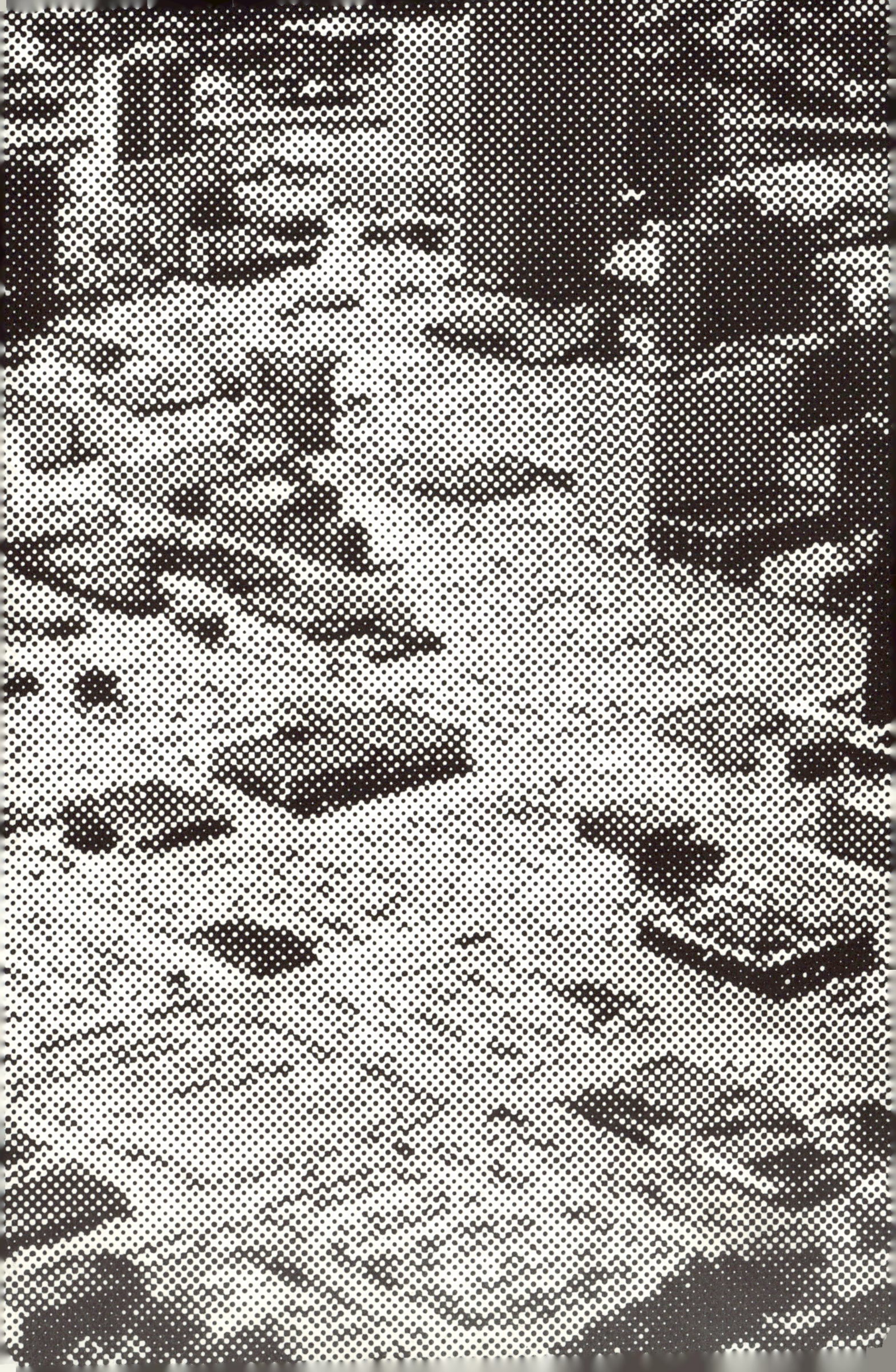

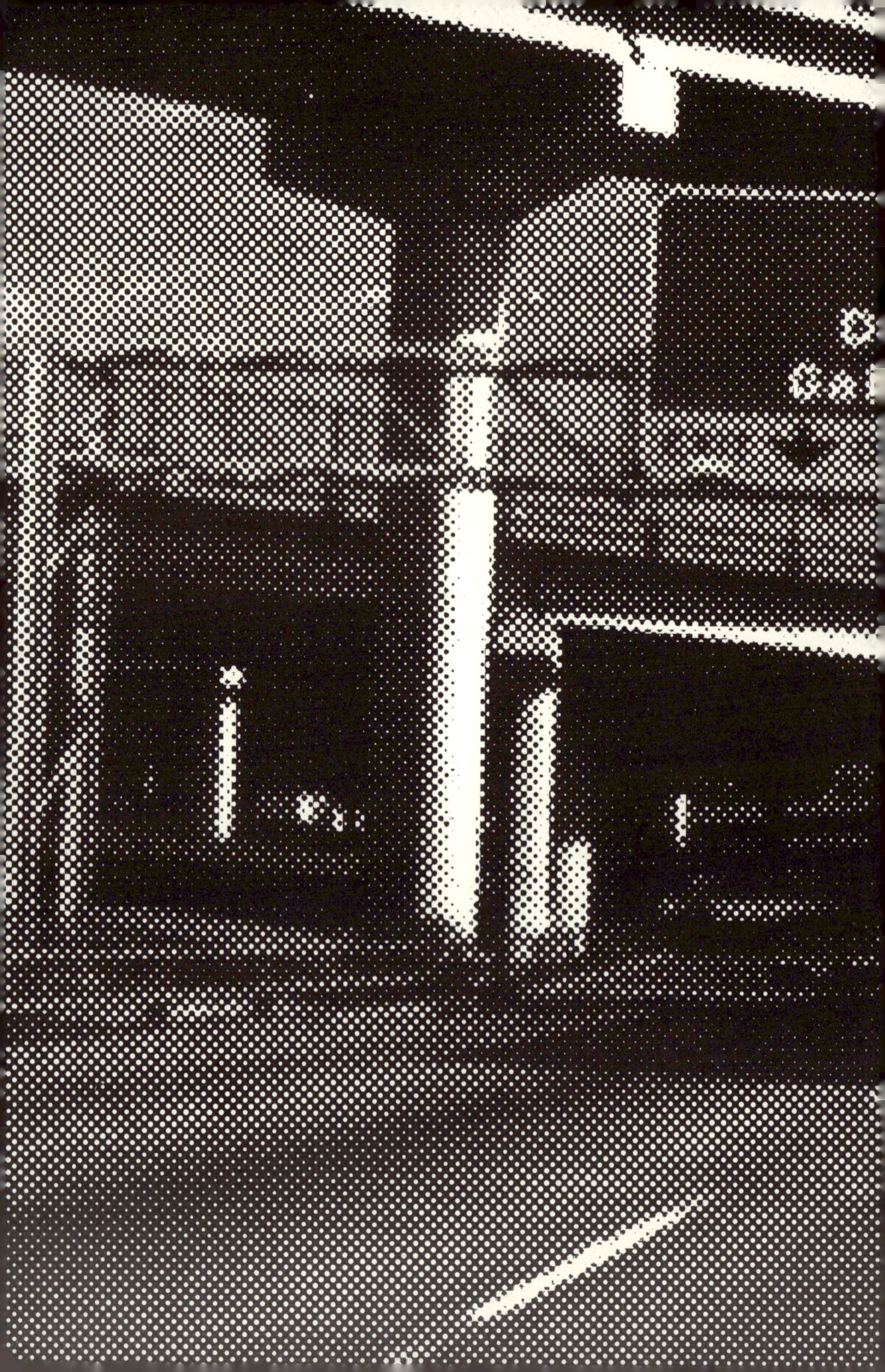

NORTH
Cleveland

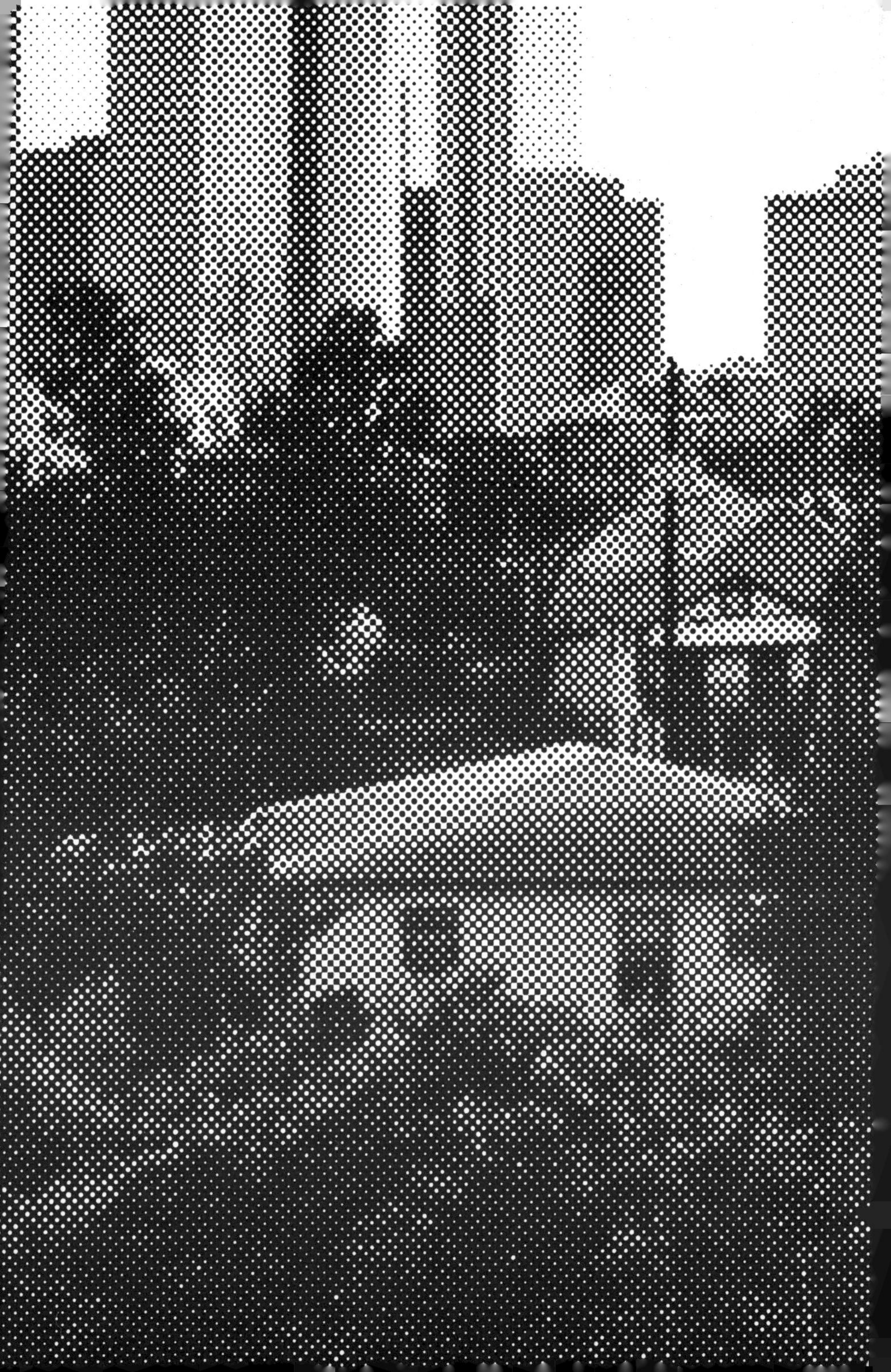

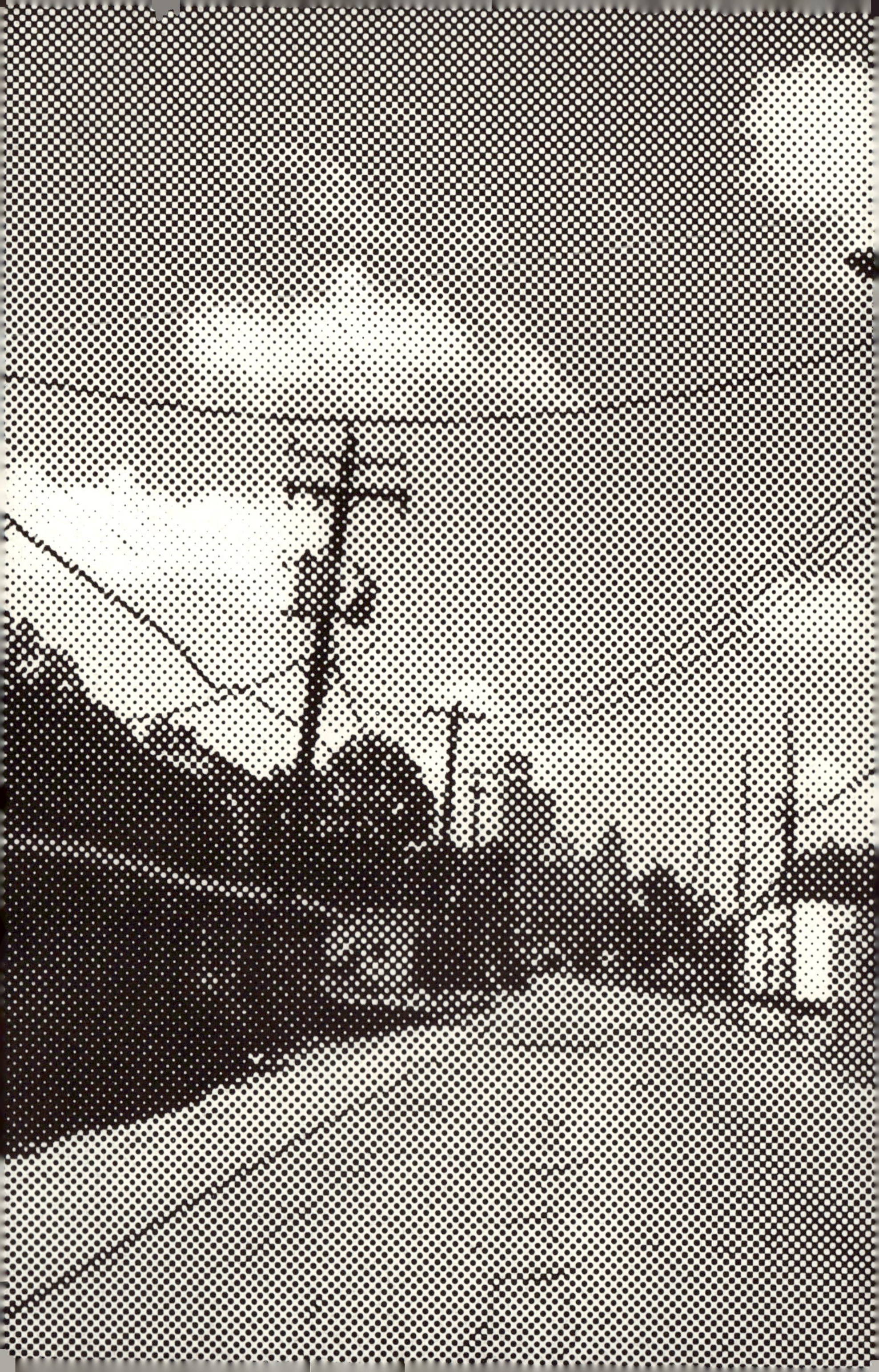

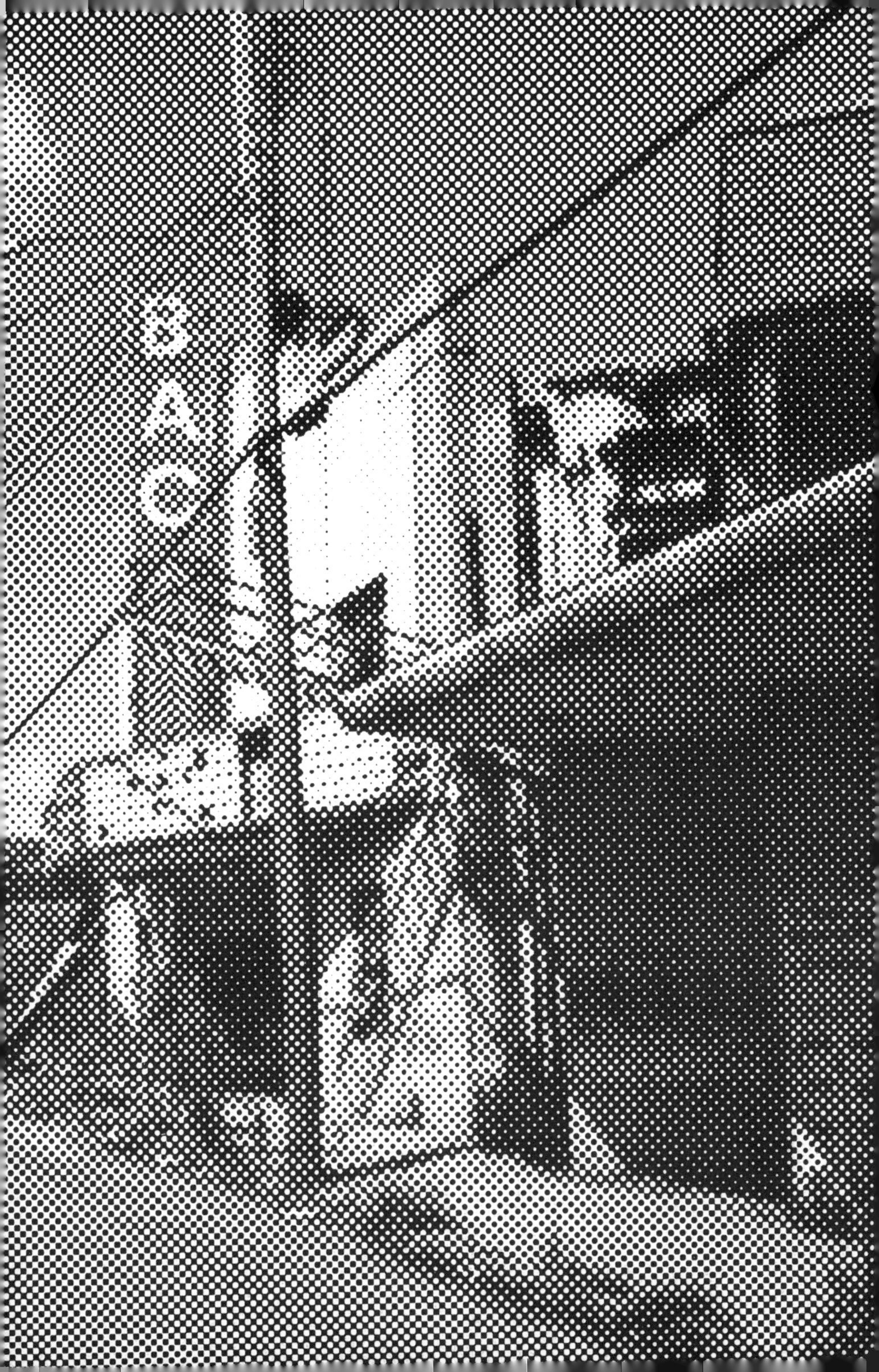

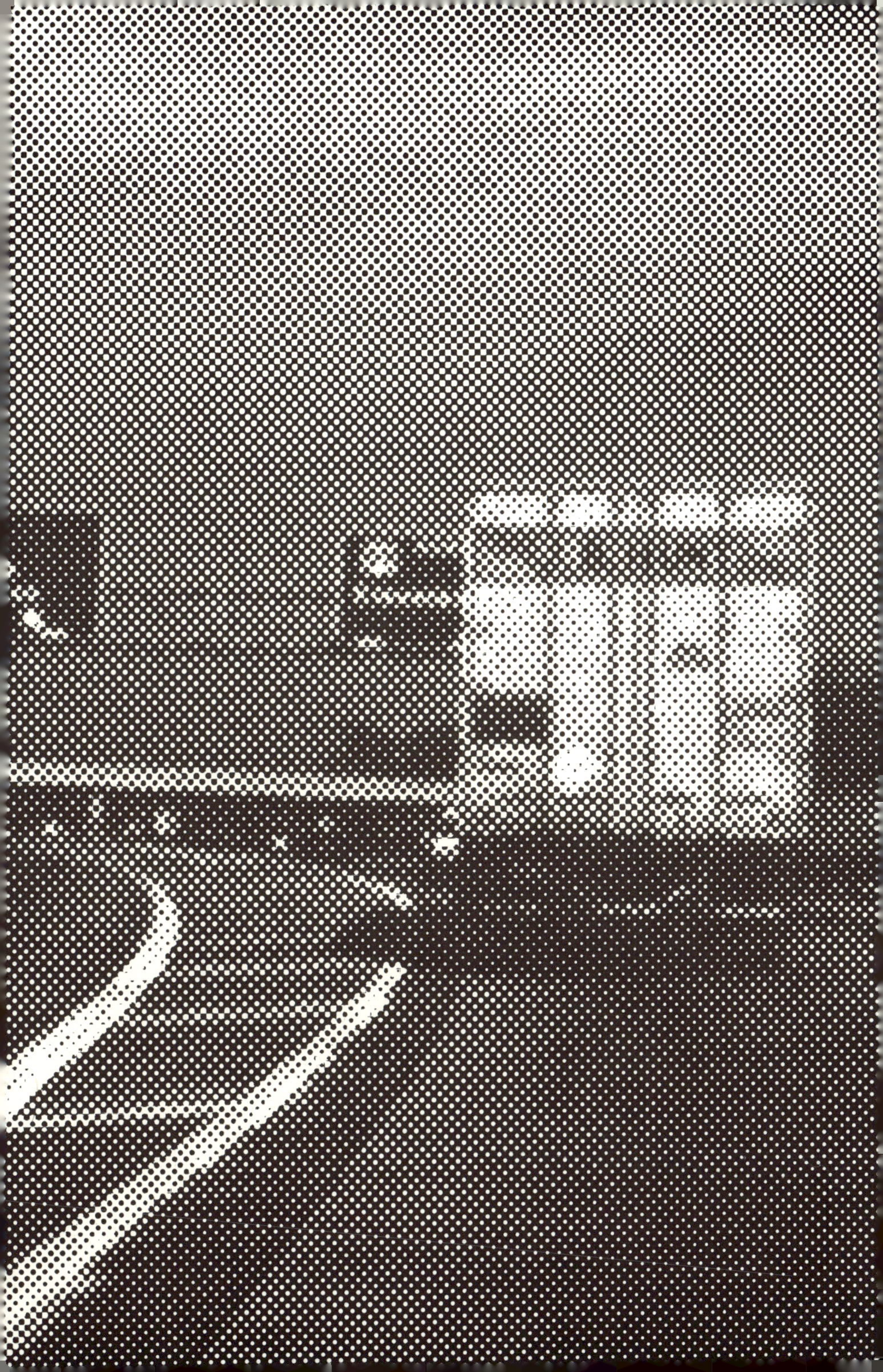

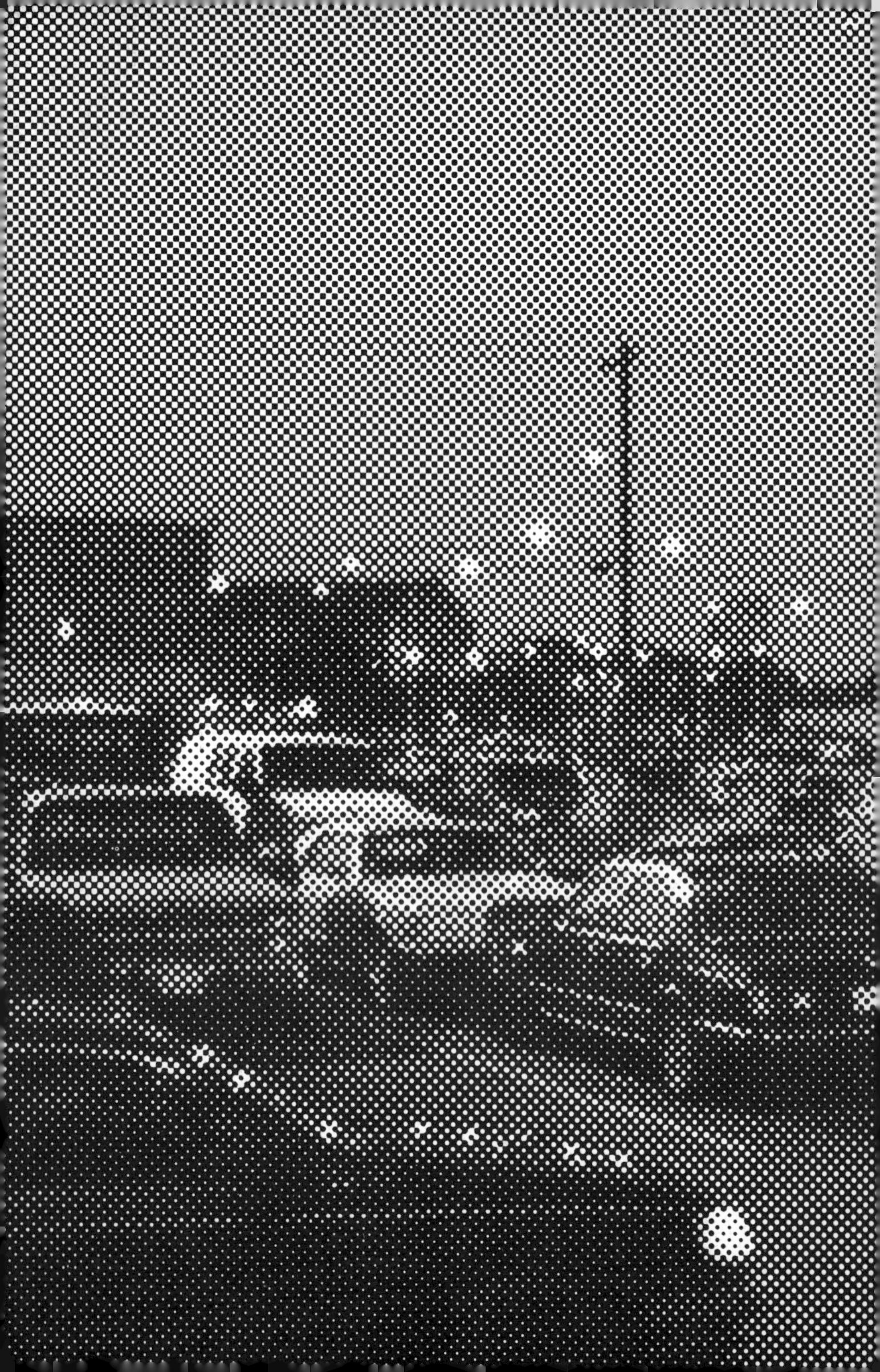

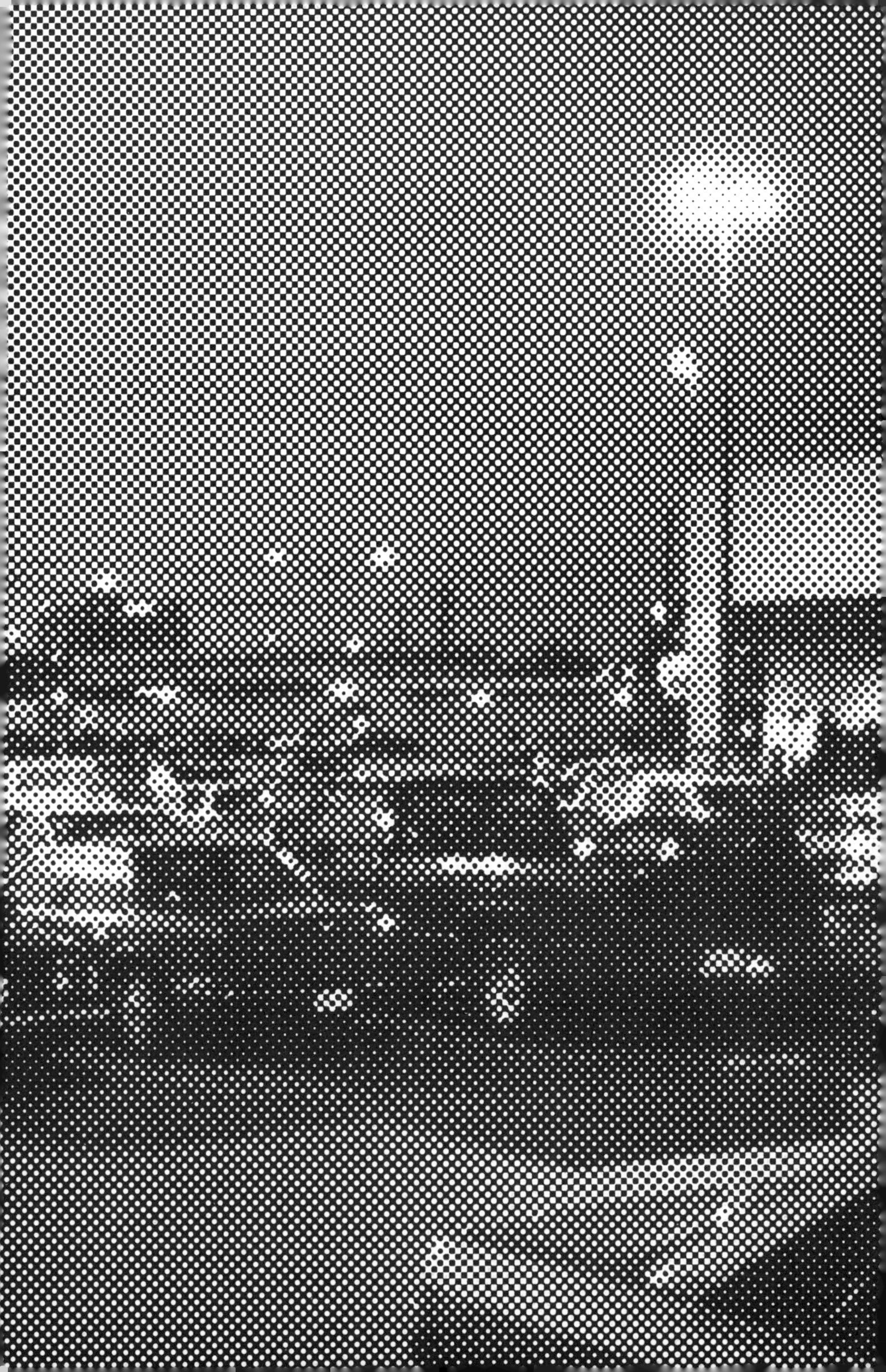

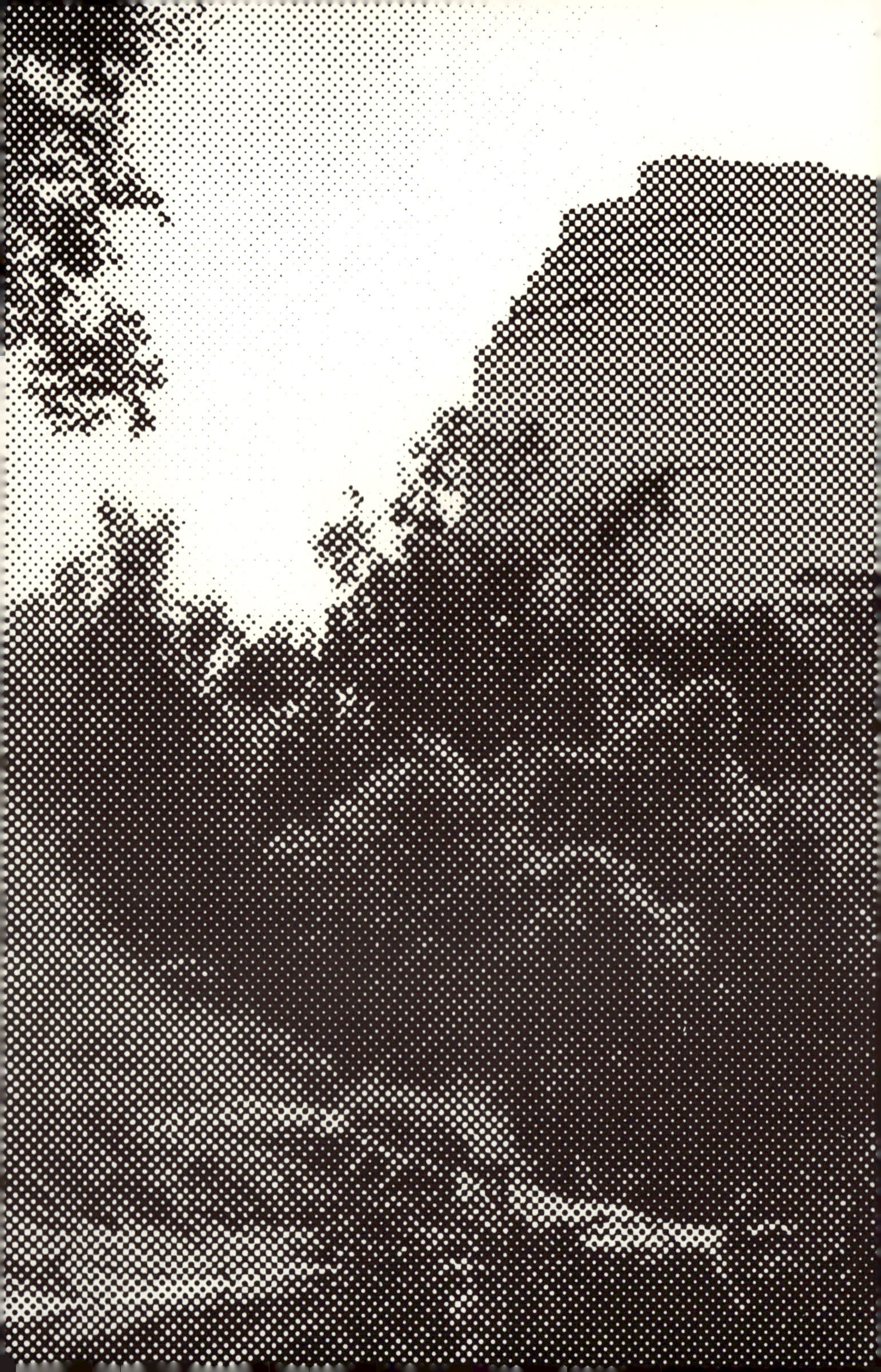

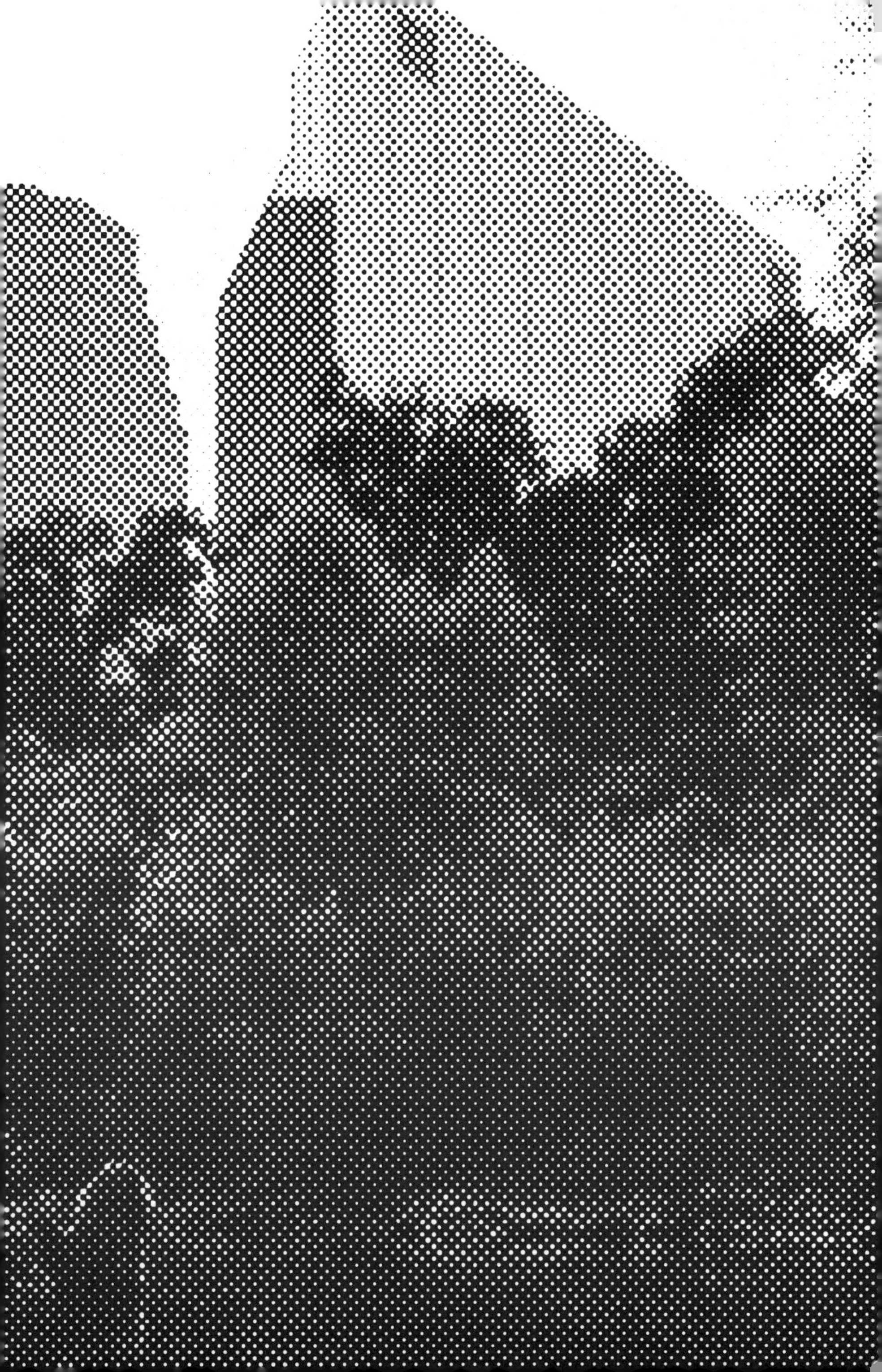

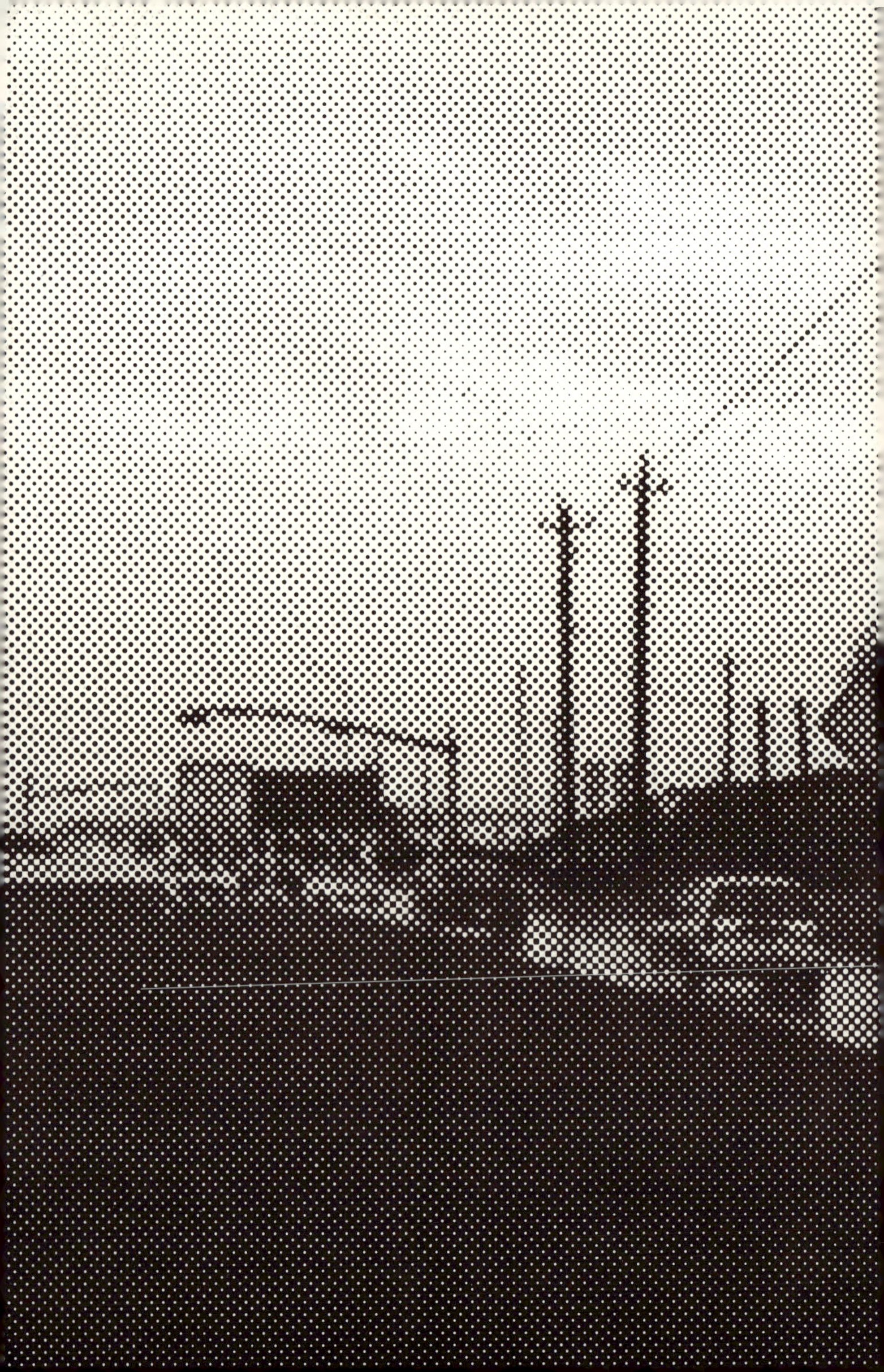

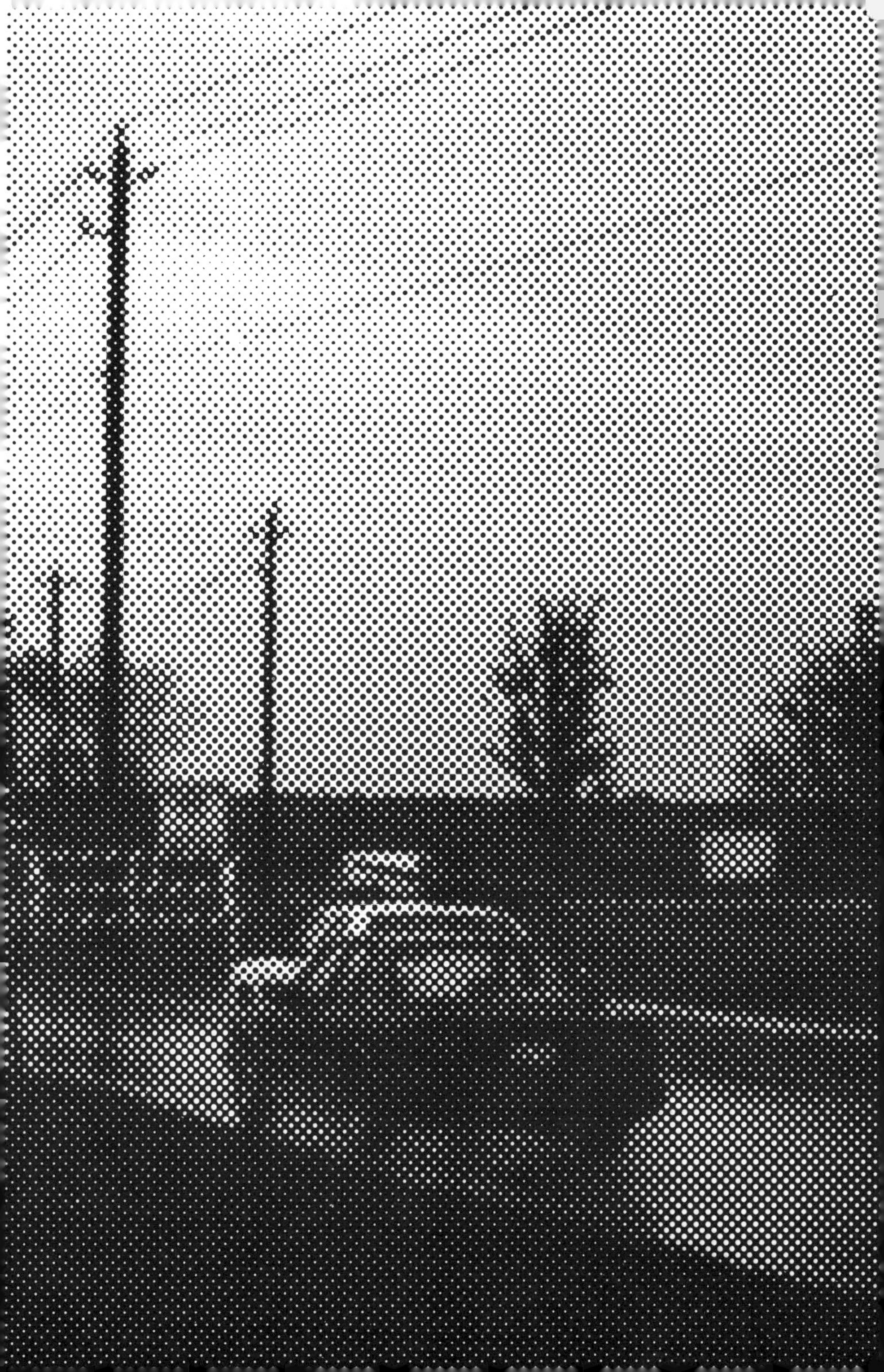

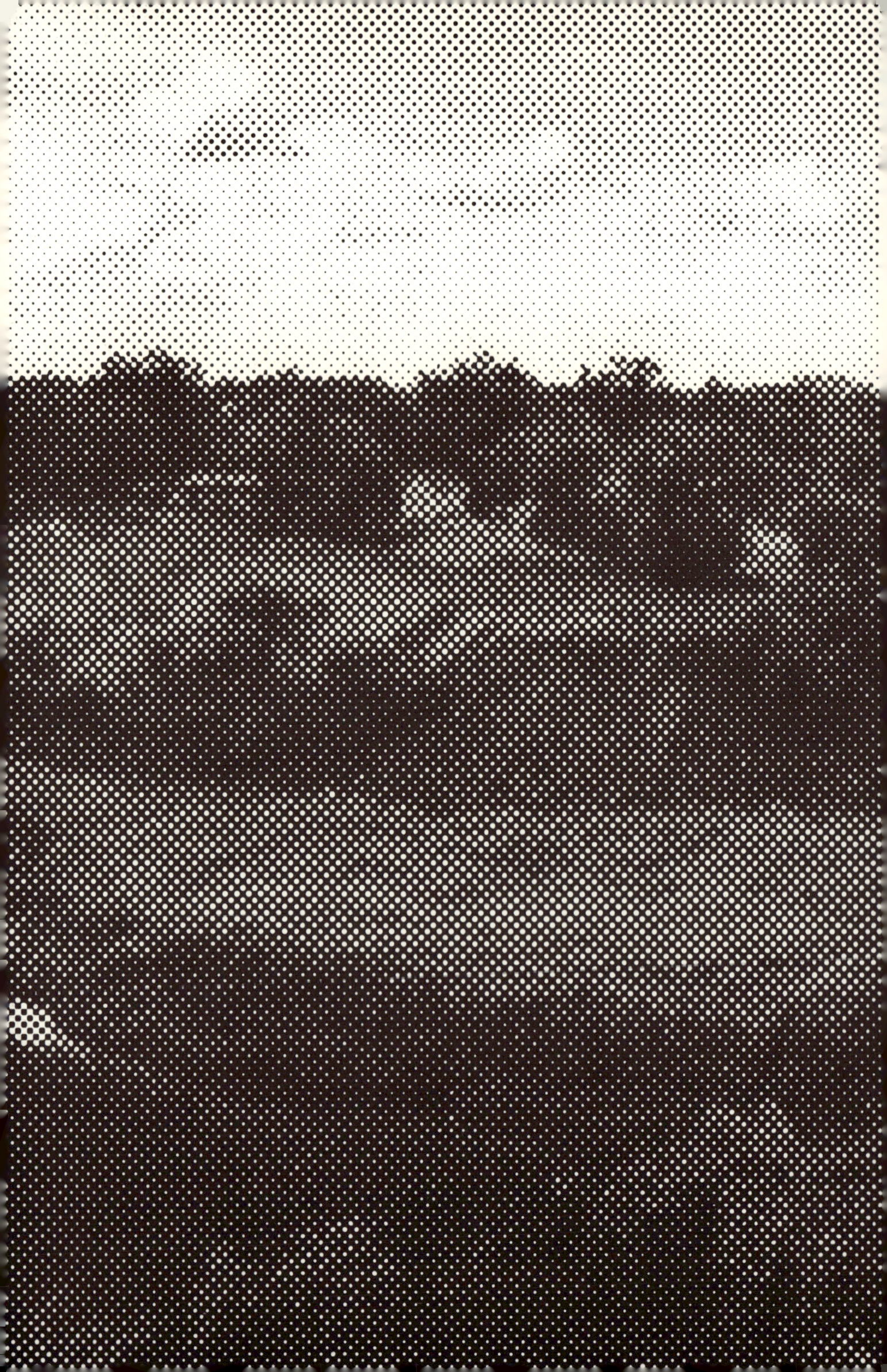

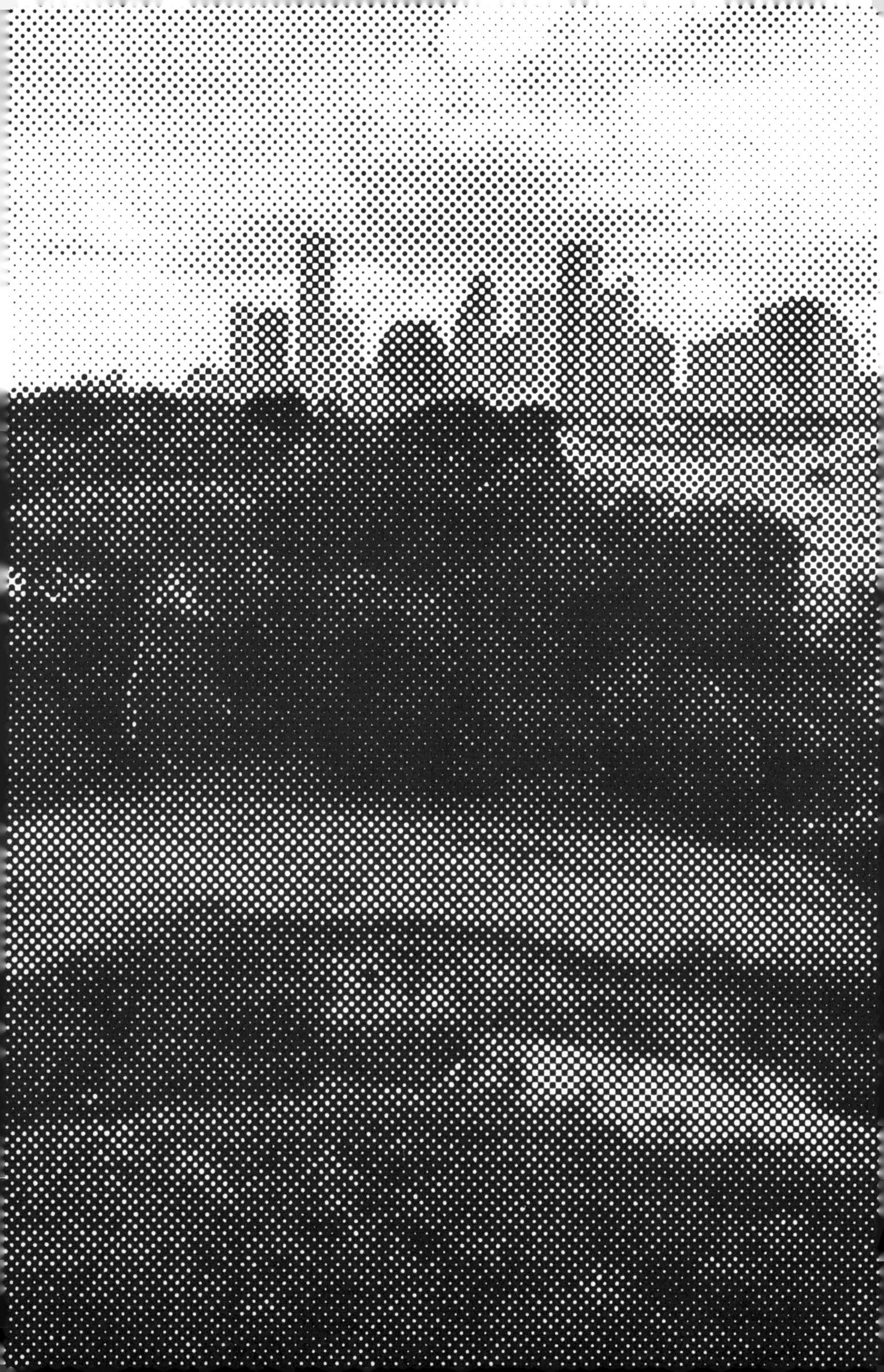

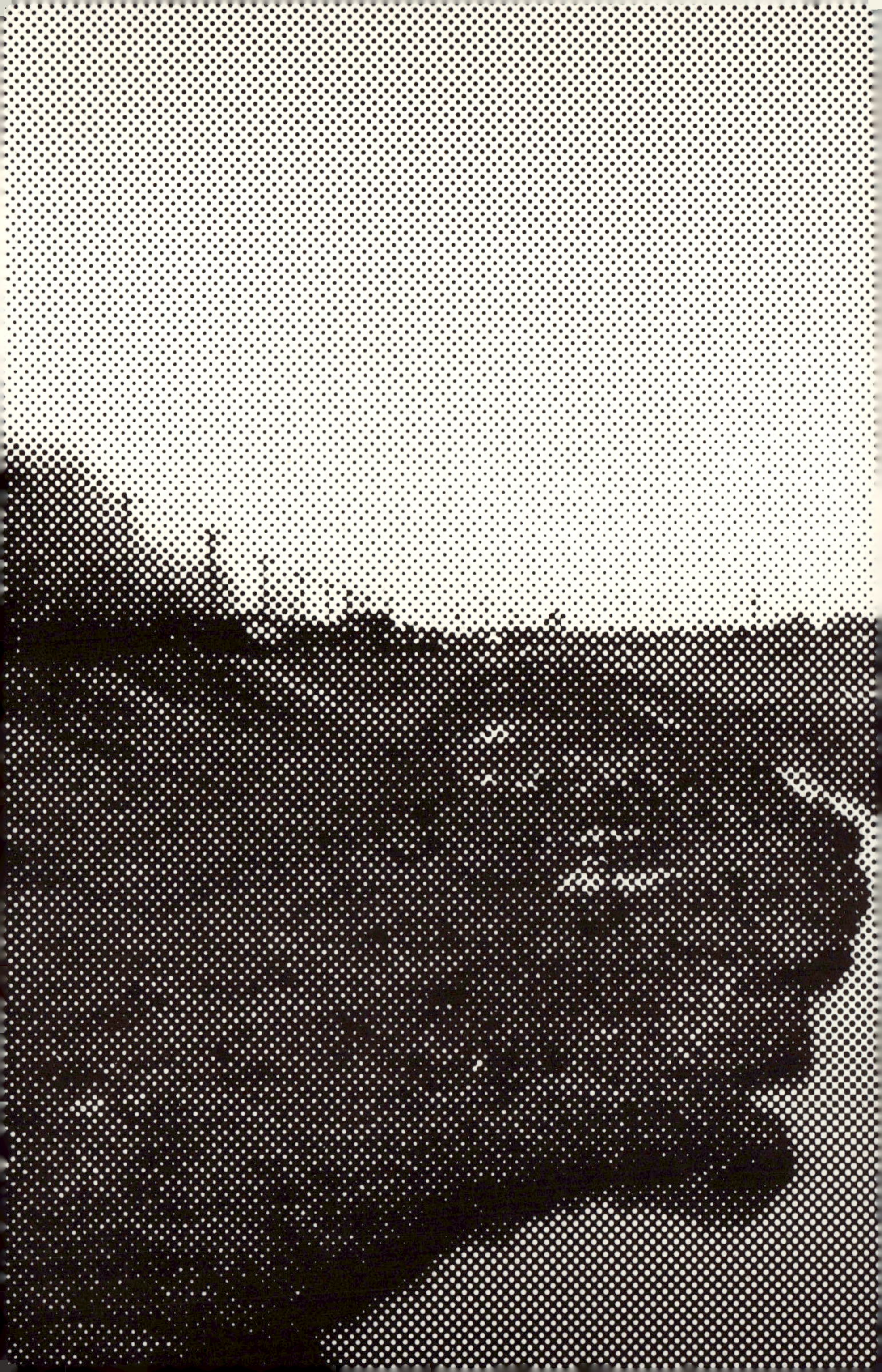

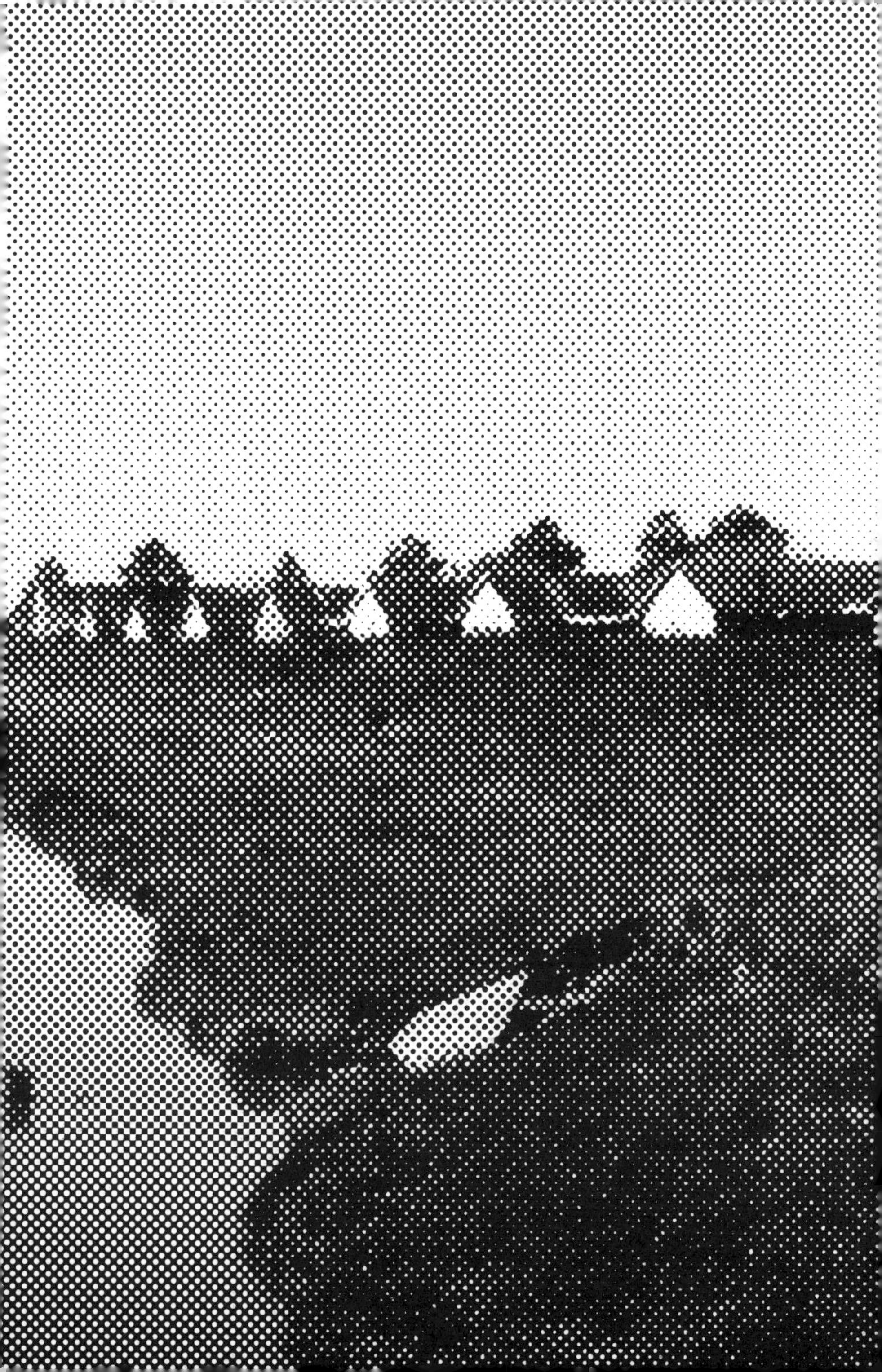

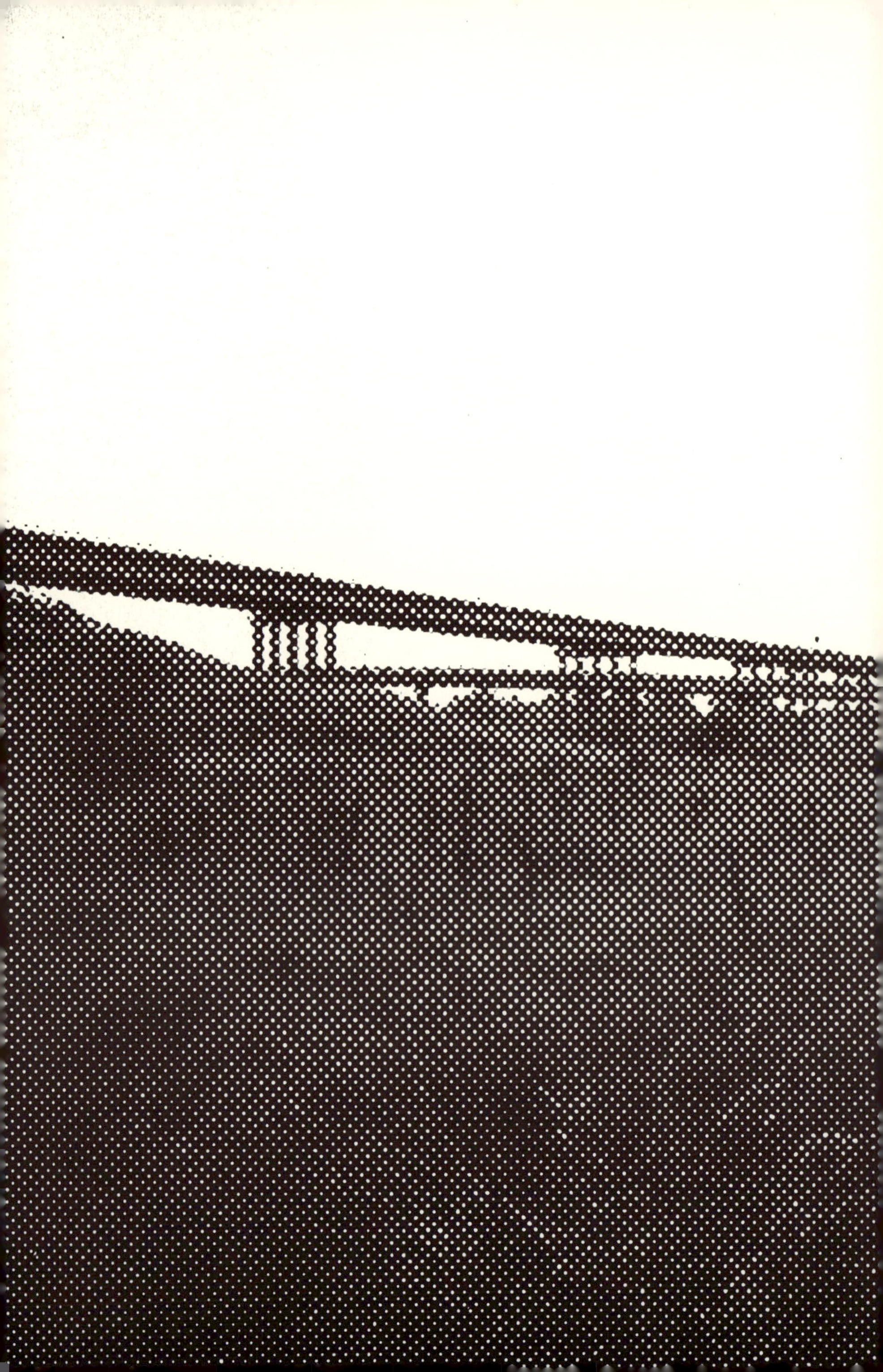

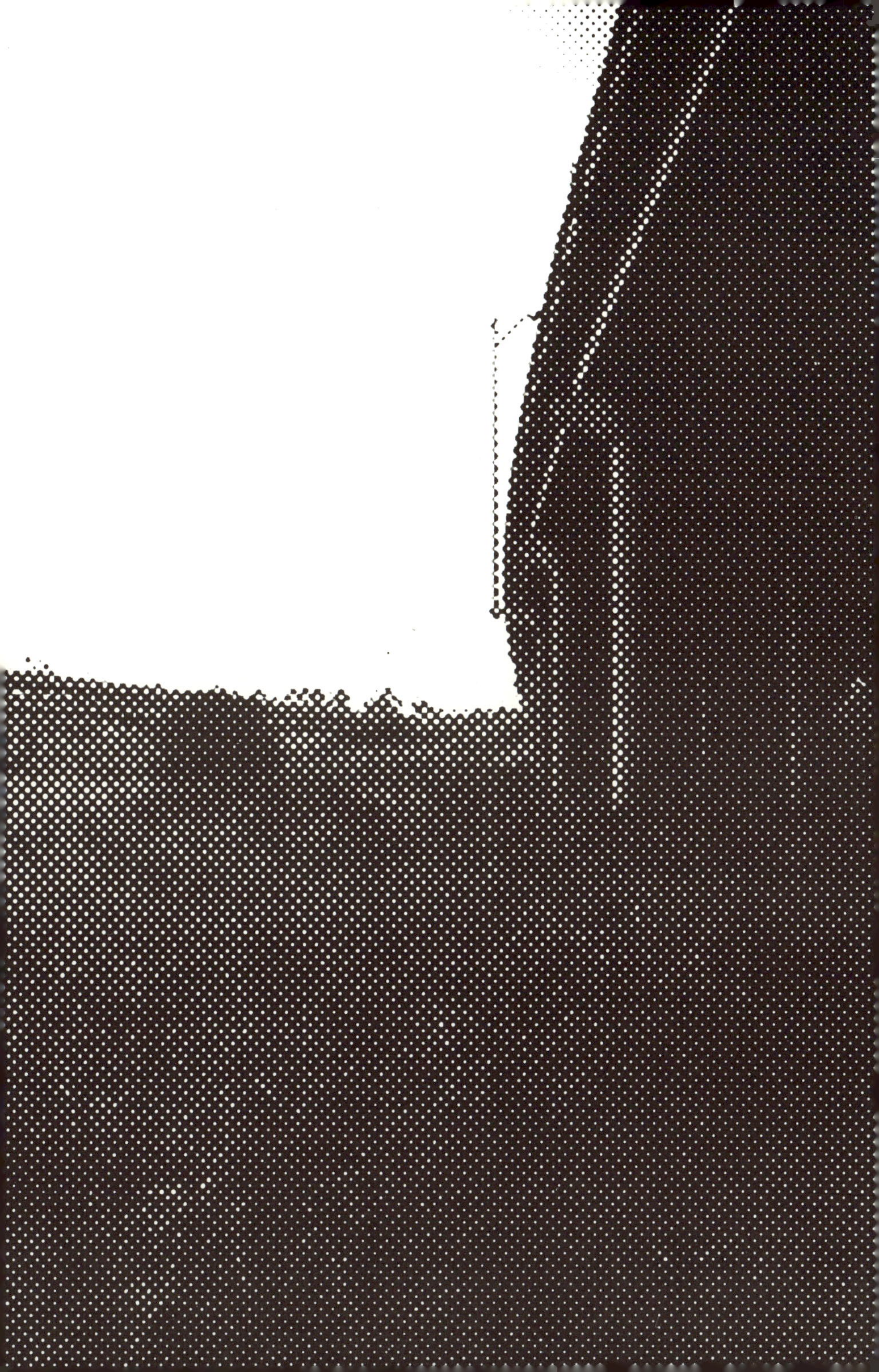

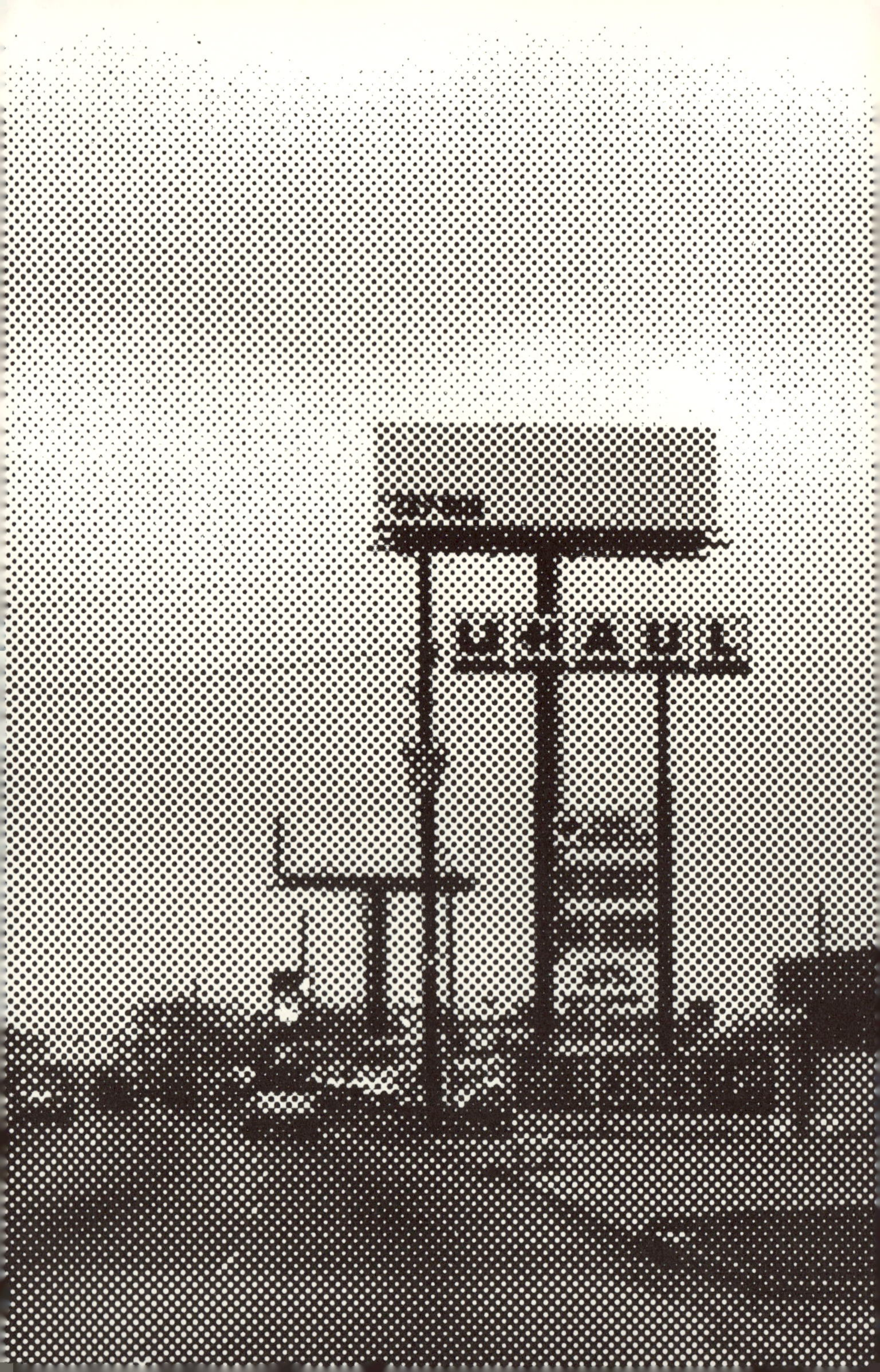

LADDERS

LADDERS

ALBERT POPE

ARCHITECTURE AT RICE 34

RICE SCHOOL OF ARCHITECTURE   HOUSTON, TEXAS
PRINCETON ARCHITECTURAL PRESS   NEW YORK

1996

Designed by Sze Tsung Leong

Published by:
Rice University School of Architecture
6100 South Main Street
Houston, Texas 77005
and
Princeton Architectural Press
37 East Seventh Street
New York, NY 10003

For a free catalog of other books published by Princeton Architectural Press, call toll free: 800.722.6657 or visit http://www.papress.com

© 1996 Rice University School of Architecture

All rights reserved. No part of this book may be reproduced in any form by any electronic or mechanical means (including photocopying, recording, or information storage and retrieval) without permission in writing from the publisher, except in the context of reviews.

Printed and bound in the United States.

Library of Congress Cataloging-in-Publication Data

Pope, Albert,
    Ladders / Albert Pope
                p. cm. — (Architecture at Rice ; 34)
    Includes bibliographical references and index.
    ISBN 1-885232-01-2
    1. City planning—United States—History—20th century. 2. Cities and towns—United States—Interpretive programs. 3. Space (Architecture)—United States.
    I. Title. II. Series: Architecture at Rice ; no. 34.
    NA1.a785 no. 34
    [NA9108]
    720 s—dc20
    [711' .4'097309045]   95-1240
                                                                       CIP

CONTENTS

INTRODUCTION: THE PRIMACY OF SPACE   0

The Primacy Of Space (2), The Primacy Of Form (3), Space/Form (7), Space/Time (9), An Idea of Form in a City Of Space (11).

CHAPTER ONE: THE OPEN CITY   14

The Open City (17), Apparatus Of Inclusion (18), Centripetal And Centrifugal Grid (22), The Historical Flow (24), Manhattan, 1811 (31), Agoraphobia (37), Queen's, 1908 (41), Centripetal vs. Closed City (44), 339th Avenue (47), Urban Transition (53).

CHAPTER TWO: URBAN IMPLOSION   54

Urban Implosion (57), Grid Erosion (58), The Ladder (61), Linear Cities (65), Hilberseimer (71), The Linear and Centric Metropolis (76), Grid Replanning (81), Modernism and Closure (86), The Superurban Stage (92).

CHAPTER THREE: INUNDATION OF SPACE   98

Inundation Of Space (101), Reorganization (102), Terminal Center (103), The Interurban Spine (105), Bridges and Tunnels (113), The Ellipsis (116), Free Space (119), Urban Architecture (123), Inside (125), Imploded Node (126), A Spatial Dominant (127), A Postmodern Sublime (134), The Closure of Late Capital (139), Native Urban Space (145).

CHAPTER FOUR: THE CENTRIPETAL CITY   148

The Centripetal City (151), Binary Structures (152), Local/Metropolitan (155), Centralized Polynuclear Expansion (157), The Emergence of the Polynuclear Field (159), Grid, Line and Center (165), The Indeterminate Center (173), The Metropolitan Endgame (176), Closure (178), The Spiral (186), Planned Disappearance (190), The Strip and the Megastructure (195), Exurban Ellipsis (199), The Disorganization of Space (201), Postwar Reversal (206), Collaborating With Entropy (211), Sprawling Babels (215), The Residue Is Not Inert (221).

CONCLUSION: MASS ABSENCE   226

Mass Absence (228), Ideologies Dance About In This Void (231), A Calculated Withdrawal (233), A Negative Sovereignty (235), Coda: The People Are Missing (238).

POSTCRIPT: LACUNAE, BY LARS LERUP   240

ILLUSTRATION AND PHOTO CREDITS   244

ACKNOWLEDGEMENTS   252

REFERENCES   254

INDEX   262

INTRODUCTION:
THE PRIMACY OF SPACE

THE PRIMACY OF SPACE

The contemporary city, the city that is, at this moment, under construction, is invisible. Despite the fact that it is lived in by millions of people, that it is endlessly reproduced, debated in learned societies, and suffered on a daily basis, the conceptual framework that would allow us to see it is conspicuously lacking. While the contemporary city remains everywhere and always seen, it is fully transparent to the urban conceptions under which we continue to operate.

These conceptions — the way we actively "think" the city — seem, at present, incapable of expanding to include the radically divergent formations of contemporary urbanism. The result is a brutal world of collective neglect, very nearly dropped from the consciousness of its inhabitants. Viewed out the window of a train or plane, on the edges of televised newscasts, or through the ubiquitous windshield, what passes for the city is a field of unloved buildings persisting at the edges of a heedless and distracted vision. The contemporary city has been not so much forgotten or deliberately ignored as it has remained unseen.

The inadequacy of a conceptual framework is tied to the process of urban development, which has been underway for the past fifty years. The contemporary city is, for the most part, understood as a sub-set of known urban conventions in the process of formation. Read as a literal extension of the conventional prewar urban core — as a sub-urb — it is implicitly understood to carry, in premature formation, the qualities and characteristics of the more mature form of urbanism found in the core. Yet, as suburban growth continues, it is apparent that the urban/sub-urban dynamic is failing. Contemporary urban development is not sub-development, rather it is alter-development. As time passes, and the sheer size of new construction approaches a critical mass, it becomes less and less plausible to regard the contemporary city in a subordinate relation to anything at all. It must finally be recognized that new development is less an extension or outgrowth of the core than a unique organism, presently at the brink of overwhelming its host.

As a form of parasite, the contemporary city possesses characteristics completely alien to its conventional urban sponsor. What was yesterday an innocuous extension of conventional form today turns out to be, not a "suburb," but an entirely unprecedented type of urban development. The contemporary city is much less about an extension of known convention than its antithesis, an inversion driven by rapidly accelerating curves of development, unprecedented demographic shifts, unique political catastrophe, and exotic economies of desire, all foreign to the forces which drove traditional urban development. It is necessary to separate this new parasitic city from its identification with the host, from its conceptual moorings as mere urban supplement and, after nearly fifty years of construction, attempt to raise it into discourse.

THE PRIMACY OF FORM

There remain, however, serious blockages to such a conceptual re-orientation. Among the greatest is that the contemporary city is not an identifiable object or "entity." Its characteristic dissipation and dispersion establish a complexity which is difficult to grasp as anything other than a statistical construct. As such, it remains conceptually transparent to participants of a design discourse bound to a fetishistic analysis and development of discrete and identifiable objects and spaces.

As proposed many times, from *Garden Cities of Tomorrow*, to *The New City*, to *Learning from Las Vegas*, to *S, M, L, XL*, it is not built form which characterizes the contemporary city, but the immense spaces over which built form has little or no control. These spaces, which overwhelm the architectural gesture,

0.1 Superstudio. "Live with objects, not for objects." Photocollage, 1972.
"When design as an inducement to consume ceases to exist, an empty area is created, in which, slowly, as on the surface of a mirror, such things as the need to act, mold, transform, give, conserve, modify, come to light." (Ambasz, 1970, p. 246)

ultimately dominate the contemporary urban environment. Vast parking, continuous or sporadic zones of urban decay, undeveloped or razed parcels, huge public parks, corporate plazas, high speed roads and urban expressways, the now requisite *cordon sanitaire* surrounding office parks, industrial parks, theme parks, malls and subdivisions are all spaces which have failed to become the focus of significant investigation. As a result the characteristic spaces of contemporary urban production remain virtually unseen and under-theorized. Without adequate conceptual access to these amorphous, unquantifiable spaces, the contemporary city remains inaccessible not only to those who live in it, but often to those who specify its design.

This inaccessibility exists for the simple reason that the characteristic spaces of the contemporary city are not identifiable entities, but rather are absences, gaps, lacunae, hiatuses, or ellipses that our commodity-bound words, buildings and "places" are unable to account for. Architects and planners stick to the discrete and the designable, even if their efforts prove to be undermined by forces beyond their control. Against such forces, designers must retreat to myopic self-examination or, more frequently in urban discourse, to a time when design was indisputably privileged. What the city has been (as a designed entity), or could be (as a designed entity), dominates academic and professional thinking as a transparent attempt to regain our formal and spatial prerogatives, our fixation with the known and designable, to the neglect of the actual state of the contemporary urban environment. There often seems no greater priority than to preserve, against all evidence to the contrary, the primacy of built form.

The difficulty in generating discourse around the actual qualities of the contemporary city stems from a near universal inability to abandon a preoccupation, not with form itself, but with the primacy of form in the contemporary urban environment. This insistence on primacy preempts the ability to conceptualize any characteristic absence or lack without transforming it into something else, that is into something architectural. The characteristic absence of contemporary urban space cannot be confronted directly by design discourse. Despite all claims to the contrary, nothing could be farther removed from contemporary urban realities than the old avant-garde tendency (operating at least since Piranesi) to construct absence, or to articulate, with all metaphysical ostentation, the architectural "Void." Such exercises imply direct design intervention into a space, a space which (by granting priority to design intention) becomes the kind of fixed and determined entity that the contemporary city conspicuously lacks.

The fallacy of constructing such a model of absence is that it produces something other than what the city is. Attempts to reinstate the privileges of design in the contemporary city do not correspond to the unconstructed kind of absence characteristic of contemporary urban production. This absence, like chaos, is not susceptible to conventional design intervention. It cannot be set up as an analytic or a design model. To state the obvious, when absence is focused on, it loses its distinguishing qualities and becomes presence. Ignoring this situation leads to the familiar, futile exercises in which developers and architects seek to formally intervene in the contemporary environment. The attempt to affect vast expanses of space with ineffectual often pathetic "design" gestures ignores rather than confronts the overwhelming scale of the context. This constitutes a paradox for the discipline, where the quality which is most characteristic of contemporary urbanism ultimately remains inaccessible to direct design intervention.

SPACE/FORM

A critique of the primacy of built form in the contemporary urban environment need not lead to the paralysis, absurdity, nihilism, irony, commercial prostitution, or the despair of an aspiring form-maker. A rejection of the primacy of form is not a rejection of urban form itself, but of its privileged status in an environment where it clearly has none. Acceding to this diminished status is not a capitulation of professional prerogatives, nor is it a betrayal of the discipline's principles. On the contrary, it opens up another set of possibilities that a continuing denial of the contemporary situation otherwise obscures. Only by abandoning the primacy of built form is it possible to reposition form so that it may effectively respond to a city dominated by space.

One of the most basic relations in the logic of conventional urban development is the working dialectic between built form and urban space. This subtle and shifting dialectic is best expressed in, for example, the association between a piazza and a campanile, a cathedral and a *parvis* or, more simply, the association between an urban street and a facade. This particular dialectic establishes, in large part, the autonomous logic of historical urban development. Despite the more recent dominance of space, such logic obtains in the contemporary city of space. The interaction between space and form continues to be a vital urban relation, but this relation may be exploited only if its recent and radical shift toward the spatial is acknowledged. The potential of significant architectural intervention in the contemporary city lies in the assertion that form can yet effect space as space continues to effect form.

The dramatic skewing of the dialectic toward the spatial is key to a revised strategy of urban intervention. Out of a rigorous analysis of the contemporary city, a so-called "post-urban" strategy of intervention emerges. Given the continued interrelation between contemporary space and form, it is possible to draft an "oblique" urban strategy that aims indirectly at the primary target of space through a secondary intervention of form. While built form is clearly subordinate, the dialectic between space and form remains operative, if not actually heightened, by the primacy of space. By forgoing attempts to regain its privileged status, built form can emerge as a strictly secondary or subordinate intervention that is nevertheless capable of engaging the primacy of space.

The idea presented here aims precisely at this inverted status between contemporary urban space and form. The intent is to identify and elaborate an operative dialectic and reposition contemporary urban space in relation to built form. What would otherwise be an obvious course of action is blocked, however, by the inability to see and understand the qualities of contemporary urban space. While a coherent logic between urban space and form does exists in the contemporary city, the traditional primacy of built form must be reversed. It is interesting today to see the most strident polemicists — many of them unabashed formalists — engaged in the questionable privileging of built form. Regardless of whether specific architectural vocabularies are revolutionary or reactionary, the privileging of form amounts to a certain paralysis with regard to effective intervention. To deny the primacy of space is to sustain a blindness to the greater urban realities whose effects remain transparent to the contemporary urban imagination.

SPACE/TIME

Before outlining this contemporary version of space/form, it is necessary to note another strategy which forcefully challenged the privileged status of architectural form. As far back as 1932, a critique of conventional urban strategies emerged from the familiar if still surprising urban polemic of Frank Lloyd Wright. In his book, *The Disappearing City*, Wright advocated an extreme dispersion of the urban environment, far more radical than any proposed before or since. Broadacre City rejected not only the centralization and monumentality pursued by Le Corbusier and others, but any significant urban aggregation whatsoever. The project suggested not simply deurbanization, but an evanescent regional dispersal: the complete disappearance of the city. In support of the ultimate dissolution of the city, Wright articulated a new analytical formulation: ". . . not only have space values entirely changed to time values, now ready to form new standards of movement measurement, but a new sense of spacing based upon speed is here. . . . And, too, the impact of this sense of space has already engendered fresh spiritual as well as physical values" (Fishman, 1994, p.46). This polemical association of urban space with time was for Wright a necessary conceptual reorientation to contemporary urban development, a reorientation still remarkably convincing. Reiterated in the 1950s by Melvin Webber (1963) and again in the 1970s by Paul Virilio (1991), this conjunction of space and time through the agency of "speed" remains powerful in its challenge to traditional urban form.

As it has evolved, the proposition suggests the dissolution of urban form into the temporal vectors of transportation and communication networks. The speed of a vehicle on a freeway, of radio and television transmission, or of digital communication has usurped the territorial domains established by form. In this regard, the contemporary urban environment is composed and recom-

9 THE PRIMACY OF SPACE

posed by each individual everyday around literal and virtual itineraries, and not in relation to a fixed arrangement of places. The city is tied together, not by space and built form, but by this itinerary executed through space in real time. In this way, time is affirmed as the legitimate increment of contemporary urban "dimension." The disappearance of the city occurs when form completely dissolves as it is disengaged from space and space is engaged by speed as it is measured over time. As space/form becomes space/time, new rules of urban development emerge supplanting the traditional dialectic between space and built form. On the overthrow of form, Virilio is clear:

Are we prepared to accept a reversal of all philosophical meaning, . . . to consider movement and acceleration not as displacement but rather as emplacement, an emplacement without any precise place, without geometric or geographic localization, as with the particles of quantum mechanics? We must at least resolve ourselves to losing the sense of our senses, common sense and certainties, in the material of representation. We must be ready to lose our morphological illusions about physical dimensions. (Virilio, 1991, p.19)

This seemingly inevitable abdication of physical form is the flip side of the privilege of form. The extremes being promoted range from the absolute primacy of built form to the absolute irrelevance of built form. There is little doubt that form is dissolving, that the city is in fact disappearing into the periphery, and that the dynamic of speed has overwritten our most fundamental urban certainties. Yet, it is also true that this dissolution of form will never be complete, that the city will not dissolve to zero. Form will never become fully transparent to our activities, be those activities muscular, mechanical, electronic or cerebral. We must remain skeptical of the Ultimate Liquidation — of "losing the sense of our senses, common sense and certainties" — and of whom this liquidation actually serves. Until the body becomes finally and fully digitized, there must always be an accounting of form and an effort to enlist its remainder into positive outcomes. No matter how intense the maelstrom of modernization becomes, how fully colonized by technologies, or how subjected we are to scientific analyses, industrial processes, corporate power, demographic upheavals, cataclysmic growth, digital revolutions, bureaucratic organization, global economic transformations, there is always a remainder of form, and this remainder belongs to us. If only it can be effectively engaged. The city — under the dramatic and often disastrous process of transformation — will not be replaced by nothing.

The polemic of "speed" and the disappearance of form will be taken up in chapter four. At this point, it is perhaps clear that the oblique strategy outlined above lies somewhere between the primacy of form and the irrelevance of form. In addressing the radical skewing of the dialectic between form and space, we are affirming the validity of formal strategies; simply because built form is subordinate, it is not irrelevant. In this case, we have chosen an approach that prefers space over time in its ability to enter into a material relation with form, the formal prerogatives which constitute the basis of architectural activity.

AN IDEA OF FORM IN A CITY OF SPACE

While it is clear that built form is secondary to the primacy of space, the logic of form itself has never been more apparent than in the patterns of contemporary urban expansion. It is necessary to emphasize this distinction between built form, which is actual construction, and form itself, which constitutes the abstract, autonomous logic of the city which both precedes and succeeds built form. This definition of urban form specifies the important separation between form and a particular design based on that form. The logic of the urban grid, for example, precedes specific grid design. An actual city grid may be rectilinear or square, it may be based on regular or irregular intervals, or it may not even be orthogonal at all. It may be curvilinear, skewed or wracked. Whatever the particular design, it remains a grid as long as it maintains its independent, internal logic. Precisely how such an internal logic is established is a recurrent subject of architectural debate. The logic is sometimes thought to be transcendent, always indexing "first causes" or the origins of urban form (Rossi, 1982). At other times the logic is thought to be established as it evolves over time and constitutes a codified urban typology unique to the discipline and its traditions (Argan). At still other times, the logic is seen to arise, not from urban construction at all, but from a wide range of natural phenomena, specifically from biological forms or biological "systems" (Thompson). Regardless of the ultimate source, each of these formal approaches attempts to discern the continuity of self-governing forces existing beneath the apparent order of things. The bottom line is that urban form and thus the city is always, to some degree, autonomous.

There has always been considerable skepticism as to whether an abstract and autonomous logic of urban form has ever existed. In the context of the postwar city, the idea is practically laughable. Given the apparent irrelevance of design interests in the decisive processes of contemporary urban development, the idea that "form follows form" strikes one as an extravagant academic conceit. In the face of such skepticism, it will be argued that urban form maintains a degree of autonomy which operates beneath and beyond the apparently comprehensive economic and bureaucratic interests which drive its development. It will be argued that contemporary urban form — in this case the urban grid itself — is presently undergoing a relatively autonomous process of transformation. It will be shown that a recent radical erosion of the grid has altered the conventional relation between contemporary urban space and built form. This grid transformation has brought about, not only the primacy of space, but a dramatic reversal of the grid's traditional organizational properties and the emergence of an altogether separate and distinct form of urban organization which will be identified as the "ladder."

The following analysis will trace the evolution of the grid through 20th-century urban development and identify precisely the point at which the contemporary dialectic between urban space and built form first emerges. It is possible to reduce this evolution to a series of precise stages. The first stage involves an analysis of the qualities of the prewar gridiron city and the existence of universal open space from 19th-century gridded construction. The second stage describes a process of grid "implosion" and the transformation of open urban systems into closed ones. This involves the erosion of the continuous grid and the consolidation of a new form of organization which is the ladder. The third stage concerns the inundation of space into conventional urban fabric resulting in the creation of a new bureaucratic battlefield, the "inner city." The final stage of development traces the evolution of the grid up to its point of transformation into a new type of urban organization which will be called a centripetal city.

Traditionally such analyses of urban form have been regarded as instrumental inasmuch as they have led to design strategies derived from the established analytical base. Such is not the case here. The value of the following analysis derives less from the suggestion of immediate intervention and more from the identification and elaboration of its unseen potential. It is most urgent that contemporary urban space and form be seen, and that a coherent identity can be conceptualized or "thought." If the city cannot be thought then, regardless of the quality of its interventions, it ceases to be an object of individual or collective concern. To discredit the idea of urban intelligibility — the idea of coherent urban form — is to promote an unspoken acquiescence to the forces which otherwise drive its development.

ONE:
THE OPEN CITY

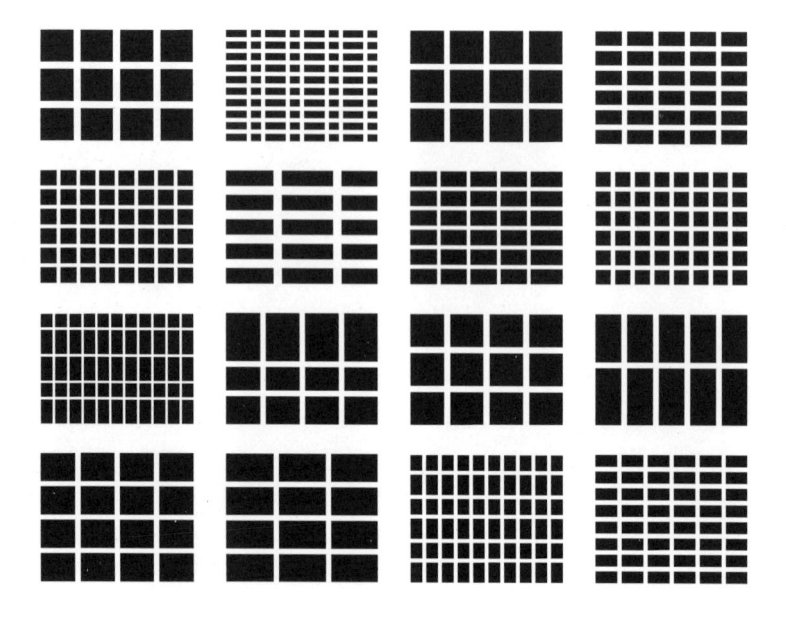

1.1 Urban Grids. From left to right, First row: Buenos Aires, Aix-en-Provence, Santiago, Aranjuez; Second row: Petra, Manhattan, Turin, San Sebastian; Third row: Montpazier, Philadelphia, Barcelona, Berlin; Fourth row: Bilbao, Madrid, Athens, Trieste.

THE OPEN CITY

In order to understand and engage the city of space, it is necessary to examine the present relation of urban space and built form. What must be confronted directly is that the relation does not presently exist; contemporary urban space and form occupy mutually exclusive positions. In spite of the rapid inundation of space into the fabric of the city, urban form has grown ever more exclusive, ever more closed to the qualities of space that dominate its production. Space and form have become polarized into discrete, non-intersecting worlds of closed urban forms and their spatial "residuum."

It is difficult to understand how a city of unprecedented spatial inundation — an urban fabric opened up by space — has produced forms that are essentially closed and exclusive. This paradox is the subject of the following chapter, which begins with a discussion of the grid and the diverse effects it is capable of inscribing onto an urban landscape. Borrowing from an analysis of modern painting, a single opposition emerges as the key distinction between two fundamentally opposed urban systems: a closed or centripetal system and an open or centrifugal system. These systems are discussed in specific historical terms relating to the 19th-century industrial gridiron, and the 20th-century attempts to reform it. With regard to recent urban evolution, the relation between open and closed urban systems will be reversed. The 19th-century gridiron city will be defined as an inherently open city, which is subsequently closed down by Garden City and *Ville Radieuse* models of urban development. The relative closure of these models will be examined in an effort to construct a more accurate account of the relation between contemporary space and form. Understanding that the vast explosion of contemporary space has produced closed and exclusive urban form is the first step in accounting for their present relationship.

APPARATUS OF INCLUSION

There is a truism concerning the urban grid which, like any truism, is as shallow, banal, and as impossible to defend as it is indisputable. The immutable relation between the urban grid and the qualities and characteristics typically associated with the urban world are summed up in the aphorism — a truism — which asserts that as the grid disappears, so does the city. To suggest such a powerful link between gridded space and urban identity is to suggest that all expectations of the city — the ways in which the city is thought — are tied to a single rudimentary form. Idealized or circumstantial, pedestrian or vehicular, curvilinear or orthogonal, the grid literally is the city.

The supposition that the city is disappearing is commonplace, even in the popular press. That this disappearance may be directly registered in the radical transformation of the urban grid may only be an obvious corollary. But the erosion of the urban grid serves as more than an index for this apparent disappearance. The transformation of the grid in the contemporary city is the sign and signal of an altogether other form of urban development that, despite the extent to which we daily confront its effects, has remained conceptually opaque. Grid transformation is the formal key to this development. It is less a transformation of traditional urban patterns than the formation of an entirely unique armature of urban organization.

If the city is disappearing, it cannot be replaced by nothing. Yet, despite the fact that all may acknowledge its radical postwar transformation — its literal dissipation and disappearance into an uncharted periphery — we have completely failed to grasp the "something else" the city is becoming. Whatever it ultimately turns out to be, this something else will not be the mysterious consequence of some immanent and unknowable future. This something else already has form and this form can be detected at precisely the moment it ceases to be urban in the conventional sense, at process of urban transformation when the grid disappears.

The bond between gridded space and urban development is rela... grid's inherent ability to generate systems of infinite complexity. Its ubiqu... tous power comes from the manner in which it conceals this complexity beneath an otherwise simplistic pattern of organization. Street layouts, modular furniture, weaving standards, fenestration patterns, bitmaps, trellises, organizational matrices, playing fields, cooking surfaces, Go boards, electrical networks, cellular lattices, surveying apparatus, Boolean networks, the Thomas Guide, Cornell boxes, and the Periodic Table only begin a veritable Chinese encyclopedia of grid manifestations. It is not the simplicity of the grid that accounts for this elaborate social topography; it is its deference to complexity that supports the wide range of its adaptive heterogeneity — to be the enabling apparatus of such an unlikely series of events.

Because of the grid's formal simplicity, its inherent complexity often remains unacknowledged. Common assumptions about the grid are often based on the reading of its strong categorical and prescriptive order: the grid as a figure or icon of order. The grid as a bureaucratic matrix, or a network of territorial control, or even the literal mesh of a cage suggests its prescriptive qualities. Yet, beyond these qualities, it is apparent that the grid is not only an icon of order; it is also a benign apparatus capable of bringing out of an undifferentiated flux an inclusive, heterogeneous field of almost unlimited complexity.

The qualities of the grid as an enabling apparatus are too often overlooked and too easily dismissed in a rush to criticize its order as reductive. The reading of the grid as an icon of reductivist order often preempts the reading of the grid as an agent of diversity and complexity. Seldom are its "weak" tendencies toward complexity and inclusion reconciled to the "strong," predictable and rigid order that is commonly associated with orthogonal grid geometry. But it is

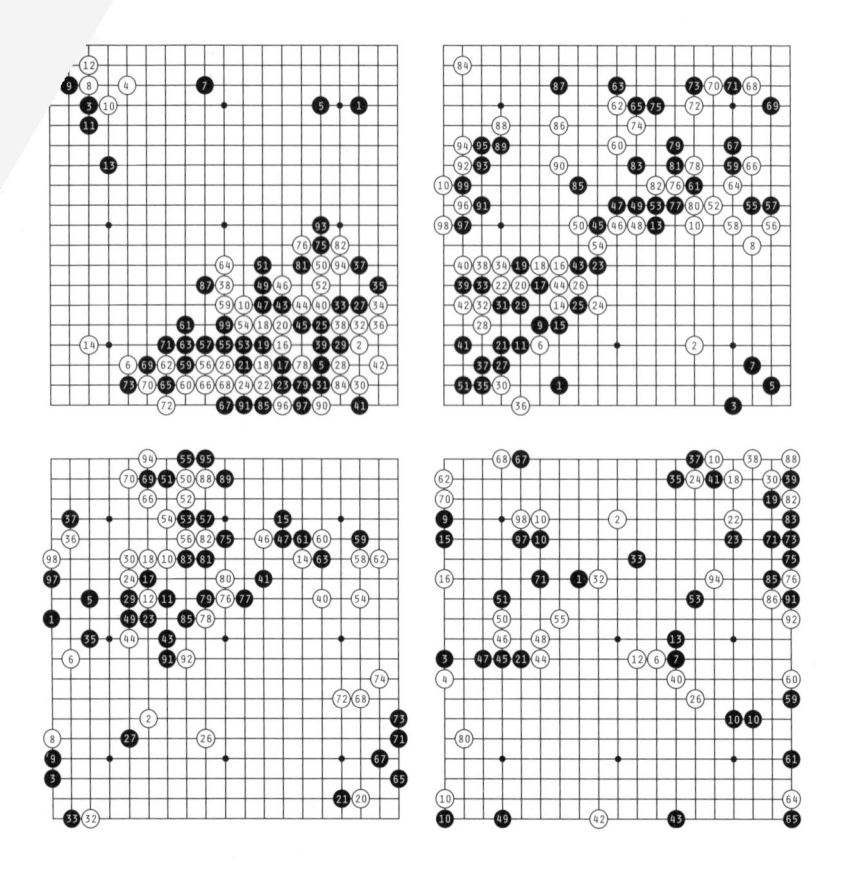

1.2 Longest recorded Go game, December 20, 1950, between Hoshino Toshi and Yanabe Toshiro, 411 moves. Sequence clockwise from upper left, 100 moves per frame.

20 LADDERS

precisely the area that lies between the heterogeneous and the prescriptive that accounts for the grid's unique power. The grid is not only predictable but indeterminate, not only prescriptive but ambiguous. It is capable of sustaining an order (urban or otherwise) that is simultaneously strong and weak.

Under the ceaseless pressures of "urban reform," 20th-century planners and designers rejected the apparently mindless deployment of the grid and eagerly promoted its disappearance. For the reformers, the grid was defined as the instrument of a reductive and banal form of social organization. The endless extension of gridiron plans suggested a brutal mechanization of urban production and the emergence of an anonymous and dehumanizing urban existence. Understood as the agent of these affects, the grid was discredited and its characteristic "weaknesses" and subtleties were subsequently ignored. The problem is that the strong reading of the reductive and mechanical quality of the grid is essentially correct. The grid can be leveling in its effect, it can be preemptive of even greater complexity, and it can and does break apart the continuities which sustain us. As such, the grid is always a threat to heterogeneity and to choice, and there is little wonder why urban reformers might wish to be rid of it. While such banal applications of the grid need to be rejected, its ability to support complex, heterogeneous environments must not be ignored. An urban environment that obtains a higher level complexity is invariably generated out of simple rudimentary forms. In the reformer's struggle against its reductive characteristics, the higher level complexity traditionally sponsored by the grid is often preempted.

Even the most cursory analysis of built urban form suggests that the link between the simplicity of the grid and complexity of the urban environment is beyond debate. If grids are the index of the most rudimentary level of urbanization, then their remarkable evolution throughout this century would figure as the key to its understanding.

CENTRIPETAL and CENTRIFUGAL GRID

The grid may be defined by the polarities of icon and apparatus, order and complexity, strong and weak, to the point of suggesting that it sustains two divergent organizational characteristics. There is another, perhaps more productive, pair of terms capable of defining its opposing qualities. Rosalind Krauss' reading of the grid's role in modern painting as both "centripetal" and "centrifugal" is unique in defining its characteristics with respect to larger spatial fields. She sets up the pair in the following way:

... *the grid is fully, even cheerfully, schizophrenic.... Logically speaking, the grid extends, in all directions, to infinity. Any boundaries imposed upon it by a given painting or sculpture can only be seen — according to this logic — as arbitrary. By virtue of the grid, the given work of art is presented as a mere fragment, a tiny piece arbitrarily cropped from an infinitely larger fabric. Thus the grid operates from the work of art outward, compelling our acknowledgment of a world beyond the frame. This is the centrifugal reading. The centripetal one works, naturally enough, from the outer limits of the aesthetic object inward. The grid is, in relation to this reading a re-presentation of everything that separates the work of art from the world, from ambient space and from other objects. The grid is an introjection of the boundaries of the world into the interior of the work....(Krauss, 1979, p.60)*

The centrifugal reading of the grid posits its infinite extension or continuity outward in all directions — the unlimited expansion of an inherently open system. The centrifugal grid form represents not so much a form in and of itself as it does the greater continuities to which it extends. Any centrifugal grid is, by definition, a fragment or synecdoche of an unbounded and unlimited field that can never be known in its entirety. It is the concrete configuration that gives access to a greater, unknowable whole. Far from the banal order with which it is often associated, the centrifugal grid, in Krauss' suggestive language, is the "staircase to the Universal"(p.52).

The centripetal grid manifests the opposing characteristics. It is by contrast a bounded figure. Its extent is known and limited. As opposed to the expansive or explosive character of the centrifugal grid, the force of the centripetal grid is contained and implosive. It is a closed, contracted system that introjects "the boundaries of the world into the interior of the work . . ." The representation of the centripetal grid is not synechdotal. Unlike the centrifugal grid, it does not represent space beyond itself. It is a discrete and thus emblematic form. In this way the centripetal grid resembles the icon of preemptive or "strong" order mentioned above.

What is most important in this centrifugal/centripetal distinction is that it takes into account the effects of each type of grid organization on the surrounding spatial field. As a discrete and closed figure, the centripetal grid is cut off from its context. This discontinuity between the grid and the spatial field creates a condition that does not exist in open, centrifugal organization. As an isolated fragment, the centripetal grid posits an outside to its own inside. The greater spatial field becomes not a site of immanent expansion, but an outside that is alien to its own interior. In an open, centrifugal organization the grid is merely the coordinates of everywhere and there is no such thing as an outside. Its vertices are single episodes amongst the uncountable indices of a universal space. This is not the same with closed, centripetal organization which, more important than its internal organization, produces a spatial context that is uniquely defined as residual. In centripetal grid organization, figure and field are polarized, and an "outside" is constructed.

This radical transformation of the surrounding spatial field, from being the coordinates of a universal continuum to becoming a residuum — the outside of a closed centripetal figure — constitutes a dramatic process of spatial inversion. Krauss uses the gridded space of Mondrian's paintings as an example, indicating that the slight gaps that often occur between the end of a grid-line and the edge of the canvas throw the whole spatial field into a violent reversal. This dramatic reversal of the spatial field is analogous to a specific type of urban transformation that shall be identified below as grid implosion.

THE HISTORICAL FLOW

It is necessary to reiterate that spatial distinctions can be linked to the status of the grid. The importance of Krauss' argument lies in the claim that the grid is a significant index of space. The possibility of extending this argument — to propose that the urban grid is a significant index of urban space — is compelling, and has already been undertaken in historical studies (Marcuse, 1987). The idea that continuous, centrifugal space is structured by a continuous grid and discontinuous, centripetal space is structured by a discontinuous grid is relatively straightforward. What makes the distinction important in contemporary analysis is that the two opposing spatial conditions simultaneously structure the present form of urban development. This dual structure breaks roughly around the time of the Second World War. The prewar city can be identified by its predominantly open centrifugal pattern of organization, and the postwar city can be identified by its predominantly closed centripetal pattern of organization. The following analysis of these opposing spatial conditions will focus, not only on these opposing grid forms, but on the remarkable mid-century grid transformation. The contemporary city is revealed in this transformation, when the open centrifugal space of the prewar city evolves into the closed centripetal form of postwar urban organization.

If the contemporary city is revealed at the moment of closure, the condition from which it emerges must be understood as relatively open and expansive. This challenges standard assumptions of 20th-century urban development where the order is exactly reversed. In the west, the prewar city is typically imagined as a closed and bounded fabric, out of which the contemporary postwar city emerged as an open matrix of space. This idea — the emergence of an inherently "open city" from a closed and obstructive urban fabric — supports the majority of historical surveys of modern urban form. In order to get beyond these ideas and to discover what they conceal with regard to the present urban formation, it is useful to propose an inversion of the sequence. An understanding of the prewar city as spatially open and centrifugal suggests that the 20th-century city evolved into a closed and exclusive urban form. In order to argue this, some significant ideological prejudices must be challenged. In effect, a defense of the 19th-century gridded city must be taken on as a defense of the open city.

Such a defense would be easier to make if the writing of 19th-century urban history had not been so ideologically driven. Considered only as the prelude of 20th-century urban reform, the 19th-century city has been routinely characterized as a closed, claustrophobic form requiring massive excision and reconstruction. The prevalent historical reading of the 20th-century city as emerging out of the depths of 19th-century industrial squalor is as convincing today as it was when it was first proposed nearly a hundred years ago. As an historical narrative, it was cast as a morality tale where the emerging urban masses were subjected to unspeakable conditions brought about by overcrowding into substandard dwellings and the lack of clean water and air. In *The Origins of Modern Planning*, Leonardo Benevolo quoted no less than six pages of Fredrick Engels' description of living conditions in the industrial city of Manchester. Engels' grisly first person account provided the ideological point of departure for Benevolo's survey of modern welfare state reforms (1971b). In a similar manner, Lewis Mumford fashioned a world out of Dickens' *Hardtimes*, summarizing 19th-century urban development in a single chapter of *The City in History* entitled "Coketown." ["Night spread over the

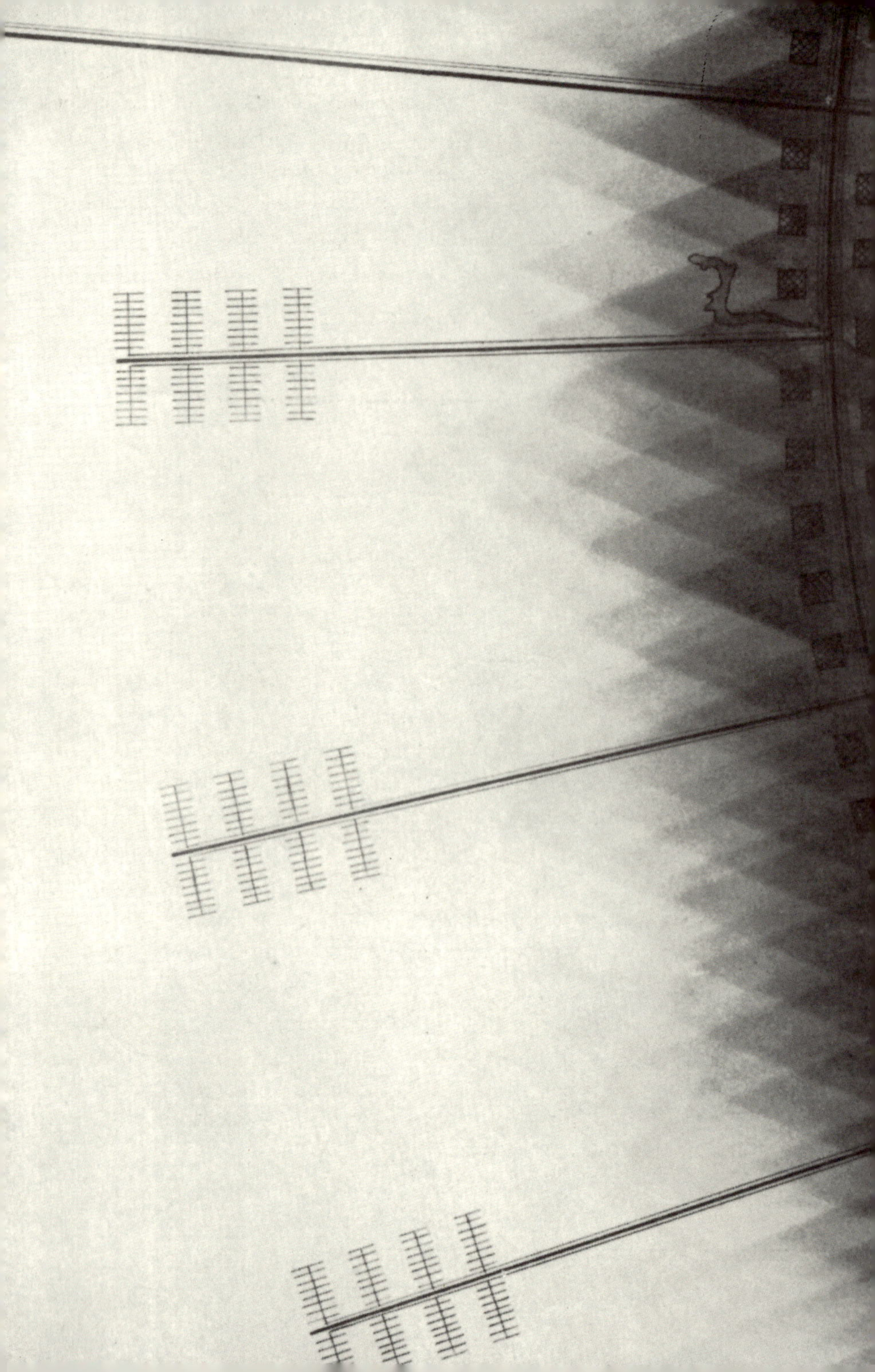

coal-town: its prevailing color was black. Black clouds of smoke rolled out or the factory chimneys, and the railroad yards" (Mumford, 1961, p.470).] Like many historians, Benevolo and Mumford sought to model the entirety of 19th-century urban development on the excesses of industrial slums such as Leeds, Manchester and Birmingham. With a few admitted exceptions, the 19th-century city was characterized as "a blasted, de-natured man-heap adapted, not to the needs of life, but to the mythic struggle for existence. . . . There was no room for planning in the layout of these towns. Chaos does not have to be planned"(Mumford, 1961, p.453). While such conditions did exist, it was an enormous distortion to suggest that they characterized the whole of 19th-century urbanization.

Mumford's prose is typical of the limited perspective of the industrial city as a condition of chaos, darkness and closure. As a student of New York, his historical omission of what must be the icon of 19th-century urban development — the 1811 Commissioner's Plan of New York — is striking given his characterization of the industrial city as so much claustrophobic "chaos." The prevalence of the open centrifugal grid in 19th-century planning was repeatedly suppressed in a blatant, ideological exercise in establishing the historical trajectory of 20th-century urban development. Assessing the general trend of postwar urban development, Ludwig Hilberseimer encapsulated what, in 1944, must have seemed like destiny. Evoking the ultimate authority of history he wrote: "Since the Gothic period, our spatial concepts have been moving steadily in the direction of greater freedom. We have become more and more concerned with widening and opening the city and merging it with open space. Today our spatial feeling tends to openness; so does our city structure. Different forces tend to dissipate the confinement of the city, to liberate the house, and with it, man"(1944, p.190). Ultimately, the arrival of the open

1.3 Ludwig Hilberseimer, The New City emerging from the "smoke shadow" of industrial production. Plan for Chicago, detail.
From: Hilberseimer, *The New City: Principles of Planning.*

of space was the deliverance of "man" from the 19th-century ɔ, finishing off a history over a century in the making.

ɪberseimer's historical narrative, similar to those of Mumford, Gideon, Pevɔner or Benevolo, was compelling fiction if for no other reason than subsequent urban transformations supported its conclusions. The postwar city seemed to offer concrete realization of historical prophecy — the emergence of an open city out of the wretched confinement of industrial exploitation. Following the war, evidence of the transformation was everywhere to be found. The replacement of monolithic masonry walls with transparent glass membranes, rigid patterns of impeded movement with the free-flow of the freeway and *autobahn*, dense urban fabric with dissipated spatial fields all brought the historical account to an irresistible happy ending. This narrative history continues to support the idea of contemporary urban development in spite of the fact that its value as prognostication has turned out to be virtually nil. Euphoria in the postwar victory of modern architecture — in the unprecedented openness of space and the dematerialization of built form — ideologically obscured the fact that that the city was, in fact, moving in exactly the opposite direction. Standing at the nexus of historical development, it was apparently impossible to see that as modern buildings and spaces began to open up, the city itself began to close down.

The widely shared misconception that modern urbanism was a direct extension of modern architecture, and vice versa, obscured the postwar emergence of closed urban development. There can be little doubt that the desired unity of "universal space" drove these misconceptions. In the heady Newtonian universe of early modernism, the macrocosm and the microcosm were to be unified into an urban *gesamtkunstwerk* — the city as a total work of art. Under such circumstances it was difficult to imagine that architecture and urbanism could operate under completely different sets of rules. There has, however, always existed an important tension or conflict between the logic of urban and architectural form. Gothic churches sit on Roman grids, Renaissance and Neo-classical architecture disrupt medieval fabric and all manner of stylistic production define the 19th-century boulevards of Paris or Vienna. In this regard, it is not difficult to argue that the conflict between architecture and urbanism was to be no more resolved in the 20th-century than it had been in the 19th. Inasmuch as the 19th-century city existed as a series of closed architectural forms in an essentially open centrifugal urban field, the 20th-century city simply inverts the relation. It will be shown how the closed polynuclear field of postwar urban development — corporate enclaves, office parks, gated subdivisions, shopping malls — is inversely related to the openness of modern architecture.

Karl Popper once suggested that historical determinism seeks to cloak the emergence of a closed society in the virtues of an open one. We apparently move toward transcendence oblivious to determinist narratives which strictly direct an opposing course. The historicist mythology of the 20th-century city runs deep and apparently dies hard. It is a measure of its persistence that contemporary urban designers and theorists continue to read the city as a series of vitalist "flows" — economic flows, informational flows, temporal flows, transportation flows, commodity flows. These readings remain rooted in the 19th-century fiction of an inevitable historical momentum moving toward ever greater degrees of openness and continuity. As those aware of urban form (as opposed to urban narrative) know, the organization of the postwar city is anything but open, inclusive, and flowing. The 19th-century city sustains a far greater degree of both physical and virtual flow than any form of urban organization that has succeeded it.

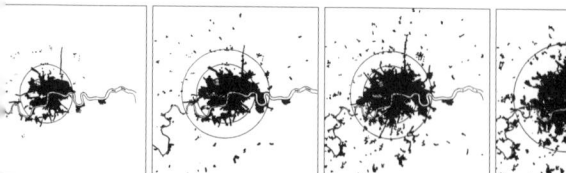

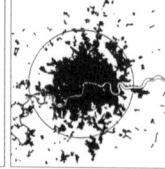

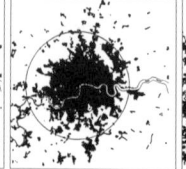

1.4 Park Avenue looking north from Grand Central Station, 1924.

1.5 Centrifugal growth of London, 1840 - 1929
From: Saarinen, *The City: Its Growth, Its Decay, Its Future.*

MANHATTAN, 1811

The long straight streets and avenues of a gridiron city do not permit the buildings to cluster like sheep and protect one against the sense of space. They are not sober little walks closed in between houses, but national highways. The moment you set foot on one of them, you understand that it has to go on . . . . — Jean Paul Sartre

The abstract properties of centrifugal grids translate directly into urban development. The street of an open, centrifugal city represents not an entity in and of itself but the greater spatial continuities to which it extends: the index of an infinite field that can never be wholly comprehended. This unbounded field — the coordinates of everywhere — cuts through and unites a sequence of scales connecting discrete urban artifacts to limitless space. Ultimately preempting local conditions (topography, pre-existent development, social, political, and economic boundaries), the open, urban grid achieves transcendence through ubiquity, becoming, as noted, "a staircase to the Universal."

A centrifugal "open" city appeared for only a brief moment in the history of urban development. In the 19th-century city, the qualities and characteristics of centrifugal organization dominated the formation of western cities. In celebrated examples, such as the Commissioner's Plan of New York, the by-law streets of London, and the Cerda extension of Barcelona, the open, centrifugal grid of the 19th-century city represented a fundamental urban transformation — an early and dramatic effect of the industrial reorganization of the city. As unprecedented economies of scale fueled an explosion of urban growth, every device of physical closure — the very idea of a closed urban system itself — was overwritten by subtle yet radical transformations of the urban grid.

The relations between social and political reorganization and 19th-century grid transformation have been analyzed by Peter Marcuse (1987). Marcuse recognizes three distinct urban grid formations, each characterized by a specific phase of capitalism. The "precapitalist city," the city of "*laissez-faire* capitalism," and the city of "mature capitalism" are stages in the development of western urbanization, each identified by subtle transformations in their respective grid formations. Marcuse argues that the "precapitalist grid" was essentially a closed grid. In his analysis, the closed grid dates backward to Miletus and forward to colonial cities in North America. Here, the closed grid is defined as a figure limited by city walls, fortifications, greenbelts, agricultural holdings, broad streets, topographic features — some sort of boundary either real or implied. The precapitalist city is interrupted by representational spaces and buildings, and their grids comprise a "complete and encompassing plan for a physically defined and bounded area."

Marcuse identifies the conversion of the precapitalist city into the *laissez-faire* city as manifest in a grid transformation largely registered in the explosion of urban space. He develops strictly economic arguments for his position. Coincident with the conversion of western economies from an agricultural to an industrial base, the urban grid broke its historical boundaries and became an unlimited field of economic expansion. Using Manhattan as the principal example, Marcuse defines the *laissez-faire* city as a response to demographic explosion, accelerated industrial production, and the rapid growth of open markets. The result was an autonomous, mechanical reproduction of the urban grid, theoretically without limit. The city was open and unbounded — directly analogous to a free market — and in this manner was always understood as ideological. The apparent agenda behind planning a simple rationalized block pattern was the "conversion of land to a commodity" where each block and parcel was standardized to expedite efficient trading. Without hindrance of successive planning procedures, a future city/market could simply be laid out in the form of an economic projection, with annexation and expansion a simple and inevitable outcome of increased productivity. In this way, the transformation of the economic, social, and political infrastructure was synonymous with the transformation of the grid. The urbanistic effect was registered in the profound explosion of the urban spatial field referred to above as open centrifugal extension.

Beyond the quantitative development of the 19th-century city, what was significant about its open centrifugal organization was the tendency to preempt traditional methods of planning. While the historically closed grids of the pre-industrial cities were often directly extended in the 19th-century, they were not intended as limited and discrete planned episodes. As they were grafted onto historical urban cores, the 19th-century grid extensions did not represent planned entities. Rather they represented the initiation of a system — a potentially interminable system — which theoretically preempted the need for future episodes of planning. If urban design had heretofore involved the planning of discrete urban districts or quarters, these new grid extensions were not simply new planning episodes, to be followed by the next. What followed was not another plan but, simply and inevitably, an extension of the system. In this manner, urban development was perceived as an autonomous process tied directly to the prospect of unlimited growth and forever preempting the possibility of economic or political closure.

If a specific example of this mode of production is needed, the Manhattan grid laid out in 1811 is exemplary. Following a series of relatively discrete gridded extensions of the original settlement (each grid skewed in a "patchwork" of disjointed urban districts), the massive gridded extension clearly marks the initiation of an entirely systematic mode of spatial production. Conceived in complete abstraction, it was imposed on the island irrespective

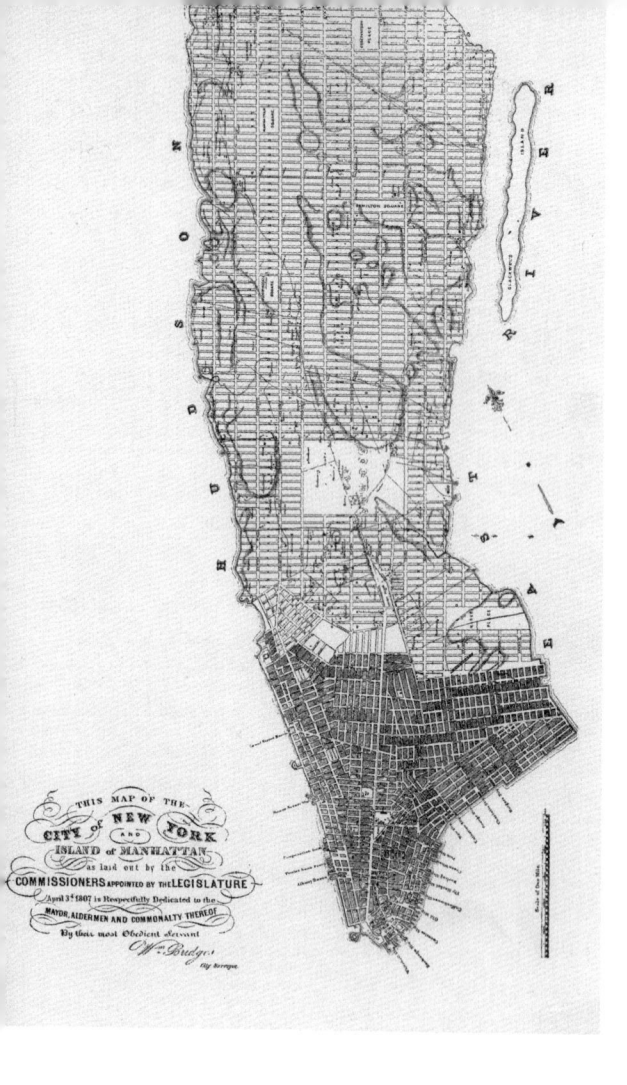

1.6 1811 Commisioner's Plan of Manhattan.

of existing topography, property lines, urban fabric, and population densities. As it was laid out, the grid extended to an area five times the size of the existing city, transforming 11,000 acres into 2,000 urban blocks. It stopped in Harlem, at the time a remote village, but that was apparently arbitrary. In its unrelenting logic, its indifference to incident, its elimination of all topological constraints and its ultimate abstraction, the Manhattan grid was a simple apparatus supporting unbounded centrifugal growth.

It is difficult to identify what still strikes us as "revolutionary" about the Commissioner's Plan (Koolhaas, 1978, p.14). Perhaps it is the size of the new grid relative to the existing city (the five-to-one ratio) suggested an overwhelming extent of growth — the forecast of an imminent demographic explosion. Or perhaps it is the sheer banality of mechanically reproducing urban fabric — the collapse of diversity and the strict univalence of the resulting system. Whatever the shock that continues to accompany its presentation, it is clear that, in this document, the city was reconceived as a process rather than a simple urban plan, and it is the difference between plan and process that ultimately defines the unique characteristic of centrifugal development. For in establishing something akin to an active urban "metabolism," the Commissioners situated urban reproduction beyond significant intervention. In the autonomy of its processes, as in the autonomy of the market economy to which it was tied, the unlimited growth of the city was assured.

Considered as an active urban process rather than a plan, the grid itself seemed to possess an independent existence. With the plan in place, it existed beyond interference, driven only by the ever-increasing speed of industrial capital. Francoise Choay defined this quality of 19th-century development as a form of critical detachment. "Following the loss of partial conscious control and of implicit subconscious control, those actually experiencing the urban phenomena came to consider it as something alien. They no longer felt inside the process of and determined by it; they remained outside, observing the transformation with the eye of the spectator"(Choay, 1969, p.9). According to Choay, the inhabitant saw the city as transformed by an "incidence of strangeness." This mode of critical detachment can be discerned in the observations of the British planner Patrick Abercrombie on a turn-of-the-century visit to the periphery of Berlin. He noted: ". . . as she grows, she does not straggle out with small roads and peddling suburban houses, but slowly pushes her wide town streets and colossal tenement blocks over the open country, turning it at one stroke into full-blown city" (Hall, 1988, p.33). What seemed to have struck Abercrombie was how the relatively rich historical episodes of urban growth and evolution were eliminated by a single stroke of mechanical urban reproduction — the inevitable outcome of some unstoppable urban engine.

Such was the stark "incidence of strangeness" of the gridded, universal continuum. Such immanent extension constituted more than a threat to the immediate hinterland. It suggested an unbounded, unlimited univalent field characteristic of centrifugal grid organization. Inevitably, such analogies to industrial growth fueled the euphoria of the 19th-century city as the prime locus of the centrifugal spatial field, and of an unbounded social, political and economic expansion. Such analogies would sow the seeds of reaction against the openness and strangeness it produced. The affinity between urban expansion and industrial production proved to be fatal as what seemed an inevitable and irreversible urban metabolism would, within the span of a century, be reversed.

AGORAPHOBIA

The transformation of the precapitalist city into the *laissez-faire* city is marked by a spatial mutation. Marcuse's use of the city grid as an index of this mutation is significant and may be extended into contemporary urban analysis. In that regard, the 19th-century grid does not support a restricted spatial field which subsequently "exploded" into the open city of the 20th-century. Rather, the grid is the index of an open spatial field which subsequently "imploded" into the closed spatial field characteristic of our cities today.

Regarding the evolution of the 19th-century city, Marcuse quoted Sam Bass Warner on the transformation of gridded space in Philadelphia. It is useful to quote Warner as a critique based explicitly on the dynamic of a grid transformation:

Philadelphia's grid descended directly from the 1682 plan of Penn and his surveyor. During the eighteenth century . . . Philadelphia's regular streets stood as America's leading example of a handsome and commodious town order. With the increase in the pace of city growth in the nineteenth century, however, other qualities of the street grid than its architectural effect came into prominence . . . falling in with the rest of the nation, Philadelphians extended their street grid indefinitely along their urban frontier. . . . The grid street, the narrow house lot, the row house, the interior alley, and the rear yard house or shack were endlessly repeated. When so repeated, however, they lost entirely their eighteenth century character and took on instead that mixture of dreariness and confusion which so characterized nineteenth century mass building. (Marcuse, 1987, p.292)

In Warner's account, the character of Philadelphia's 18th-century colonial grid was overrun by "endlessly repeated" mass construction, producing a radical transformation of the character of the city grid. Like many 19th-century extensions, the extension of Philadelphia appears similar if not identical to the form of the older pre-industrial grid. What is described by Warner is not a formal transformation, but a spatial transformation from the closed colonial

1.7 "By-law Streets," London.
From: Benevolo, *The Origins of Modern Town Planning.*

city to an open, infinitely extensive industrial city. Beyond the elimination of hierarchical axes, representational sites and public squares, what Warner determines to be the decline of urban character cannot be precisely identified, yet his reaction seems to be motivated by something like Choay's "incidence of strangeness." The banal, mechanical reproduction of the social fabric of cities along with their subsequent semantic impoverishment are finally subsumed in the sudden and dramatic lack of discrete spatial closure.

The inversion of the spatial field — from a closed discrete plan to an open and indefinite autonomous process — reveals a common anxiety in the face of 19th-century urban development. All of the "dreariness and confusion" of the new urban landscape of Philadelphia, New York, Berlin or London seems to be the result of a sudden overexposure to a new type of universal urban space. As the explosion of the urban spatial field overwhelmed the relatively modest scale of pre-industrial closure, various turn-of-the-century reform movements were able to mount successful critiques against these new spatial qualities. Because the fabric of many cities in the United States was predominantly of 19th-century origin, it was more often the immense scale and excessive openness that provoked the critics. In these newer cities, the deleterious effect of industrialization was not the grotesque overpopulation of medieval urban cores which "Haussmanization" was intended to open up. While the European critique of the industrial city focused on the overcrowding, disease and squalor of an industrialized medieval fabric, the American critique tended to focus on the banal and dehumanizing form of universal urban space.

The critique of 19th-century urban space was typically made in tandem with an assault on its economic practices. It invariably resulted in a vilification of the 19th-century "speculative grid" as boring, monotonous, rigid, uniform, provincial, inefficient, unfocused, lacking occasion, event or representational opportunity, indifferent to topography, historical preconditions, variety and diversity. For Frederick Law Olmsted, the grid was simply the "epitome of evil commercialism"(Pluntz, 1990, p.303). From the advocates of the Garden City to the mid-20th-century cult of "townscape," the critique of the 19th-century gridiron invariably referred to the excesses of unbridled capitalist development, all assessed from the overt ideological position of an emerging welfare state.

In response to these arguments, one could speculate that the economic and political practices which brought the open centrifugal city into existence were far more acceptable than its revolutionary spatial characteristics. The homogenous uniformity of open centrifugal development — the unlimited, all-encompassing spatial field that it implied — suggested the existence of a singular, ubiquitous continuum. The absence of an exception or escape from this continuum was as oppressive as the mechanical reproduction of its countless urban blocks. It may be that the social will to universal space never existed in the 19th-century, despite its inscription in urban form. For this reason alone, the viability of centrifugal development would have been limited. Yet the unrestrained attack on the 19th-century city seemed to stem from something more immediate than contemporary political or economic practices. The retreat from the open city of the 19th-century was, as it remains today, a visceral affair. Past all the rhetoric of political and economic excesses and subsequent welfare state reform, it was a reaction to the vast openness and uniformity of space which signaled the end of the open city.

Proof of such a sweeping generalization is ultimately found in the antidotes proposed by the turn-of-the-century reform movements. The Medievalists, the 19th-century social utopians, the advocates of the Garden City, the City Beautiful, and the followers of Patrick Geddes simultaneously rose in protest against the 19th-century city. While each forged different historical perspectives and targeted their own specific points of criticism, they all eventually merged in a common attack on the 19th-century urban development. Whether in the form of closed monumental axes, picturesque planning techniques, imposed population limits, superblock and *cul-de sac* development, the revival of medieval typologies, or complete civic secession, each "remedy" aimed at some form of truncation or closure to the universal spatial field. It was a phobia of space inherent in these turn-of-the-century reforms that laid the groundwork for the modern "implosion" of urban form and the postwar emergence of closed urban development.

QUEENS, 1908

The 19th-century gridiron is perhaps the ultimate diagram of the open city, and it remained the driving force of urban development well into the 20th-century. The description of its demise is the description of the emergence of contemporary urban form. The implosion of the open centrifugal grid and the emergence of a closed centripetal urban organization mark the decisive juncture in the development of contemporary urbanism.

Returning to New York City, the grid laid out in 1811 would not last a century before its seemingly inevitable inertia began to show symptoms of decline and reversal. In the intervening century, the grid was filled and expanded to the adjacent boroughs, exceeding even the bold expectations of the commissioners. In 1908, at the same time Patrick Abercrombie was making his observations of Berlin, Frederick Law Olmsted, Jr. challenged the open centrifugal development of the city with a radical reorganization of a 33-block tract in Queens. Begun as a philanthropic enterprise based on the English Garden City, Forest Hills Garden was described in its prospectus as the antidote for "bare streets" without proximity to natural settings, playgrounds and recreational facilities. In a statement from its sponsor, the Russell Sage Foundation, "the constant repetition of rectangular blocks in suburban localities" was "abhorred," and an alternative model of urban development was sought in the Olmsted plan (Plunz, 1990. p.118).

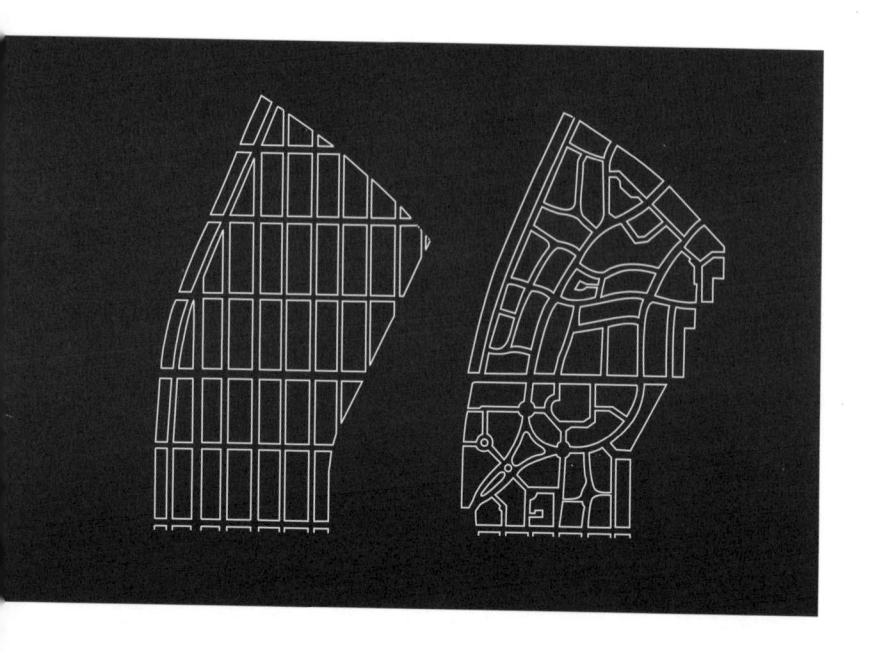

1.8 Frederick Law Olmsted, Jr. and Grosvenor Atterbury, Forest Hills Garden street layout (right) compared with the New York City gridiron as initially planned for the area (left).

Anticipating a trend that would soon overtake centrifugal produc[tion and] radically alter the metropolitan region, Olmsted reconfigured the p[rior] gridiron of Queens by eliminating all but one of the site's fifteen through-streets. In its place, he designed a hierarchical plan with a primary entry gate (a medieval "Station Square") and axis leading to a center planned as a "flag-pole green." Closed off from the surrounding metropolis, this Garden City has been recognized as the first major transgression against in the gridiron of New York. As a gap or lacuna in the continuity of the fabric, it marked an implosion of the grid which radically reinterpreted the entirety of its surrounding as an *external* condition. In an attempt to fashion an alternative to the universal spatial continuum of the 19th-century city, Forest Hills Garden established the open centrifugal grid as outside its borders, the initial step in a planned disappearance of the city. In opposition to the singular continuum of the centrifugal city, Olmsted instigated what would soon become a binary or polynuclear field of isolated urban nuclei fashioned in opposition to an increasingly hostile metropolitan residuum. It would be only a half century before this process of (centripetal) urban development would culminate with the production of the ultimate urban "exterior" — the imperiled "inner city."

Concerning the project, Olmsted wrote: ". . . the monotony of endless, straight, windswept thoroughfares which represent the New York conception of streets will give place to short, quiet, self contained and garden like neighborhoods, each having its own distinctive character" (Plunz, 1990, p.118). The nascent urban dynamic could not be more clear. The trajectory of development from open to closed city was set into motion as the first major challenge to the inertia of the 1811 plan. The centripetal implosion of Forest Hills interjected the "boundaries of the world" into the interior of the city. In a strange way, Olmsted's intervention is an inversion of the "Haussmanization" of the pre-industrial, medieval cores of European cities. Rather than open systems

CRITICAL! SN FC!

being superimposed onto closed ones, Forest Hills superimposed a closed system onto an open universal matrix of space.

It is well established that turn-of-the-century reform movements, especially the planning strategies of the Garden City, established precedents for the Modern City. What is not so well established is that their legacy is one of closure being translated directly into contemporary urban form. This contradicts the conventional understanding of urban evolution as the progressive opening up of 20th-century city. In effect, the 19th-century city was already wide open, so much so that the majority of 20th-century urban reform was directed specifically against the open city.

CENTRIPETAL VERSUS CLOSED CITY

To suggest that such a modest intervention as Forest Hills Garden would transform the mode of urban spatial production may seem bizarre. It implies that such interventions were formidable enough to challenge the combined social, political and economic forces of centrifugal urban development. What single idea could be imagined as powerful enough to stop the engine of 19th-century urban reproduction, to thwart its apparent inevitability? The intention of Forest Hills Garden to position the vast extent of the city as "outside" its Medieval gate seems to be ludicrous in hindsight. But the sudden transformation of the great metropolitan continuities into the field of ghettoes now identified as the inner city has occurred and does suggest a force of such dimension at work. The question remains whether the idea of Forest Hills Garden, and similar episodes of centripetal planning, have something to reveal concerning the nature of these forces.

It has already been suggested that the power of this intervention came from a reversal or inversion of the urban spatial field. As defined above, the closed centripetal grid is a literal inversion of the continuities of centrifugal development. Contained and closed within the boundaries of a prescribed spatial field, the centripetal grid establishes an exclusive, emblematic order. In centripetal development, all continuities are blocked into a distinct figure representing nothing if not the limits (and the power) of closure against an unknowable expanse. This closure produces a significant urban exterior by the imposition of a boundary condition. Such an outside is alien to centrifugal urban development which, as a universal continuum, cannot establish a condition external to itself.

It is important to note that the Centripetal City is not entirely synonymous with the closed pre-industrial city described by Marcuse and others. Before the 20th-century, clear instances of actual centripetal urban development were rare. What may seem to be examples of closed centripetal organizations, such as walled towns, actually appear as closed and bounded grids, capable of constructing discrete figures and significant outsides. Yet one can see that, over time, fortified walls, tax barriers, or agricultural allotments were frequently torn down and rebuilt or simply built over by subsequent, often fast-paced, urban development. The strongest fortified walls have never been able to stop an intrinsically expansive urban growth. What is most important is not the momentary conditions of closure, but the processes of urban expansion itself. The traditional boundaries of cities were built and rebuilt in such rapid succession that, in retrospect, the continual re-engineering of urban fortifications seems an astonishing feat. And while certainly distinct from the character and speed of 19th-century expansion, this traditional pattern of growth is unlike the fixed limits of closed centripetal expansion.

What may be the historical exceptions to this rule are the radical or unplanned transformations of urban form generally resulting from catastrophic events and massive demographic displacements. Such dislocations,

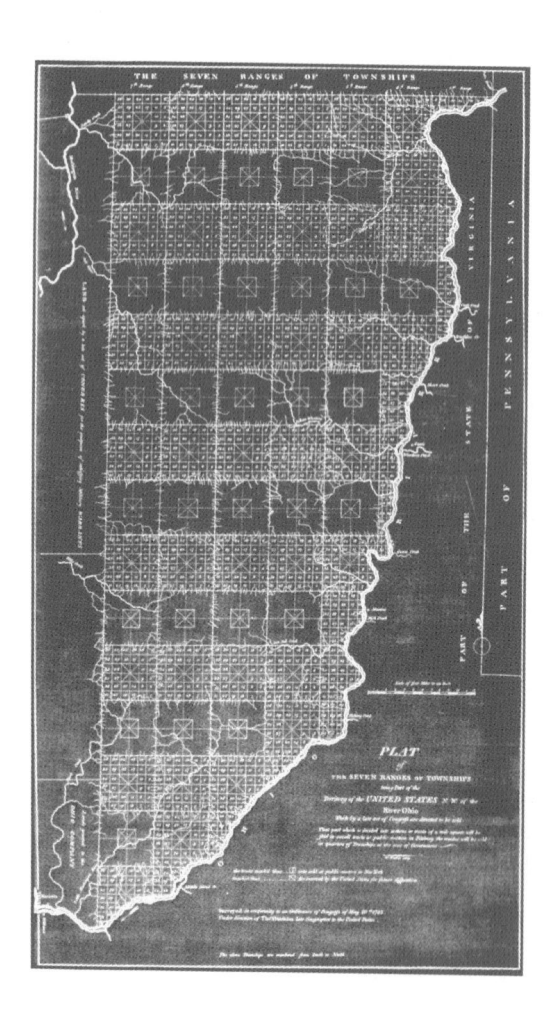

1.9 "The Seven Ranges of Townships," surveyed in Ohio, 1796.
From: Reps, *The Making of Urban America*.

caused by natural and man-made disasters, demonstrate a rapid transition from a centrifugal to a centripetal urban order — a process subsequently described as urban implosion. A city which undergoes a dramatic loss in population, such as medieval Rome or postwar Berlin, are historical examples of catastrophic implosion.

Historical developments based on a centripetal order are rarely found in cities at all, but in analogous urban constructions such as palaces, prisons, schools, monasteries, asylums and forts. In these instances, the grid organization is not an expansive apparatus of urban development — an inherently generative system — but derives from another agenda altogether. It is not a coincidence that these examples of centripetal development are emblematic of imposed order, often an authoritarian organization indicative of a closed, militaristic or bureaucratic system. Historically, these grids of confinement are exceptions to the rule of centrifugal development. Actual cities were rarely conceived in this way and, despite substantial degrees of closure, were by necessity thought of not as terminal or pathological conditions, but as essentially open systems.

339th AVENUE

The distinction between closed and open grids depends on a specific reading of urban form and space. What is important in this distinction is the reading of the urban spatial field that each grid generates. While the form of the centrifugal and centripetal grids often coincide, their respective spatial fields are invariably opposed. When considered as the effect of formal density, the 19th-century city is actually congested and closed, while the 20th-century city is relatively dispersed and open. When considered as the effect of the urban spatial field, however, the open continuities of centrifugal grid expansion conflict

1.10 "Speculative row houses on West 133rd Street," New York, 1882.
From: Silver, *Lost New York*.

field, however, the open continuities of centrifugal grid expansion conflict with the spatial boundaries or residuum of centripetal grid closure.

The difference between, for example, an office building located in a gated suburban office park and another identical office building located on the busy street of a central business district is not a difference in architectural form, but a difference in the surrounding spatial field. The distinction in character between the two identical buildings is in the perception of the surrounding space — the suburban office park being a closed field which creates an excluded exterior, and the central business district being an open field which is infinitely extensible and linked to the world. Whether approaching the building by car or on foot, moving through its core, or sitting at a desk by a window, one confronts the dramatic distinctions between spatial containment and spatial continuity. The characteristics of these fields have a determining influence on what would otherwise be identical programs and identical architectures.

So significant is the urban spatial field that any discussion of architecture is irrelevant before its terms are established. This is another way of saying that architecture has been absorbed, if not outright precluded, by the spatial field of the contemporary urban metropolis. While such conclusions are debatable, the discussion of the urban spatial field is usually ignored, lost somewhere between discussions of architectural and urban form. Although the subject of urban space is often addressed and addressed well, it is usually confined either to the architectural scale of "place-making" strategies or to the planning scale of regional dispersions. The absence of precise spatial analysis at a scale between the plaza and the region reflects the old urban/rural and architecture/planning division of academic labor. This division produces an artificial separation between city and landscape that is nowhere more pronounced than in the failure to account for the expanded spatial field of the 19th-cen-

1.11 *New Mexico, 1957.*
Photograph by Garry Winogrand.

50 LADDERS

than in the failure to account for the expanded spatial field of the 19th-century city.

This field assumed shape, literally, in the United States, with the continental gridding of the Land Ordinance Act of 1785, also known as the Jeffersonian Grid (Reps, 1965, p.219). Anticipating the explosion of the American industrial city, the Ordinance ruled the surveying and allotment of all land from the western boundary of Pennsylvania to the Pacific coast. The mechanical deployment of the surveyor's grid indicated not only a democratic allotment, but also the national manifest destiny, literally inscribed in the configuration of the landscape. Starting at the unit of measurement of five "chains," or 330 feet (approximately the size of a single city block), the Ordinance established the graduated gridding of the continent, specifying boundaries from the scale of township schools up to the borders of adjacent states and nations. In many cases, the surveyor's grid became the actual framework for the specific platting of cities (Rowe, 1991, p.27). It is this continuity between the urban and the continental scale established by the Ordinance that accounts for the expansive spatial field of American gridiron development. The pre-industrial boundary between city and "country" was finally eradicated in the 19th century as urban space merged with larger fields of national and international space. Buildings and sidewalks, rural roads and agricultural fields became the arbitrary, circumstantial coordinates of a singular, universal spatial continuum.

As may now be imagined, the unbounded centrifugal explosion of the 19th-century gridiron plans seemed to constitute more than just an imminent occupation of its immediate natural surrounding. The real utopia of its production was to liberate the city from the oppression of local conditions and to establish, even in the most mundane environments, the "coordinates of everywhere." As the spatial field expanded past all previous boundaries, the

American city could not help but project an affinity with the geographic scale of the continent that was ultimately drawn to it.

Driving west out of Phoenix on Interstate 10 toward Los Angeles, nearly ten miles past any signs of inhabitation, you unexpectedly come across an exit for 339th Avenue. The exit is marked by a standard green interstate sign indicating a narrow, paved right-of-way which quickly recedes to the horizon and vanishes. It is an arrogant claim on the open desert, staked out in defiance of all probability, waiting for the inevitable expansion of the city to catch up. One may smile at a city's ambition, the arrogance of the kind of planning that would imagine such a fantastic extent of growth. But on reflection, it is certain that this sign is nothing but an outmoded bureaucratic reflex, an anachronism which sprang out of another set of possibilities, and a way of imagining the city which is now forty years extinct. For in Phoenix, as in every other American city or town, the idea of an open city — the city as part of a vast unity which is the world — is defunct.

The continuities of space moving through the original gridiron of Phoenix and connecting it to the expanse of the desert frontier have been lost to the urban imagination. The grid has long since imploded, its continuity preempted by a myriad of closed corporate subdivisions now ringing its original centrifugal growth. In 1995, Phoenix was ranked among the five fastest growing urban regions in the United States, pushing out into the desert at the fantastic rate of one acre per hour. Yet this expansion is being made not toward, but altogether in spite of the desert horizon. Now on the "outside," 339th Avenue has been cut off by a sea change in urban thought — out of fear, distraction, laziness, greed or an intolerance of exposure. It is a phantom urban block, occupying the desert as a monument to another set of possibilities — to a time when those continuities were so obvious, so inevitable, as to generate out of a small desert town no less than 339 streets.

URBAN TRANSITION

The city which underlies our present urban imagination is the open centrifugal city. Urban environments which are routinely represented in films, magazines, television, books, newspapers, travel brochures, documentaries, political speeches and academic essays reflect an open system, a continuous field, an unbounded urban world. It is a field of dramatic action where nothing is preempted, where anything can happen. The latent possibilities represented by the open city support the necessary aspirations of a "free society" which cannot tolerate an absolute and complete closure of political, economic, or social form. Yet, it is clear that the city of our imagination is absurdly out of synch with the city of contemporary construction. We live out our social and political fantasies on the remnants of a 19th-century stage. The gridded space which we actually produce is not an open vitalist field connected to the world; it is not centrifugal. It is rather the abbreviated, closed, enclave of centripetal organization. The contemporary world is imploded, leaving behind nothing more than spurious representations of otherwise indispensable continuities.

For the purposes of this investigation, the centripetal urban grid will be referred to as a grid in the process of turning into something else, an index of the city that is in the process of turning into something else. This other urban form will be referred to as a ladder. As a unique urban structure, the ladder has emerged as the fundamental armature of postwar redevelopment and reconstruction. It is literally an invention of reconstruction — the centripetal reconstruction of the postwar city. Yet the real evidence of this urban order is not the visible mark of urban form, but the emergence, almost as a by-product, of a unique type of contemporary urban space.

TWO:
URBAN IMPLOSION

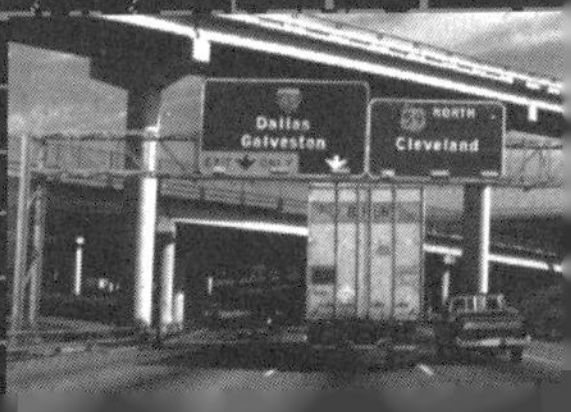
Dallas
Galveston
NORTH
Cleveland

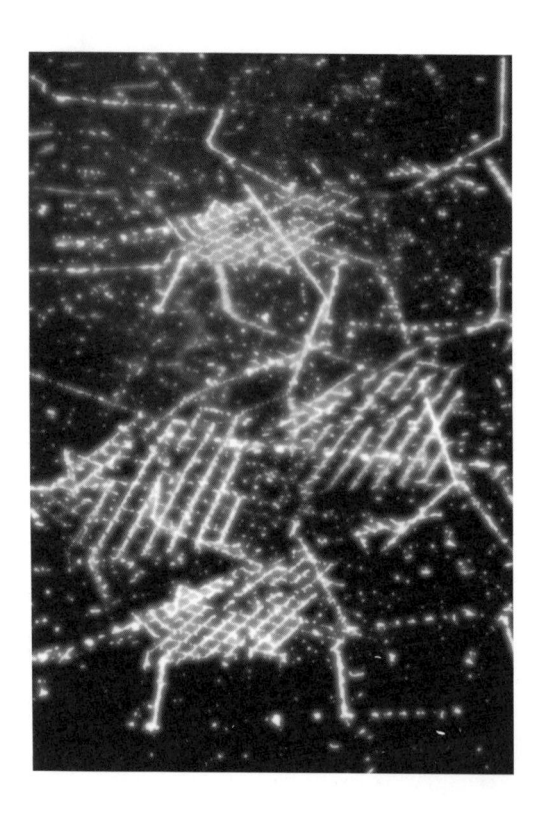

2.1 Minneapolis - St. Paul, Minnesota. Aerial view at night.

URBAN IMPLOSION

An alternative trajectory of urban evolution has been posited. This trajectory attempts to reverse the historicist suggestion that the city is evolving in ever greater degrees of openness and freedom. A rudimentary spatial analysis tied to the transformation of the urban grid indicates that the city is not opening up, but is, in fact, closing down. The sources of contemporary urban closure will be identified and described in this chapter.

Initiated at the turn of the century by the Garden City movement, strategies of closure were subsequently adopted and advanced by modern architects and urbanists working in the 1920s and 1930s. There is an historical succession of schemes moving in greater degrees of closure from the Garden City, to the Modern City, directly to the built reality of postwar urban construction. Contrary to the routine association of modernism with emphatic spatial continuities, the majority of modernist proposals inverted and closed the 19th-century urban spatial field. The most consistent and didactic body of work on modern urban closure comes from the German theorist, Ludwig Hilberseimer. Hilberseimer's projects provide a focus, both in the production of new urban settlements as well as the replanning of existing gridiron constructions. They also provide an important guide to the processes of postwar spatial production, specifically spatial "implosion."

GRID EROSION

The postwar transition from an open centrifugal to a closed centripetal organization — what has been referred to as a spatial implosion — was foreshadowed in the turn-of-the-century renovations of the urban grid. It may be overly simplistic to suggest that an erosion of urban form produces a corresponding implosion of urban space. While the relation of form to space is often quite direct, grid erosion will be used to here designate a more subtle and precise operation. Grid erosion does not result in the immediate liquidation of form into space, but a powerful and indeterminate ambiguity between form and space.

Contemporary urban evolution suggests that the disappearance of the grid coincides with the disappearance of the city, yet it is apparent that this disappearance is never really complete. In the contemporary city, just enough of the grid remains to sustain conventional urban associations. There is a grid, yet there is no grid, just as there is a city at the same time there is no city, but rather a form of spatial organization that only resembles a conventional urban environment. Any map of postwar urban development will indicate that grid erosion is no theoretical abstraction. In practically any contemporary street layout, whether a *cul-de-sac* housing tract, a peripheral slab city, a gutted, skywalked CBD or an upscale suburban office park, the traditional open urban grid is there, and it is not. The grid exists in fragmentary form as the remnant of a recognizable urban order. These eroded fragments establish, not traditional urban associations, but oblique suggestions, subtle omissions, minor exclusions, and incompletion. They produce a city of insidious presence/absence, as obscure in form and identity as the unaltered grid is the very matrix of clarity.

If grid erosion can be characterized as the subtle distortion of urban convention, its effects are far from subtle. The contemporary city sustains "amenities" with enough conventional urban associations to sustain civic illusions, yet not enough for these illusions to be effective in reconstructing a conventional urban existence. If the historical city is a necessary social construct, its erosion is not simply a formal transformation, but a lapse in indispensable social relations. It is interesting to consider the significance of a city constructed over many years, but with only a partial development or subtle repudiations of the urban known. Lacking the substance of known forms, such a city would fail to engender an adequate identity of its own. Like a dream from which one is unable to wake, the inhabitants would struggle with archaic memories of civic monuments, public parks, and pedestrian streets, never knowing why they fail to account for the new and unknown world that establishes their lives. Given such a premise, the city could vanish and no one would even notice.

If it is true that as the grid disappears, so does the city, then there must be a moment in which the city, as it is historically understood, ceases to be. This moment is the point at which the space of the city implodes, which is the point at which the grid transforms into a ladder. While there is no simple criteria against which to check the movement from grid to ladder, centrifugal to centripetal, open to closed, it is possible to isolate a threshold beyond which only so much of the grid remains to sustain conventional urban associations. In the process of erosion, grid and ladder exist simultaneously. Yet, for all intents and purposes, the grid has been transformed into another form of development structured by centripetal organization. The meaning of open centrifugal development is extended to the very threshold of its complete transformation.

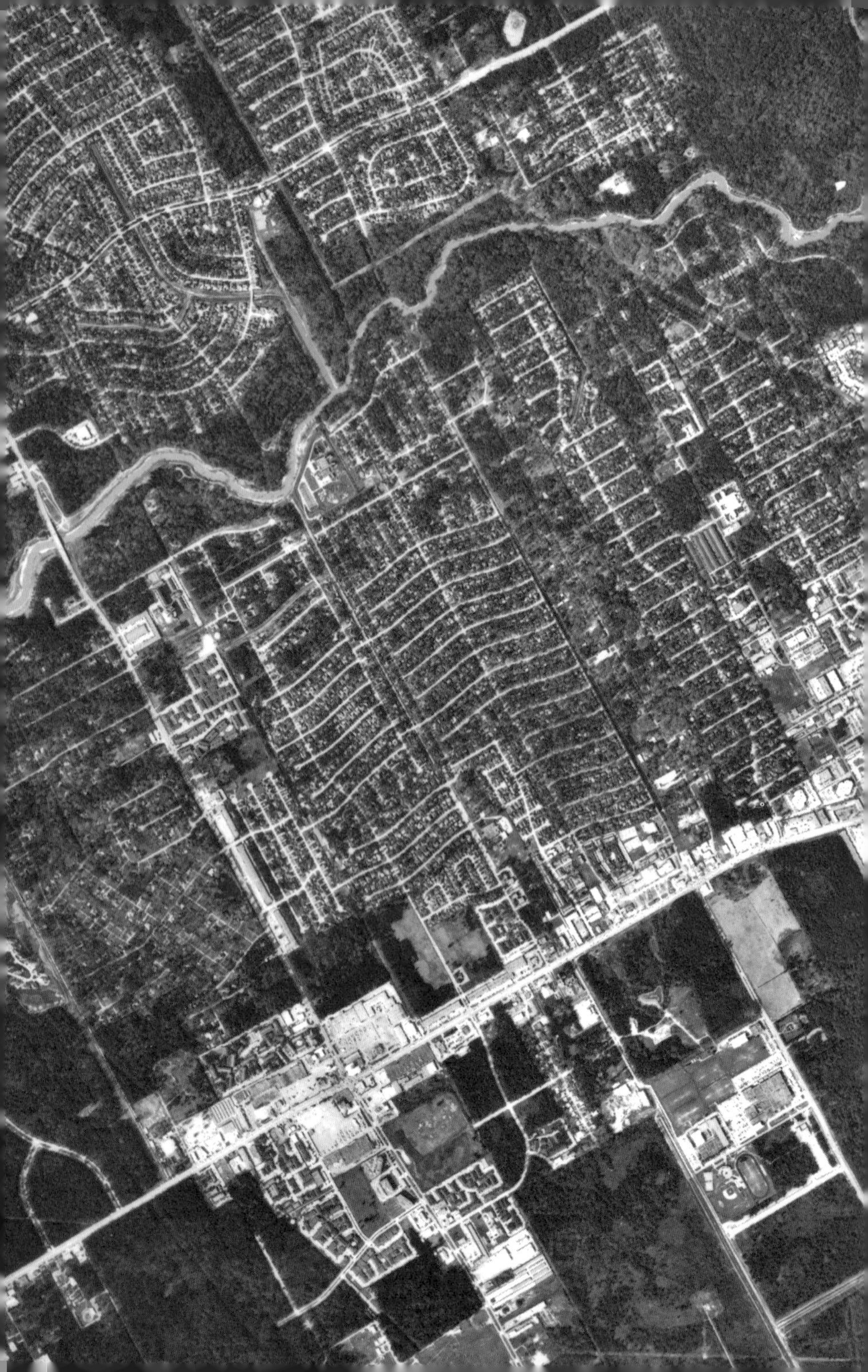

THE LADDER

The erosion of traditional urban form is linked to the implosion of urban space. As space displaces larger and larger sections of the open centrifugal grid, the universal continuum of the 19th-century city collapses, and the qualities and characteristics of the contemporary city begin to emerge. To understand this spatial displacement, it is necessary to adopt an oblique strategy, to investigate not the space itself but the increasingly fragmented grid which is the residue of its production. This residue is associated with the emblematic figure of the ladder, the remainder of a partially eroded grid. As a finite grid fragment, cut off from its surrounding spatial field, the ladder manifests the characteristics of closed centripetal organization

The distinction between an open, centrifugal and a closed, centripetal organization is established by their respective spatial fields. The simple isolation of a grid fragment from the extensive field of centrifugal development produces a radical transformation of urban structure. As erosion interrupts the continuities of the urban grid, an exterior condition or spatial residuum is produced. While the resulting form of the isolated ladder is grid-like, its characteristics as urban infrastructure are completely transformed. In the ladder, vestiges of traditional urban form survive, yet its spatial qualities are antithetical to those of open centrifugal urbanism.

The effect of these antithetical qualities becomes apparent when the ladder is compared to a continuous grid. When overlaid, the characteristics of the two forms of organization are indistinguishable. At first glance, the ladder appears to be nothing more than a simple fragment of the grid, a single spacing or fringe element extracted from its continuous pattern. A comparison, for

2.2 Subdivision and Strip, Farm to Market Road 1960, Houston Texas.

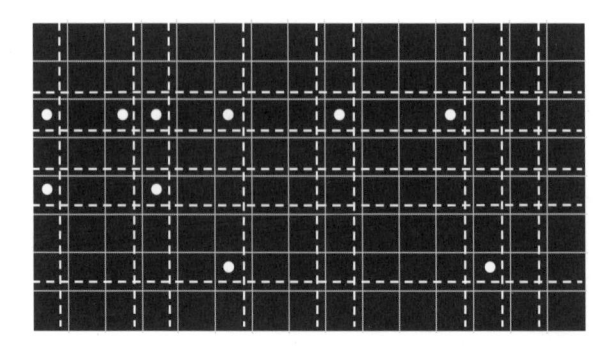

diagram 2.1
Ten Grid Points

Among a group of ten points on an open grid, several different routes can be shown to interconnect each point. The number and sequence of the gridpoints visited can be adjusted to a variety of itineraries, responding to any number of plans, often at cross-purposes. On the open grid, the number of available options multiplies. Grids function as non-hierarchical networks open to diverse response and are capable of structuring complex associations. The open patterns of movement generated by the grid demonstrate these qualities.

example, between the single street of a grid and the principal axis of a la reveals that the two patterns coincide. This coincidence dissolves, however, when placed in the context of the larger spatial field. Far from duplicating the qualities of the centrifugal grid, the ladder seems to constitute an inversion of its properties. In contrast with the infinite continuity of the open grid, the ladder is a finite, indivisible, hierarchical structure. As a closed isolated fragment, it lacks the potential for integration into an extensive urban field. In contrast to the grid, the ladder forms a singular and exclusive route/root system that generates a fundamentally closed pattern of organization. Measured against the continuous spatial field — an infinitely vast reservoir of potential integration — the singularity of a ladder constitutes a closed system.

A simple tracing over the two types of organization will clarify the difference. Among a group of ten points on an open grid, several different routes can be shown to potentially interconnect each point. The number and sequence of the grid-points visited can be adjusted to a variety of itineraries, responding to any number of plans, often at cross-purposes. On the open grid, the number of available options multiplies. Grids function as non-hierarchical networks open to diverse response and capable of structuring complex associations. The open patterns of movement, or flows, generated by the grid demonstrate these qualities.

These open patterns become more apparent when seen in contrast to the exact same configuration of ten points arrayed on a ladder structure. Among an equal number and spacing of ladder-points, only one route exists which interconnects these points — one itinerary, one plan, and the virtual suppression of cross-purpose. At its most fundamental level the ladder is an exclusive system and, inasmuch as it eliminates greater continuities, a closed system. In comparison to the multiple interconnections generated by the grid, the ladder is the agent of a mechanical unity, of division, classification, and prescribed

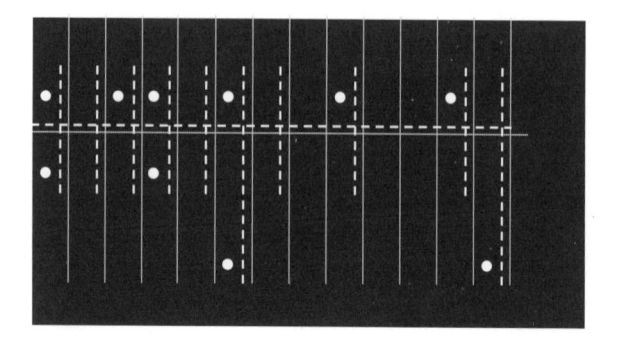

diagram 2.2
Ten Ladder Points

Among a group of ten points on a ladder, only one route exists which interconnects them — one itinerary, one plan, and the virtual suppression of cross-purpose. At its most fundamental level the ladder is an exclusive system and, inasmuch as it eliminates options, a closed system. In comparison to the multiple interconnections generated by the grid, the ladder is the agent of a mechanical unity: of division, classification, and prescribed response. While seeming to share a basic morphology, the ladder and the grid generate opposing patterns of order.

response. While seeming to share a basic morphology, the ladder and the grid generate opposing patterns of order.

It is difficult to account for this radical divergence in what appear to be coincident ordering systems. How can the simple extraction of a grid fragment from a continuous spatial field draw out latent hierarchies, eliminate choice, imply boundaries and ultimately generate a closed system? And how can it stage such a dramatic reversal with such subtle changes in form? The collapse of the continuous field constitutes a contextual reorganization, the effect of which is primarily spatial. The reversal of the centrifugal spatial field amounts to what Krauss identified as the "introjection of boundaries" into the interior of the city. These new boundaries, the product of spatial implosion, are of vital importance to any analysis of contemporary urban development. They constitute an unprecedented and unique type of urban space.

LINEAR CITIES

The closed centripetal organization of the ladder appears to be a reductive, if not regressive, urban morphology. In that regard it may be surprising to find its prefiguration in the organizational strategies of modern architecture and urbanism. Although buildings organized around circulation spines and so-called "linear cities" existed before the 20th-century, so numerous are the examples, and so susceptible are they to machine-age metaphors (transportation flow, assembly-line production, functional distribution), that they often appear as strictly modernist propositions.

Long important to contemporary urban theorists, the linear city occupies a significant position in the development of the Modern City. The enormous number of variations produced in the 1920s and 1930s comprises one of the most remarkable and inventive moments in urban history. Beginning in 1882

with the Spanish theorist Arturo Soria y Matta, the linear city was conceived as a unique variant of a Garden City built along a tree-lined, residential boulevard, with rail and roadway forming a dominant central armature. In the 1920s and 1930s, Soria y Matta's linear city emerged as an alternative to the English Garden City which had taken the form of autonomous new towns arranged concentricly around existing urban cores (Collins, 1959b). While Garden Cities focused on limited-size simulations of provincial towns, the linear city was conceived as an open-ended, limitless extension of the metropolis. Responding to the imperatives of urban transportation, the linear city attempted to translate an active urban process rather than adopt the traditional, hierarchical morphologies promoted by the Garden City. Machine-age programs and processes projected into a metropolitan infrastructure would replace the centralized hierarchical typologies common to both 19th and 20th-century urban models.

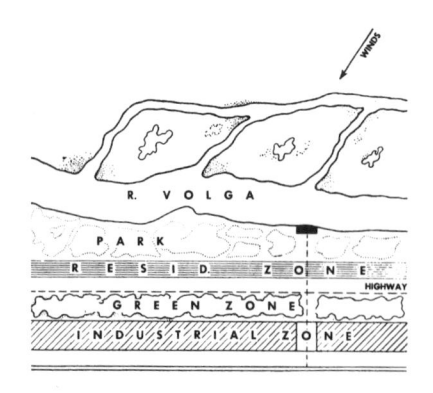

2.3 N.A. Milutin, Proposal for a Linear City on the Volga River, 1929, Site Diagram.

From the beginning, many variations of the linear city were proposed, each of which falls into one of two broad categories. The first is the "band type," developed in the 1920s by the Russian theorist N.A. Milutin. Initially conceived as a critique of a proposed settlement for a tractor assembly plant outside of Stalingrad, Milutin's plan was arranged, like the plant itself, as a series of six parallel zones, layered astride a transportation armature. Each band was divided according to functional criteria in an arrangement that Milutin claimed was directly analogous to assembly-line production. The railway, the industrial zone, a greenbelt, the residential area, the park zone and the Volga River were established as independent parallel bands, each capable of infinite extension. In connecting existing cities or independently stretching out into unsettled territory, the bands theoretically unrolled across the landscape with no significant transverse breaks (cross-axes), or variations in the basic sectional arrangement. Le Corbusier, having explored a variety of linear and non-linear urban proposals, finally settled, in 1940, on a variation of Milutin's parallel bands which he called a "linear industrial city," one of *Les Trois Etablissements Humains*. A more architecturally developed variation of the banded city was proposed by Ivan Leonidov in his 1930 competition entry for the steel-producing settlement of Magnitogorsk. Although similar to Milutin's basic scheme, it excludes the industrial zone from the band and, as a form of linear grid, allows for programmatic interaction among the remaining functions. In its high degree of abstraction, its absence of hierarchy, its unique interface between parallel zones, its access to open landscape, Leonidov's project continues to be an important theoretical model.

A second type of linear city also appeared in the 1920s based on features similar to Milutin's linear bands. This second type is organized around a centralized, hierarchical spine. The hierarchical spine configuration has obvious antecedents in the 19th-century city, particularly in institutional ensembles

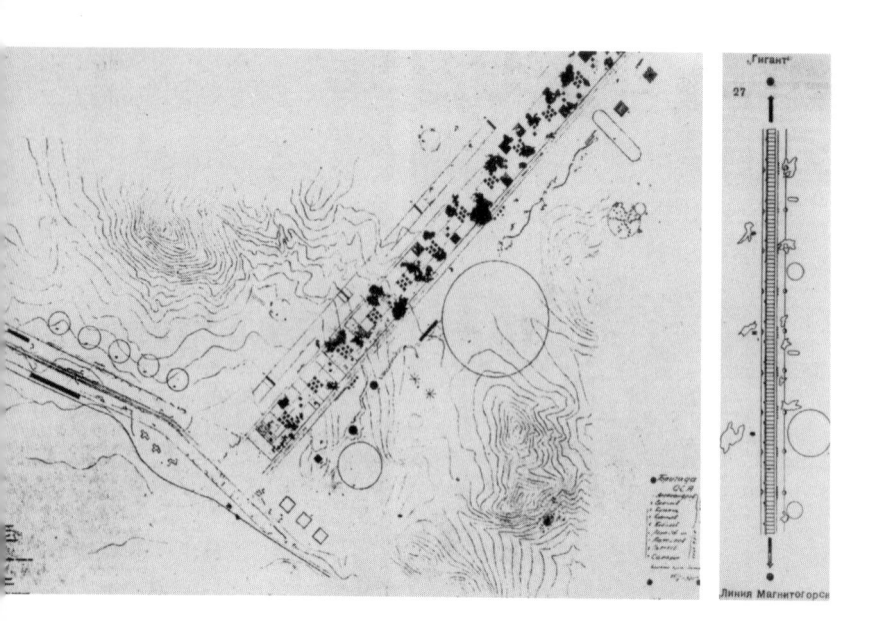

2.4 Ivan Leonidov, Competition design for Magnitogorsk, 1930, Site Plan.

such as prisons, schools, public hospitals and asylums. Surprisingly, the model reappears in the twenties in a very different ideological role: at the forefront a radical and progressive urban agenda.

As opposed to a series of parallel bands which are theoretically "unrolled" to an indefinite length, the linear spine is composed of relatively independent axial parts that are overlaid in a succession of scales forming the major pattern of urban circulation. In contrast to the linear band, where the main armature lies to one side of the linear zones, the spine is always organized in direct relation to a path of transportation. Being arranged around a single dominant route, significant cross-axes extend off the major artery forming new spines of development. Against the equivalent repetition of band zones, these lateral spines may generate a succession of overlapping figures. In this way, the spine alleviates the relentless continuity of the parallel band scheme by generating flexible patterns of secondary and tertiary development. These relatively autonomous spinal configurations can be built up incrementally, as autonomous units, into a wide variety of metropolitan patterns.

As a form of development, the linear spine proved to be far more adaptable to the realities of postwar construction. In this regard, the legacy of the 20th-century linear city was handed down through this specific arrangement. The ladder is the linear model ultimately associated with the organization of contemporary urban development.

2.5 Ludwig Hilberseimer, The Settlement Unit.
From: Hilberseimer, *The New City*.

HILBERSEIMER

As Milutin is identified as the prophet and prime theorist of the linear band, Ludwig Hilberseimer must be named as the prophet and prime theorist of the ladder. Best known as the architect of a series of grim urban proposals dating from the 1920s, Hilberseimer had a long and productive career attempting to render what he took to be the essential form of contemporary urban development. Rarely considered an author of significant paradigms, his work remains as a disturbing, if not altogether accurate, vision of impending urban conditions. Joseph Rykwert once remarked: "one can only take note in astonishment of Ludwig Hilberseimer's success. His barren, gloomy, menacing drawings prophesy a city without streets, even worse, if that is possible, than that which has actually been realized. This success is a sociological phenomenon of the strangest kind" (Pommer, 1988, p.17). In response, it can simply be said that Hilberseimer remained a realist, uncompromising in his rejection of the utopian tendencies of modern urbanism and focused in his attempt to render the salient qualities and characteristics of an emergent urban production.

Following his Berlin period, Hilberseimer's architectural and urban investigations shifted dramatically. Until that time his work was preoccupied with the urban cell and the effects of its mass deployment into a anonymous metropolitan condition. Michael Hays refers to these effects as the "inscription of the posthumanist subject" into the space of the Modern City (Hays, 1992, p.241). These studies of the urban cell took the form of the German *zeilenbau*, or row building, consistently arrayed on an open centrifugal grid — specifically the open centrifugal grid of Berlin. Beginning with a 1927 sketch entitled, " Metropolis as Garden City," Hilberseimer abandoned both the grid organization of his *zeilenbau* proposals, and the cellular articulation of his architecture. In his new phase, which coincided with his appointment to the faculty of the Bauhaus, he replaced the relentless punched openings of his urban walls with transparent skin structures arrayed, not on a grid, but on a series of parallel urban spines. In making this transition, Hilberseimer moved away from the cellular "inscription" of the subject. What emerged in its place was the *urban* inscription of the subject, where inscription affected not only a modification of the architectural cell, but a modification of infrastructure itself.

Following his immigration to the United States in 1938, Hilberseimer developed this spinal configuration into what he called a "settlement unit," which became the primary organizational element in each of his subsequent urban proposals. The settlement unit was the centerpiece of his 1944 book, *The New City*, in which he defined its qualities and projected it into a wide range of circumstances. The book established the settlement unit through a series of determined criteria, including sun orientation (relative to both room arrangement and site massing), wind patterns (what he referred to as the "wind shadow" of the air pollution produced by heavy industry), and traffic control (where he compared the relative merits of centric and linear urban arrangements relative to efficient traffic flow). Behind all the analysis of insolation, pollution and traffic, the relentless form of the settlement unit emerged, a form that he was to repeat in all of his subsequent urban proposals. This form, a centripetal configuration, structured everything in Hilberseimer's urban world. Its ubiquity was tempered only by its inevitable dispersion and disappearance into the natural landscape which Hilberseimer referred to as "camouflage"(1944, p.126).

In contrast to his earlier use of the open grid, the "settlement unit" was conceived as a finite urban element, an autonomous centripetal figure defined generically in a 1940 sketch as "The Elements of City Planning." In a seemingly endless number of permutations, the settlement unit was presented at the most general typological level of urban organization almost, it seems, as a replacement for the primary urban grid. Making some unusual claims for its adaptability, Hilberseimer stated: " . . . like a brick — always typical and yet so various in use — such a settlement unit could be used for every requirement that might arise in any city of whatever type and size or topographical character. It would provide the greatest possible flexibility in itself, and the greatest possibility for useful combination. No matter how such units were combined, the same favorable conditions for one unit would remain in all its combinations"(1944, p.113).

In its permutations and combinations, the settlement unit was arrayed with the same sequence of six zones: industrial zone, freeway, feeder, commercial and administration zone (within a greenbelt), residential zone and a park zone (combined with schools and community areas), which could be combined into an infinite number of metropolitan configurations. Linked along a route of transportation, subsections developed off significant cross-axial spines. Each subsection led to a progressively smaller scale of spinal configuration, leading to the pedestrian scale of the settlement unit itself. Each settlement unit was to be autonomous. Hilberseimer claimed that its size was based on comfortable walking distances, making it an early version of the "pedestrian pocket." The cross-axial development effectively partitioned the metropolitan spine, created an autonomous local condition and, according to Hilberseimer, effectively eliminated the need for metropolitan commuting.

Demonstrations of enormous metropolitan configurations of settlement units fill the pages of *The New City*. Giant Superblocks of units were proposed for the flatlands of the midwestern prairie. Sinuous linear groupings were adapted to the mountain ridges, valleys and coastlines of both existing and hypothetical urban situations. London, New York, Washington, and Chicago were all completely reorganized into massive linear agglomerations following

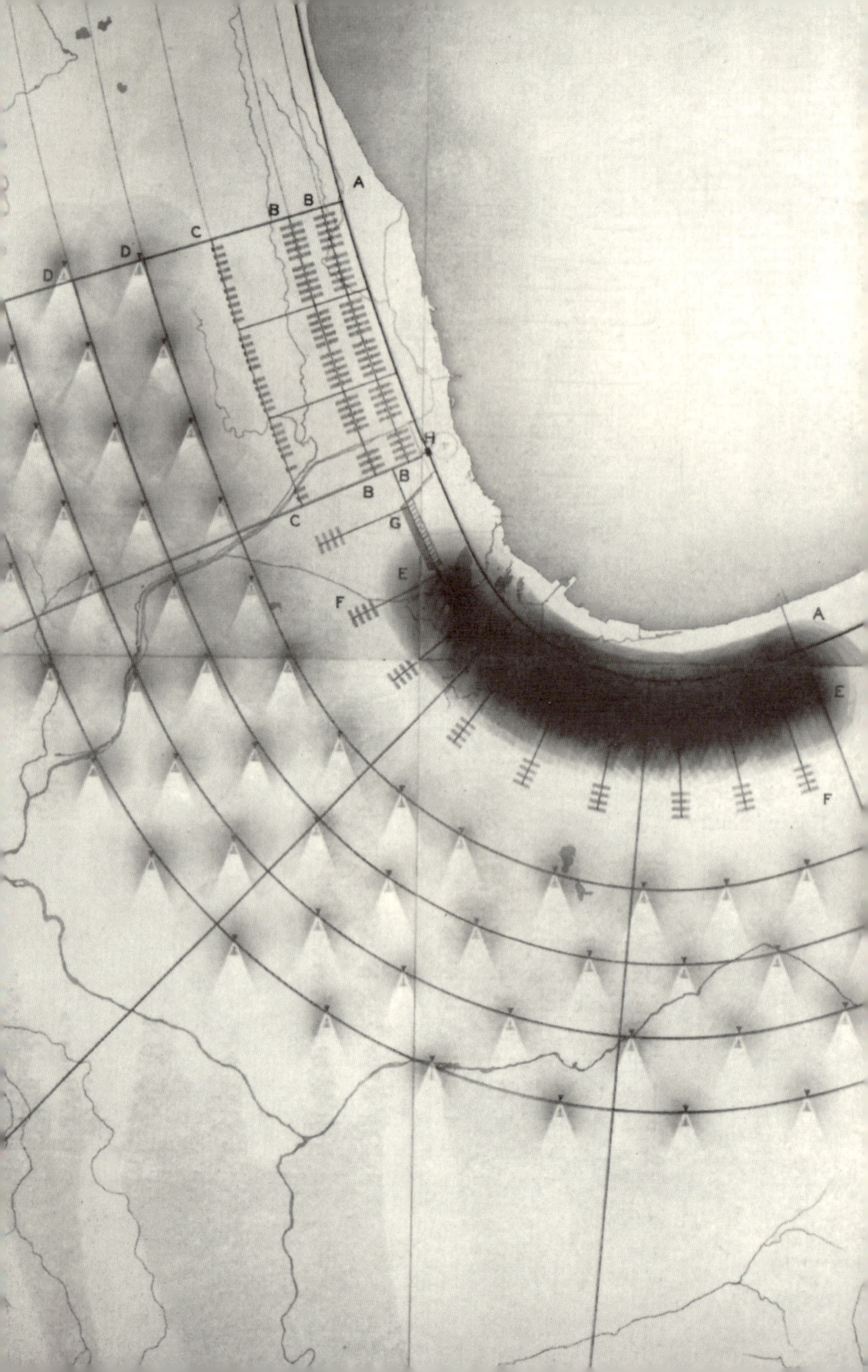

A
B
B
B
C
D
D
H
B
B
C
G
E
F
A
E
F

the shape of an island or the course of a river. In the settlement unit, Hilberseimer was proposing nothing less than an alternative to — a modernist equivalent of — the ubiquitous urban grid. The new metropolis was proposed as a mutation of traditional urban forms sustaining all the flexibility of the conventional gridiron structure while offering pedestrian neighborhood units, increased adaptability, coherent form and, most important, large urban open spaces.

Given the subsequent evidence of the built environment, it is clear that among modern theorists Hilberseimer came closest to approximating the form of the postwar environment with his discreetly formed settlement units. The Milutin banded linear city has remained theoretical, requiring a scale of bureaucratic organization and a level of global investment that, fortunately, has yet to emerge. Unlike Milutin's scheme, Hilberseimer's strategy allowed for the incremental growth of autonomous units. The increments of growth could be adjusted to various extents and complexities of development, which were not restricted by a single predetermined metropolitan configuration. The inherent flexibility of the structure allowed local configuration a relatively high degree of autonomy. As a result, the comprehensive scale of his proposals were theoretically more complex and less prescriptive than either the parallel bands proposed by Milutin or the "towns" proposed for the English Garden City.

2.6 Ludwig Hilberseimer, Proposal for the replanning of Chicago.
From: Hilberseimer, *The New City*.

THE LINEAR AND CENTRIC METROPOLIS

The combination of the autonomous "settlement unit" with a continuous transportation artery made Hilberseimer's proposal a relatively accurate prefiguration of contemporary urban organization. Hilberseimer attacked centralized metropolitan configurations preferring either linear or superblock combinations of settlement units. Hilberseimer spoke of his metropolitan arrangements as an urban hybrid combining the best qualities of both the centric and the linear models of urban expansion. "The linear or ribbon system, especially when it is combined with point-formed settlements, . . . is far superior to the centric system for the needs of our day"(1944, p.74). This combination of the "point-formed" local organization and line-formed metropoli-

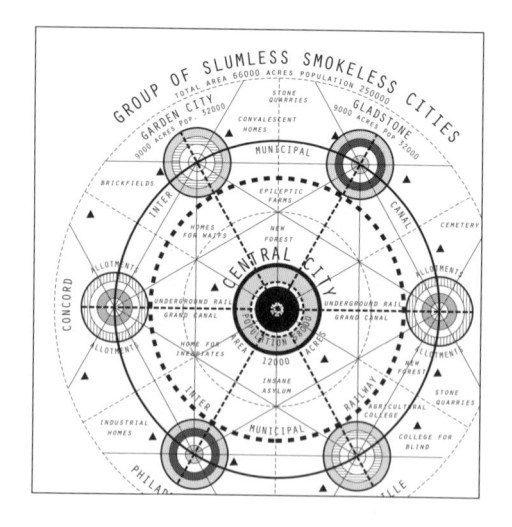

2.7 Ebenezer Howard, Diagram of the "Social City," showing a "Central City" surrounded by six smaller Garden communities.
Centralized Polynuclear Expansion.

tan organization can be contrasted with all centralized metropolitan models including the 19th-century city as well as the centralized polynuclear model advanced by the proponents of the Garden City.

In the 1920s and 1930s, the modernist attack on centralized hierarchical models of organization went well beyond the publicized assaults on the architectural academy. The defeat of traditional, mostly classical, models of architectural organization has been acknowledged and recorded by the standard histories. In the wake of that victory, the arguably more important attempt to defeat traditional, mostly classical, models of *urban* organization has been abandoned and, for the most part, forgotten. Unlike the architects, modern urban strategists were never able to supplant the hierarchical city center or urban core with their radical proposals of distributed points, lines and fields. The persistence of hierarchical metropolitan centers up to the present day suggests the negligible success of these alternative models in displacing the centralizing hierarchical motifs of traditional urban organization. A particularly interesting and early episode of the debate between the virtues of a traditional centralized and a modern linear metropolis is found in Hilberseimer's discussion of the Garden City.

In *The New City*, Hilberseimer freely acknowledged a variety of influences from the Anglo-American Garden City movement. Ebenezer Howard, Raymond Unwin, Henry Wright and Clarence Stein were all credited by Hilberseimer, particularly with regard to settlement unit. Unwin's influential advocacy of the superblock and Wright and Stien's plan for Radburn are noted as the source of what Hilberseimer referred to as the "closed-end street"(1944, p.107). Illustrating a plan of Radburn in *The New City*, Hilberseimer acknowledged the affinity of the settlement unit with these early innovations in suburban planning. Hilberseimer breaks with his immediate predecessors in regard to the metropolitan consequences of their superblock and *cul-de-sac* developments. Radburn, unlike Hilberseimer's settlement unit, was not projected into a larger metropolitan configuration. All major through traffic was to bypass the superblock, but it was never clearly specified where that traffic was going, not even in Wright's 1926 regional plan for New York State. One can only imagine that Radburn led to another Radburn placed at an equally discrete distance from the metropolitan core. For the majority of Garden City planners, the implicit model of metropolitan expansion took the form of a series of closed polycentric sub-developments surrounding a hierarchical metropolitan core.

Centralized Polynuclear Expansion was first conceived as a model of metropolitan growth by Ebenezer Howard in his book, *Tomorrow; A Peaceful Path Toward Real Reform*. In the book he included four diagrams that defined his idea of the Garden City. In regard to a metropolitan order, the crucial diagram is the one he called the "Social City," showing an aggregate of six autonomous garden cities surrounding a hierarchical core. This diagram has had a remarkable effect as prognosis, and in some cases as the literal model for contemporary urban expansion (Hall, 1988, p.169). Also referred to as the "New Town" model, the "Social City" was reiterated as an alternative to centrifugal expansion by urban reformers throughout the first half of the 20th-century. As a diagram of a centralized hierarchical expansion, the "Social City" came fully into its own with postwar reconstruction and expansion of western cities. As a model of metropolitan growth, Centralized Polynuclear Expansion remains the primary form of urban organization operating today.

As represented in Howard's rudimentary diagram, Centralized Polynuclear Expansion established a radical innovation in metropolitan development. Instead of extending the urban edge, Howard suggested that the line of existing centrifugal development be jumped over, and new discontinuous or closed centers of growth be established as autonomous Garden City communities. Cut off from its field of immanent expansion, centrifugal growth would be preempted by these new nuclei of autonomous development. Instead of a traditional single center of expansion, a series of concentric nuclei would initiate new growth. Each of these nuclei would be segregated by greenbelts — Howard suggested 5,000 acres for each settlement of 32,000 people — that were large, mechanically linked, green spatial reservoirs.

It is important to note that, despite the wholesome, domestic appeal of the Garden City, these were not modest proposals. Garden cities were conceived from the outset as radical interventions with agendas ranging from the paternalistic control of industrial populations to the formation of nascent anarchistic societies. Their driving force was their subversive relation to the existing city. Patrick Geddes exclaimed "towns must now cease to spread like expanding ink stains and grease spots." He meant that the industrial city was analogous to an uncontrollable toxic creep, and that what was really at stake was not so much the character of development as the manner in which it expanded. Change the way the city evolves and, regardless of the specific ideology of the counter-proposal, radical renovation will follow.

A distinguishing feature of centralized polynuclear expansion is that it is inherently contradictory, simultaneously asserting both traditional and innovative modes of urban organization. While the new nuclei of Garden City development challenged the hegemony of the dominant center, they were simultaneously configured in hierarchical relation to it. New developments contested the status of the centrifugal core and sought to truncate its expansion, yet they ultimately relied on it for both their placement as well as their overall metropolitan coherence. As opposed to the strategists of the linear city, Garden City proponents imagined the 19th-century city to be a stable hierarchical core around which the new, autonomous nuclei would gather in perpetuity. In retrospect, it is obvious that the metropolitan core could never have

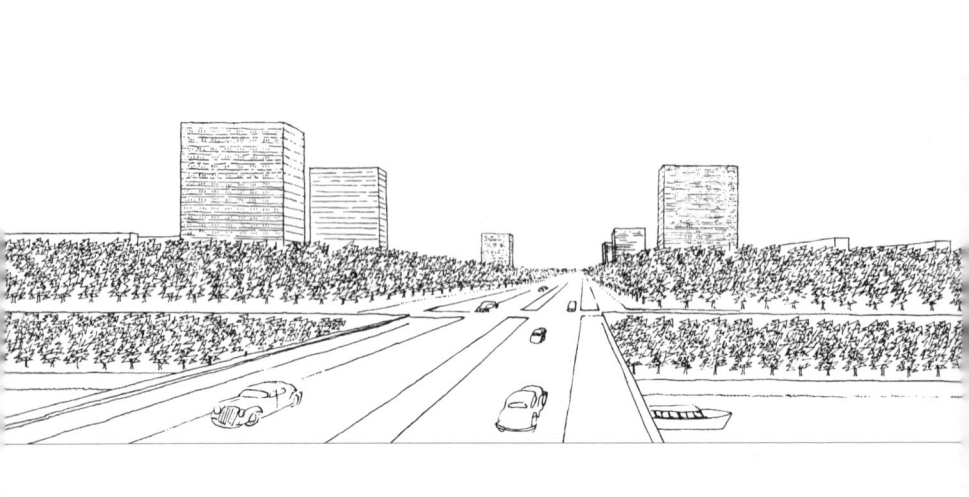

2.8 Ludwig Hilberseimer, perspective view of the University of Berlin from the Heerstrasse, Competiton, 1937.
The City of Space.

remained stable in the face of its altered pattern of development. Once centrifugal expansion was terminated — once the city was cut off from its potential field of expansion — the urban core would decline. Hilberseimer acknowledged rather than ignored this inevitable decline. As a realist, he would not leave the bulk of 19th-century urban development untouched, confining himself to new settlements and suburban extensions. While Radburn would serve only as a sub-urban model, implicitly presuming the existence of a coherent metropolitan core, Hilberseimer's strategy recognized that the closed centripetal organization of the settlement unit would undermine the core, and he accounted for this in his strategies. The settlement unit was thus not only a tool for new urban growth, it was also a tool for the "replanning" of the open centrifugal city. As a closed centripetal grid fragment, Hilberseimer's settlement unit was conceived as the catalyst of spatial implosion.

GRID REPLANNING

A crucial chapter of *The New City* is devoted to what Hilberseimer euphemistically called "replanning" projects. Unlike the majority of modern urban theorists who worked on the design of entirely new cities, the focus of Hilberseimer's polemic became increasingly involved with the reorganization of existing urban grids. Hilberseimer, like Mies, always made his best case, and maximum impact, by way of contrast to existing urban environments. (The surrealist photo-collage was a favorite device of Hilberseimer's, as it was of Mies.) His preferred method of historical juxtaposition was the transformation diagram. Each of Hilberseimer's replanning proposals projected a sequence of discrete phases, staging the total reorganization of existing urban conditions. This reorganization involved the transformation of open urban grids into a discrete series of closed settlement units. As applied to a number of American and European cities, these transformations dramatically demonstrated a spatial implosion, a sudden staged conversion from centrifugal to centripetal urban development. In these studies, Hilberseimer precisely described the process of urban transformation, which, by 1944, was already on the verge of transforming the conventional city.

Starting with existing grid, Hilberseimer proposed the strategic elimination of key streets and the majority of intersections, transforming the continuity of the open grid into a series of radically disassociated closed figures. In an emblematic example, Hilberseimer proposed the transformation of the Marquette Park district of Chicago, demonstrating the effects of the process when carried out on an active urban community. In a sequence of three phases of development, a three-square-mile section of urban fabric was replanned through a simple erosion of the gridded infrastructure. As intersection after intersection was eliminated in each of the phases, the ladder emerges in the

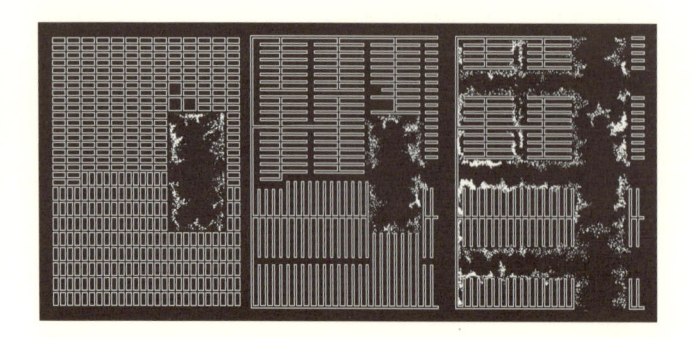

2.9 Ludwig Hilberseimer, Replanning of Marquette Park, Chicago. Grid demolition in three stages, c. 1950.
From Hilberseimer, *The Nature of Cities*.

GRID EROSION

interstitial space of grid erosion. The process continued until a primacy of space was achieved — that is, until a greater balance of space surpassed what remained of built form. In the final frame, the entire three-square-mile section of urban fabric had imploded into six discrete settlement units floating in an open spatial field. This imploded pattern of development is identical to the centripetal organization of postwar urban construction.

In *The New City* (revised in 1955 and retitled *The Nature of Cities*), Hilberseimer applied his replanning strategy to two hypothetical examples of provincial towns, as well as to three specific metropolitan conditions. In each case, a continuous gridded infrastructure was transformed into a series of centripetal figures. The rationale behind these transformations was presented as an elaborate defense of the settlement unit. Gridded intersections were understood to be life-threatening for pedestrians and vehicular traffic alike. With the elimination of each successive intersection, the community would apparently become safer. The significant amount of land saved by the elimination of streets would be given over to children for parks and playgrounds. The easy walking-distances within each mixed-use settlement unit would eliminate the waste of commuting. The isolated figures of the units were easily adapted to conditions of topography, insolation, and the prevailing winds. Being that it was 1944, Hilberseimer also evoked the threat of aerial bombardment in support of his plans. The production of urban firebreaks was a consideration. Deadly pollution, traffic fatalities, inadequate distribution, fire, aerial bombardment: this was Ludwig Hilberseimer's city — an emerging catastrophe demanding equally catastrophic action. Yet beyond these carefully, often exhaustively pursued circumstances, there lurked an obsession — it would seem purely aesthetic — that the highest priority must be put on the production of open space.

Hilberseimer's relentless transformation of the continuous field may

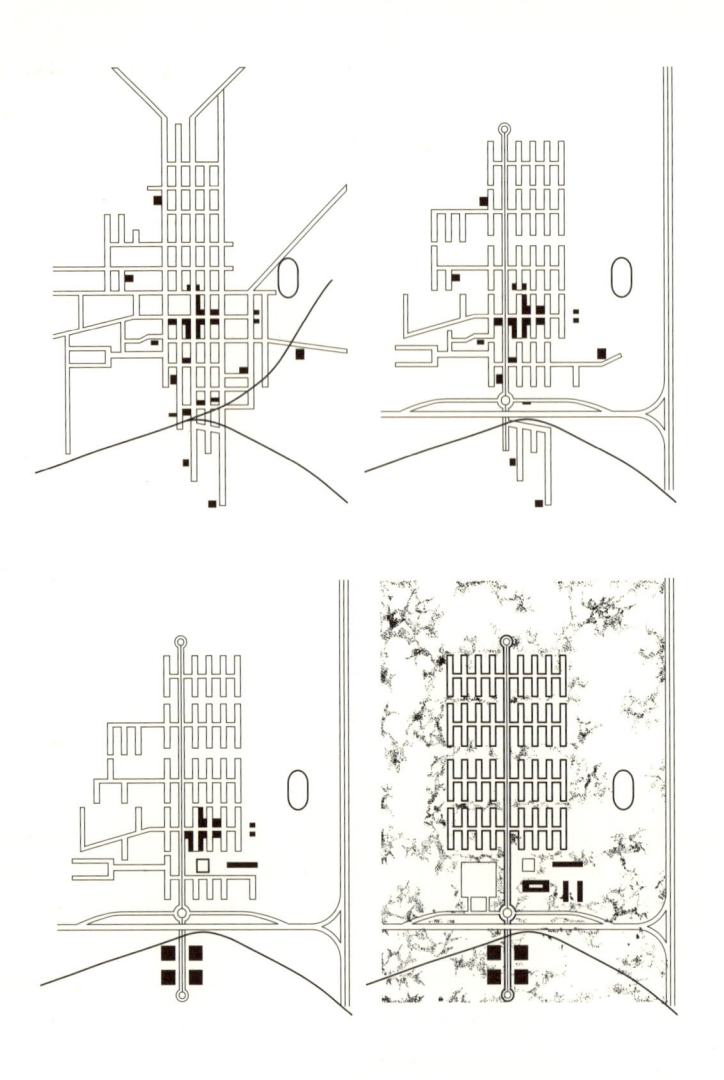

2.10 Ludwig Hilberseimer, Elkhorn, Wisconsin replanned in four stages. 1, Existing plan. 2, Grid demolition, Freeway and feeder connection. 3, Industrial park constructed. 4, Final grid demolition, commercail and parking relocated.

seem in hindsight an overt act of repression. The centripetal organization of the settlement units appears to be conceived more as a machine for the elimination of choice — the censuring of urban activity — than any progressive act of modern urban emancipation. But urban censure was obviously not the intention of the planner. In replanning these cities, the elimination of choice, the coarsening of the urban fabric, the fragmentation of the community into a series of closed and controlled ghettos, the dissection of an extant political body were all the means to the greater end of urban open space. In hindsight, the erosion of the grid demonstrated in Hilberseimer's replanning of Chicago can be seen as prefiguring the waking nightmare of Cabrini Green or the twenty block desolation of the Robert Taylor Homes. Yet the old, well-rehearsed outrages against the forces of contemporary development should not blind one to the analytical or didactic procedure being described in the plan.

In Hilberseimer's transformation of the urban grid, we witness a precise description of the implosion of the postwar, postgrid, posturban contemporary city. The erosion of the grid described a sequential process — the precise stages of spatial implosion — collapsed into a single site. If we invert our vision with the intention to see, not the production of six closed ladder forms but the production of space, the salient urban operation becomes obvious. It may be argued that what Hilberseimer was interested in was not so much the elimination of form as the production of contemporary urban space. Describing his mixed-height housing development of 1930, he stated, "Like the individual building, the entire city can be open and spacious. The separate high-rise buildings in the midst of the park, with its low single family houses, have the effect of shaping the space. A feeling of amplitude and openness of the urban space is optically evoked through them. Leaving behind the traditional narrow, closed space of the streets and city, the urban space emerges free and open on all sides"(Pommer, p.45). That this "free and open urban

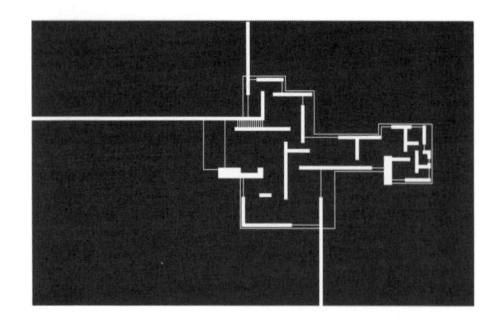

2.11 Mies van der Rohe, Brick Country House Project, 1923.

space" would be bought at the expense of closed and exclusive urban form introduces the paradox of modern planning that has yet to be reconciled.

The implosion of the grid, the dramatic relinquishing of the centrifugal field, and the subsequent production of a new form of interurban space all attend, and at the same time surpass, the effect of closed centripetal development.

MODERNISM AND CLOSURE

In a 1965 essay entitled "A City Is Not a Tree," Christopher Alexander argued that what he called "artificial cities" — the modern cities of Brasilia, Levittown, Chandigarh — lacked a level of complexity necessary to sustain a legitimate urbanity. He attributed the failure of these cities with their strict hierarchical organization into a configuration that he called a "tree." The initial analysis was striking and has yet to be adequately answered, for what Alexander revealed was a remarkable and unsuspected unity in the form of the Modern City. Presented as a conspiracy against the native intelligence of conventional urban development, these "artificial cities" were characterized as willful, reductive exercises in form, carried out against an unsuspecting urban body.

Alexander's analysis was bracing. Unfortunately, his remedy was mired in the sensibility he so forcefully criticized. Had he done even the most routine analysis of the form of his so-called "natural" cities (Liverpool, Kyoto, Manhattan), it would have been revealed that each possessed powerfully gridded infrastructures. His invention of the "semi-lattice" — a severe, hierarchical grid presumably derived from set theory — would have been completely undermined by his citation of these "natural cities" that are themselves impressive full "lattices" or non-hierarchical, open grids. (It was, no doubt, their grids that "naturalized" them.) Alexander's tree is not a formal system, but the analysis he did do on the Greater London Plan (Abercrombie), Greenbelt (Stein), Mesa City (Soleri), Tokyo Plan (Tange), Chandigarh (Le Corbusier), Brasilia (Costa) and, Hilberseimer's Settlement Unit ("the most beautiful example") leaves little doubt that modern planning is virtually synonymous with the tree-like spinal configuration described here as closed centripetal development. The problem remains — and this is why the essay is so provocative — to reconcile the reductive order of Alexander's "tree" with the progressive values one typically associates with modern architecture and urbanism.

Closed urban systems limit urban choices by enforcing a movement into strict hierarchical spines or roots. In addition to being hierarchical and prescriptive, a grid fragment isolated from its spatial field automatically defines this field as external to its own condition. Hierarchy, prescription and exclusion can thus be counted among the more disturbing effects of a modern urbanism which is otherwise understood to offer the increasing openness, choice and inclusion of a city dominated by space. Said in another way, Hilberseimer's implosion of the grid flies in the face of modernism's most basic ideological assumptions concerning the value of open systems, the continuities of architectural and urban space, and the radical dematerialization of built form. It is difficult to reconcile what seem to be regressive characteristics with the apparently progressive agenda of modern urbanism.

It would not be an exaggeration to say that the invention of a radical spatial continuity was among the prime accomplishments of modern architecture, as well as the impetus behind much of its novelty and success. From Wright's Prairie Houses, to the early projects of Rietveld and Van Doesburg, to Gropius at the Bauhaus, to Le Corbusier's development of the *piloti*, ribbon window and roof gardens, spatial continuity is among the most decisive innovations of modern architecture. Interpenetration between rooms, and between rooms and landscapes, and between landscapes and cities, and between cities and regions established an agenda of progressive liberation from the primacy of closed architectural form. It was the projection of these spatial continuities, the "destruction of the box," that ultimately broke the figurative, anthropomorphic order of traditional architecture and urbanism. A unique substratum of "Universal Space" suggested an open, expansive, centrifugal continuity, and it was this radical continuity that the furniture and buildings indexed. In, for example, Rietveld's furniture or Mies' Brick Country House, form only serves to index the local coordinates of a much greater, unknowable spatial field. It is only to state the obvious that these characteristically modern continuities were expansive and centrifugal — explosive rather than implosive.

While the aesthetic significance of continuous Universal Space is clear, it was nonetheless made to bear an enormous ideological burden, much of which is still with us today. Powerful convictions link the development of spatial continuities with a corresponding diminution of all forms of political, economic and aesthetic coercion. The conventional, prewar city continues to be imagined as a closed and bounded form, out of which the Modern City would emerge as an open matrix of space. In this regard, the desire to break the city open to light and space is as much a manifestation of political will as an architectural strategy. For the true believer, the formula is a brutally simple inversion. The traditional city is seen as a morass of restrictions, the concrete manifestation of a moribund political, economic and cultural system. The antidote could be found by simply opposing form with space. The new city would be a liberating environment, composed of free and fluid space. In a celebrated passage from *Urbanisme*, Le Corbusier states that in "my settled opinion, which is quite a dispassionate one, . . . the centers of our great cities must be pulled down and rebuilt, and that the wretched existing belts of suburbs must be abolished and carried farther out; on their sites we must constitute, stage by stage, a protected open zone, which when the day comes will give us absolute liberty of action. . ." (Le Corbusier, 1971, p.98). Fifty years later the ideology of the void is very much intact: "Where there is nothing, everything is possible. Where there is architecture, nothing (else) is possible. . . . Only through a revolutionary process of erasure and the establishment of 'liberty zones,' conceptual Nevadas where all the laws of architecture are suspended, will some of the inherent tortures of urban life — the friction between program and containment — be suspended" (Koolhaas, 1995, p.201). Throughout this century, modern architecture and urbanism have been driven by a powerful teleological trajectory, an historical destination which will, someday soon, arrive at the complete transparency of form. Moving us along this trajectory is the idea that form is inherently an encumbrance to the free play of ideas

2.12 Mies van der Rohe, Campus Plan, Illinois Institute of Technology, 1939, Chicago, Illinois, Aerial photomontage.
Photograph by Hedrich-Blessing.

and actions, institutions and activities, and that the demateri͟
will result in the elimination of these encumbrances. The eradica
form, and the resulting liberty of action are the results of a specific ͟
cal agenda translated directly into the metaphysics of (open, urban) space.

Hilberseimer's agenda "to dissipate the confinement of the city, to liberate the house, and with it man," (1944, p.190) drove his obsessive production of space. The literal dematerialization of the urban grid precisely echoed the dematerialization of furniture, doors, walls, foundations, and the ultimate destruction or dematerialization of the building envelope itself. The modern dematerialization of form emerged at the right time, as the right strategy, for all the right social and political reasons. Yet, in a headlong pursuit of *"beinahe nichts,"* the dramatically uneven effects of dematerialization were disregarded. As noted, the openness of architectural form does not guarantee the openness of urban form. It is only in sloppy aesthetic fantasy that the characteristics of a microcosm duplicate and reflect the characteristics of a macrocosm. By now it is clear that the dramatic spatial continuity of modern architecture sponsors the closed urban ghetto more than it sponsors any liberating openness of universal urban space.

It is remarkable that the idea of a progressively dematerialized city — the dispersion and disappearance (or return) of the city into the natural landscape — remains so culturally potent even when confronted by the retrograde effects of the ubiquitous grid fragment. This is the paradox of the primacy of contemporary urban space. Contemporary environments structured by freeways and feeder roads, airports, shopping malls, amusement parks, office parks, industrials parks, pedestrian bridge-and-tunnel schemes, and planned residential developments are all based on the grid fragment that is the result of grid erosion. Paradoxically, the centripetal figure can be seen as the regressive by-product of a seemingly progressive pursuit of space.

Contemporary urban space advances as the remnants of the gridded city ecline. Space emerges by the same processes and at the same moment that urban activity is censured. This is the absurdity of contemporary urban development: where dreams of escape are built as prisons, where contemporary corporate enclaves are built against an embattled landscape of spatial dreams turned nightmare in the harsh reality of a sunbelt subdivision. What seems remarkable, historically, is that the early moderns were blinded, at a metaphysical level, by Space. It is nearly impossible to imagine that they remained ignorant of the material consequences of their spatial ambitions. Their faith, however, that space would ultimately prevail is their legacy, never so strikingly apparent as in the evidence of the contemporary urban environment. Its primacy of space continues to be driven by something like that faith.

It remains to be seen how contemporary urban space stands to recuperate the strange morphology that it has created.

THE SUPERURBAN STAGE

The centripetal ladder possesses characteristics incompatible with the gridded continuities of conventional urban development. What yesterday was an innocuous extension of the urban known turns out today to be an other form of urbanism altogether. Once the characteristics of centripetal organization have been isolated, it is apparent that "suburban" development is not what our language suggests it to be. Neither secondary, subservient, supplemental, nor subordinate, centripetal development is an aggressive inversion of traditional urban form.

As the construction of centripetal growth continues, now at the threshold of exceeding all prewar development, what has been understood as a subordinate structuring relation has become less and less stable. While Centralized

Polynuclear Expansion has been the predominant mode of 20th-century urban growth — defining what we continue to know and expect of a metropolitan experience — it is undoubtedly a terminal condition. The integrity of the prewar core cannot be sustained because open centrifugal development collapses when cut off from its field of imminent expansion. With the decline of a single center of expanding urban growth, the contemporary city has evolved into two distinct types of organization. These two types are no longer related as city-prime and city-sub, but are two equal and opposing entities: the vestiges of a prewar centrifugal core and a myriad of surrounding centripetal figures. A simple diagram of this dual morphology would show an interrelated series of prewar centrifugal grids and postwar centripetal ladders. Using Houston as a demonstration of this morphology, the prewar inner city is characterized by an aggregation of grid structures laid out in separate but ultimately contiguous developments. Surrounding these grids is the Loop — a continuous forty-two mile freeway encircling the precise boundary of the prewar gridded city. Fully penetrating into the gridded structure and extending out from the Loop are the major through freeways, off of which tract developments, office parks, industrial parks, and shopping malls are structured. In this diagram, as in the actual city of Houston, outerloop "suburban" development has usurped the primacy of the urban core.

For many years it has been possible to ignore the precise relation between centripetal and centrifugal development; this despite the fact that the center/peripheral structure of Centralized Polynuclear Expansion has become radically unstable. We have already moved from the early stages of suburban growth — where traditional centrifugal development is primary and "suburban" centripetal development is secondary — to the present stage, where the two forms of development are somewhat balanced. It is now apparent that growth in Houston and other cities has outstripped the ability of the center to

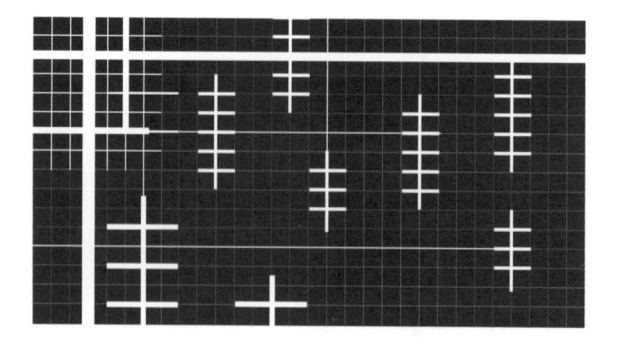

diagram 2.3
The Superurban Stage

With the decline of a single center of expanding urban growth, the contemporary city has evolved into two distinct types of organization. These two types are no longer related as city-prime and city-sub, but are two equal and opposing entities: the vestiges of a prewar centrifugal core and a myriad of surrounding centripetal figures. A simple diagram of this dual morphology shows an interrelated series of prewar centrifugal grids surrounded by a field of postwar centripetal ladders. The prewar inner city is characterized by an aggregation of grid structures laid out in separate but ultimately contiguous developments. Surrounding these grids is the interurban beltway encircling the precise boundary of the prewar gridded city. Fully penetrating into the gridded structure and extending out from the beltway are the major through freeways, off of which tract developments, office parks, industrial parks, and shopping malls are structured.

provide a coherent metropolitan order. It can be argued that juncture we are entering a "superurban" stage, where centripe͟ fully dominates the hierarchical centrifugal core. Initiated as a sub-u͟ asite, contemporary development is now at the point of overwhelming its hos͟ completely altering the terms under which the city is conceived.

While many may now agree that the crisis of the centralized metropolis is upon us, it can be argued that we have not begun to grapple with its social and political consequences. For example, it is scarcely recognized that the collapse of centrifugal development will have a far greater effect on the so-called suburbs than on the declining metropolitan core itself. Once defined against the logic of the open centrifugal core, the exclusive suburban enclave is already attempting to compensate for its ultimate decline. Over the past two centuries, enclaves have been defined against expansive, open urban development. It is a truism that closed systems can only be read against relatively open systems. There is a dynamic balance between closed and open development that has historically allowed for the existence of introverted worlds such as monasteries, prisons, exclusive suburbs, hospitals, or the university campus. Given this dynamic, prewar, pre-centripetal enclaves made sense only in relation to the expansive, open, centrifugal development of the city. As in monastic societies, the appeal of the enclave has been historically grounded in the presence of an outside, unbounded, and opposing world against which it could define the terms of its exclusion. With the collapse of the open system of centrifugal urban development, these terms have had to change.

In the absence of a dialectic with open urban systems, centripetal developments are not independent and isolated parts of the world. They are themselves now obliged to be the "world," for the "world" is no longer constructed in the idea of the open city. In its attempt to be the world, the suburban enclave must fail because the world is nothing if not an open system and an en form, an extensive potential where anything can happen. Closed centripetal developments can never replace these qualities, they can only project simulations, caricatures, and contrivances. While the familiar architecture of the historical enclave (such as the university campus) may remain unchanged in its specific form, it undergoes dramatic political and cultural transformation with the inversion of the greater metropolitan field. With great unease, one comes to discover that the terms of understanding the historical enclave have been altered by the absence of open urban development and the collapse of its vital continuities. Historically open urban centers degenerate into tourist sites, Main Street becomes a "festival marketplace," the campus becomes a theme park, traditional suburbs become xenophobic enclaves, and one is (still) left wondering how it ever happened.

One explanation lies in the recent transition to a superurban stage of urban development, where the working dialectic between closed and open systems has collapsed. If a closed world only exists in relation to an open world, then the collapse of centrifugal development leaves closed urban systems in a crisis. Open urban systems continue to be represented by the vestiges of the 19th-century city which, however gentrified or derelict, still allow unforeseen political, economic, and cultural events to unfold. This potential is preempted by a closed urban environment, and so must be supported in other ways. In order to sustain their social viability, closed urban systems must simulate the possibilities of open urban systems. The single overriding ambition of each of these closed systems is to enhance and refine their ability to simulate an open one. The result is an acquired rather than a native form of urban space.

As urban space implodes, there is a moment in which the city, as it is historically defined, ceases to be. This moment occurs in the transition from the grid to the ladder. While it is impossible to locate this moment precisely, the transition is a certain outcome of the process of grid erosion. The critical balance between vestigial grid and the emerging ladder, where enough of grid remains to support conventional urban associations, is becoming precarious. It is at this moment that the city, characterized by centrifugal urban development, begins to disappear, and development has gone superurban. The superurban stage occurs when closed centripetal development overwhelms the open centrifugal city, and native urban space fades in relation to its acquired simulation. It is the moment when the space of the open centrifugal "world" implodes.

"CRUCIAL SN/PC"!

⇒ SUPERURBANITY

CLOSED CENTRIPETAL DEVELOPMENT

THREE: INUNDATION OF SPACE

3.1 Downtown Houston, c. 1970.

INUNDATION OF SPACE

This chapter will examine the postwar reorganization of the open urban grid. The analysis will focus on the transformation of the historical urban core into a series of closed centripetal figures. These centripetal figures, or ladders, structure a variety of urban phenomenon across a wide range of scales. From the interurban freeways, to parking garages, to pedestrian bridge and tunnel systems, to the sections of speculative high-rises, the ladder is understood as the agent of grid reorganization and a dramatic spatial inversion. The remarkable unity of these forms suggests the transformation of the city into a closed corporate *gesamtkunstwerk,* a totalizing order superimposed upon the open formation of the prewar urban core. The residue of this order is defined as a unique type of imploded urban space that will be referred to as the inner city ellipsis. The inundation of this space into the urban core is the defining characteristic of the postwar transformation.

In order to clarify the idea of the inner city ellipsis, it will be contrasted to Fredric Jameson's seminal analysis of postmodern urban space: the "postmodern sublime." Centered on a discussion of an inner city atrium, Jameson's analysis is critical in situating the postwar transformation of the city into the economic infrastructure of Late Capital. Jameson identifies this global infrastructure as the real and only subject of contemporary urban representation. His argument establishes an important connection between the closure of centripetal form and the economic infrastructure which supports it. The qualities and characteristics of the atrium as described by Jameson ultimately provide a counterpoint to the qualities and characteristics of the inner city ellipsis. The space of the atrium serves as the strategic foci for closed centripetal networks while the space of the ellipsis represents its excluded, abandoned exterior. Stressed to the extremes, the corporate interior and the inner city ellipsis form the opposing poles of the renovated urban core.

of the urban core is a global phenomenon preceded by the war and the subsequent advances of postwar economic development. Allied bombers, aggressive freeway engineers, ruthless entrepreneurs, minor bureaucrats in the Department of Housing and Urban Development, celebrated architects and the precise trajectory of the V2 rocket have all served as the agents of this radical urban transformation. This list of contributors would suggest that, whatever its cause, the transformation of the postwar city overruns the many political, economic, and cultural agendas which have supported it. The most widely cited evidence of its scope is in the comparison between cities which suffered massive eradication in the war with cities which suffered massive eradication in the processes of reconstruction and "urban renewal."

The postwar globalization of capital is the most common explanation of this world-wide urban reorganization. There is little argument that multinational or "Late Capitalism" was accelerated by the political and economic upheavals of the Second World War. If one agrees with certain historians, economists and novelists that the war was as much a celebration of markets as an armed ideological conflict, then it is only a short step to conclude that the outcome of war resulted in a global consolidation of these markets, now capable of overreaching local power-bases, including those responsible for urban construction. This vision of an abstracted, transnational urban space has been identified and analyzed by many critics including Henri Lefebvre:

Capitalism and Neocapitalism have produced abstract space, which includes the "world of commodities," its "logic" and its worldwide strategies, as well as the power of money and that of the political state. This space is founded on the vast network of banks, business centers and major productive entities, as also on motorways, airports, and information lattices.

Within this space, the town — fountainhead of wealth and center of historical space — has disintegrated. (Lefebvre, 1991, p.51)

Lefebvre and, more recently, Fredric Jameson suggest that urban representation is now equivalent to the representation of the global infrastructure of multinational capital. The ability of this infrastructure to override indigenous practices provides one of the most compelling accounts of contemporary urban development. Before engaging this account, however, it is important to note that formal analysis must be skeptical of all exclusive connections between form and the economic infrastructures which support them. Form, urban or otherwise, always maintains a degree of autonomy and obeys laws which are not scripted by economic event. The disintegration of the historical space of the city into "abstract space" does not always parallel the vicissitudes of capital. To note the obvious example, the implosion of cities in centralized economies — economies presumably immune to the transformations of capital — is well documented. The postwar transformation of the traditional city seems to respond to no single determining factor and one is left to account for this global reorganization of form as the effect of forces beyond the prerogatives of war, money, or politics.

TERMINAL CENTER

Hilberseimer's attack on the urban grid — a real prophecy of what would shortly take place in cities large enough to have a consolidated core — seems in hindsight nothing short of bizarre. Considered as a transformation of the urban infrastructure, Hilberseimer's planning could be understood as a preposterous metaphysical conceit. The deliberate destruction of active urban communities in an incessant quest for what? Space? This could be dismissed as willful aestheticism had it not been so accurate in prefiguring the actual formation of contemporary urban development.

Garden City proponents imagined the 19th-century city to be a stable hierarchical core around which new, autonomous sub-urban nuclei would gather in a polycentric arrangement. In retrospect it is obvious that the metropolitan core could never have remained stable in the face of altered patterns of development. Once open centrifugal development was terminated — once the city was cut off from its potential field of expansion — the urban core was transformed by the same form of organization that obstructed its growth. In this way, the centric expansion of the Garden City model was a terminal strategy which, by its very production, created the condition of its own decline.

It must have been possible to predict the implosion of the 19th-century metropolis. In fact, much of what passes for modern urban planning is imagined in the face of such an inevitability. The destruction of existing cities carried out in the name of modern urbanism today seems so brutal as to be inconceivable. It is, however, possible to understand these willful gestures as important preemptive propositions. It is conceivable that modernists anticipated the decline and collapse of the 19th-century city and, in crisis mode, sought to alleviate the adversity of its demise. This may be directly attributed to an anticipation of the ultimate effects of centripetal development. It is important to reposition the often shallow critiques of modern interventions into historical urban fabric as attempts to manage the effects of an inevitable transformation.

Hilberseimer's case may prove the point. Among all other urban polemicists, Hilberseimer seems to have been most driven by the knowledge that the 19th-century city would no longer be stable once its specific mode of expansion ceased. It has been suggested that the proponents of the Garden City were irresponsible as regards the metropolitan consequences of their plans. Their rural fantasies relied on the illusion of an intact metropolitan core — a place of greater economic, political and cultural consequence — to sustain the isolated and parochial world of the "town." Following the inevitable collapse of the historical urban core, the Garden City would posses no viable metropolitan strategy. The approaching superurban stage, where there is no open urban referent against which to read closed centripetal development, suggests that we have already reached the endgame of their strategy. Hilberseimer and most other modernists rejected the hierarchical centric development of a Garden City metropolis and sought to address its deficiencies by accounting for the necessary reorganization of the urban core. His strategy not only accounted for the inevitable collapse of the core in his "replanning" proposals, but projected a mode of linear metropolitan expansion derived from the terms of centripetal production. While the subsequent developments of the postwar city did not follow the simple, elegant and sterile transitions imagined in his proposals, they arrived at essentially the same place.

THE INTERURBAN SPINE

The reorganization of urban form, from a prewar gridded city to a postwar laddered city, can be traced in the architecture of the urban core. In the messy postwar renovation of the core, this reorganization was chaotic and difficult to isolate and identify as a discrete process. Hilberseimer's replanning projects are useful in this regard, describing the reorganization in neatly phased diagrams showing the massive eradication of urban fabric and the subsequent rebuilding of the city around a new centripetal infrastructure. Hilberseimer speculated that such an orderly process of transformation would take two generations to accomplish. What instead happened over this period of time is not the methodical demolition and reconstruction of the urban core, but the construction of centripetal configurations on top of, or beneath, the existing

3.2 Boston: centripetal reorgnization.
From: Benevolo, *History of Modern Architecture.*

urban fabric. With the simultaneous, superimposed existence of both centrifugal and centripetal order, the urban center is the scene of an ongoing process of grid erosion and spatial implosion. Because open centrifugal development is overlaid rather than destroyed , and its traces survive the reconfiguration, the architecture of the center city provides a precise demonstration of spatial implosion.

In previously urbanized sites, implosion occurs as a succession of closed centripetal figures are placed on top of or underneath existing gridded space. The most prominent demonstration of this process is in the insertion of an interurban freeway through a conventional urban core. From freeways, through parking garages, and into pedestrian bridge and tunnel systems, the city center is systematically restructured by a succession of centripetal overlays. As these formations begin to redistribute the patterns of urban activity, the existing fabric evaporates into another type of urban organization fully dominated by space. This process of spatial production leaves in its wake the astral residue characteristic of "blighted" urban cores. Blight is only the pejorative description of the effects caused by the rapid implosion of contemporary urban space.

There is little debate about the primary role played by the interurban freeway in the reorganization of the postwar city. While its relative influence may be undisputed, its precise role in the mechanics of grid erosion is not well understood. With the introduction of the freeway, the continuities of gridded space were thrown into a fantastic reversal. As the first in a series of successive centripetal interventions, the overlay of the freeway signaled a full-on reorganization of both the urban core and the urban periphery. What made the freeway intervention so powerful was its ability to bypass the existing limit of centrifugal development — to leap over its edge of growth and begin new autonomous nuclei of expansion. The ability to overreach and subsequently

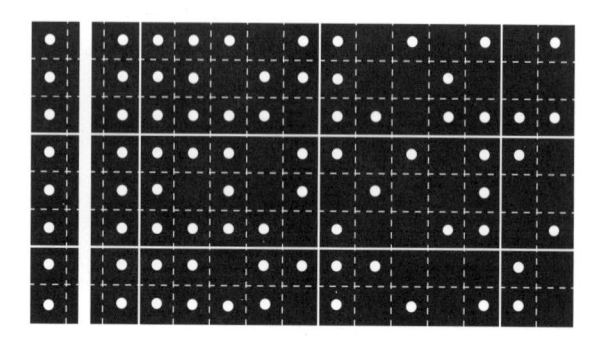

diagram 3.1
Remapping the urban core 1

Overlaid onto a finely gridded block and street pattern, the freeway downgrades or eliminates those streets of the grid not corresponding to its exit spacing. A freeway typically has a single exit every two or three miles. Over that same distance, a typical urban grid provides between thirty and fifty cross-street connections. With regard to urban transformation, what is most significant about a freeway is not what it connects on an interurban scale, but what it disconnects on a local scale. Like the small rural town that disappears for want of a single Interstate exit ramp, the crude scale of freeway intervention often eliminates significant chunks of the urban fabric which fall between its exit spacing. In the case of the existing urban grid, its heretofore evenly distributed pattern of activity is redirected onto those streets that correspond to s regional scale. The impact is the downgrading of a significant portion of the grid into a series of interstitial voids.

obstruct the greater continuity of the city is decisive. Following the closure of the centrifugal frontier and the preemption of its expansion, the reorganization of the existing city became inevitable. Surrounded by an antithetical form, the existing core could only transform or decline.

As was noted above, the order of a centripetal spine is different from the order of street grid in that it limits choices by enforcing a strict hierarchical movement along a primary route of transportation. Bypassing the local scale of the grid, the freeway dramatically coarsens the existing urban fabric. Overlaid onto a finely gridded block and street pattern, the freeway downgrades or eliminates those streets of the grid not corresponding to its exit spacing. A freeway typically has a single exit every two or three miles. Over that same distance, a typical urban grid provides thirty to fifty cross-street connections. With regard to urban transformation, what is most significant about a freeway is not what it connects on an interurban scale, but what it disconnects on a local scale. Like the small rural town that disappears for want of a single Interstate exit ramp, the crude scale of freeway intervention often eliminates significant chunks of the urban fabric which fall between its exit spacing. In the case of the existing urban grid, its heretofore evenly distributed pattern of activity is redirected onto those streets that correspond to an interurban scale. The impact this has on the grid amounts is the downgrading of a significant portion of its area into a series of interstitial voids.

Evacuation of freeway interstices and the ensuing dereliction of the urban core produce a radical transformation of the urban center. The concentration of vehicular activity around the axes of regional intervention and the subsequent destabilization of urban fabric establish a series of abandoned interstitial zones which, in American cities, were quickly eliminated under the slum clearance provisions of the 1949 Federal Housing Act. The replacement of urban fabric with isolated slabs, surface parking or, more frequently, with

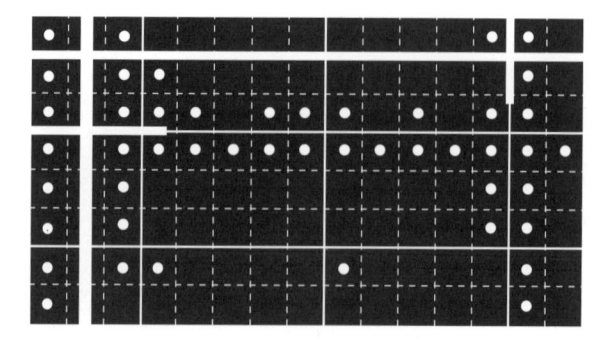

diagram 3.2
Remapping the urban core 2

Evacuation of freeway interstices and the ensuing dereliction of the urban core produce a radical transformation of the urban center. The concentration of vehicular activity around the axes of regional intervention and the subsequent destabilization of urban fabric establishes a series of abandoned interstitial zones which, in American cities, were quickly eliminated under federal slum clearance provisions. The replacement of urban fabric with isolated slabs, surface parking or, more frequently, with nothing at all, generated an enormous inundation of urban open space. The urban core was transformed from the "fountainhead of wealth and center of historical space" into isolated corporate development fortified against its spatial residuum now designated the "inner city". The freeway, directly set off not only the destruction of the grid fabric but the emergence of a distinct type of contemporary urban space.

nothing at all, generated an enormous inundation of urban open space. The urban core was transformed from the "fountainhead of wealth and center of historical space" into isolated corporate development fortified against its problematic spatial residuum now designated the "inner city". The freeway, as well as other centripetal formations, directly set off not only the destruction of the grid fabric but the emergence of a distinct type of contemporary urban space which may be characterized as implosive.

The cycle of production runs in precise stages: 1) Overlay of the freeway onto the 19th-century grid; 2) A subsequent concentration of activity which coarsened the urban grid; 3) The downgrading of the interstices; 4) The dereliction and destruction of the interstitial fabric; and 5) The subsequent emergence of an urban residuum which exists "outside" of the new patterns of use brought into play by the centripetal reorganization.

Only fifty years separate Patrick Abercrombie's report on the centrifugal explosion of Berlin and its inversion: the equally grand spectacle of centripetal implosion in the reorganization of the inner city. Marshall Berman was present for the postwar reorganization of the South Bronx:

For ten years, through the late 1950s and early 1960s, the center of the Bronx was pounded and blasted and smashed. My friends and I would stand on the parapet of the Grand Concourse, where 174th Street had been, and survey the work's progress — the immense steam shovels and bulldozers and timber and steel beams, the hundreds of workers in their variously colored hard hats, the giant cranes reaching far above the Bronx's tallest roofs, the dynamite blasts and tremors, the wild jagged crags of rock newly torn, the vistas of devastation stretching for miles to the east and west as far as the eye could see — and marvel to see our ordinary nice neighborhood transformed into sublime, spectacular ruins.
. . . when the construction was done, the real ruin of the Bronx had just begun. Miles of streets alongside the road were choked with dust and fumes and deafening noise — most strikingly, the roar of trucks of a size and power that the Bronx had never seen, hauling heavy cargoes through the city, bound for Long Island or New England, for New Jersey and

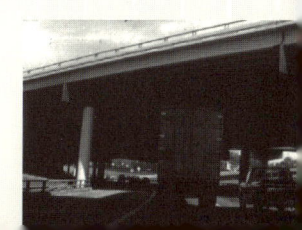

all points south, all through the day and night. Apartment houses that had been settled and stable for twenty years emptied out, often virtually overnight; large and impoverished black and Hispanic families, fleeing even worse slums, were moved in wholesale, . . . spreading panic and accelerating flight. At the same time construction had destroyed many commercial blocks, cutting others off from most of their customers and left the storekeepers not only close to bankruptcy but, in their enforced isolation, increasingly vulnerable to crime. . . . Thus depopulated, economically depleted, emotionally shattered — as bad as the physical damage had been, the inner wounds were worse — the Bronx was ripe for all the dreaded spirals of urban blight. (Berman, 1988, p.293)

The emplacement of the Cross-Bronx Expressway onto the continuity of urban fabric at once established major urban territories "outside" of an insular flow of traffic. This insular flow established an unprecedented interurban artery feeding a vast regional reorganization. The metropolitan continuities of the gridiron which once sustained the Bronx suddenly overshot it, crushing the intricate local conditions and depositing a vacuum in its wake. This vacuum is the residue of space effectively bounding the South Bronx as a fully isolated urban ghetto. Recalling the definition of centripetal organization as the introjection of boundaries into the center of the city, the role of the interurban freeway in the mechanics of the new spatial production become clear.

As an aside, Berman's book, *All That Is Solid Melts Into Air*, contains his remarkable assessment of Modernism as a high cultural movement irrevocably bound up with the attempts of countless people to come to terms with the destructive "maelstrom" of modernization. His description of the reorganization of the South Bronx, his home, by Robert Moses' Cross-Bronx Expressway is one of the most poignant demonstrations of his thesis, if only because Berman ultimately yielded to the authority of the transformation. However difficult it may be to embrace the autocratic destruction of personal history,

Berman acknowledged the ultimate importance, if not sacrifice, of sustaining a link to the "maelstrom" which he knows to be the unique and vital wellspring of the modern project. Unlike the unanimous assault on contemporary urban development from architects, social critics, and political journalists, Berman did not seek refuge from the maelstrom which destroyed his city, for this would break the crucial bonds between Modernism and modernization. Given the growing force and brutality of the maelstrom, there seems, as yet, no graceful way to sustain those bonds. Yet Berman persuades us that they must be sustained if for no other reason than the tools of cultural destruction are identical to the tools of cultural survival and resistance. The processes of contemporary urban production which Berman described in narration and Hilberseimer described in form are beautiful if ultimately graceless attempts to engage the maelstrom which sustains the modern project.

BRIDGES AND TUNNELS

The overlay of the freeway spine and the subsequent emergence of imploded urban space are decisive stages in the transformation of the gridded city. What follows the overlay of the freeway are a series of linked interventions which extend and accelerate the reorganization of the urban core.

As the freeway erodes the gridded urban fabric, the discrete space of the conventional urban street begins to disappear. In an extension of the initial intervention, the newly imploded space is bridged over and tunneled under in a successive overlay of centripetal figures. These alternate pedestrian armatures, which are configured as interblock spines, reroute the activity of the grid into new connections provided above and below street level. The impact is to drive the remaining pedestrian activity into an interior world of skybridges, atriums, and tunnels. These elevated or subterranean pedestrian pas-

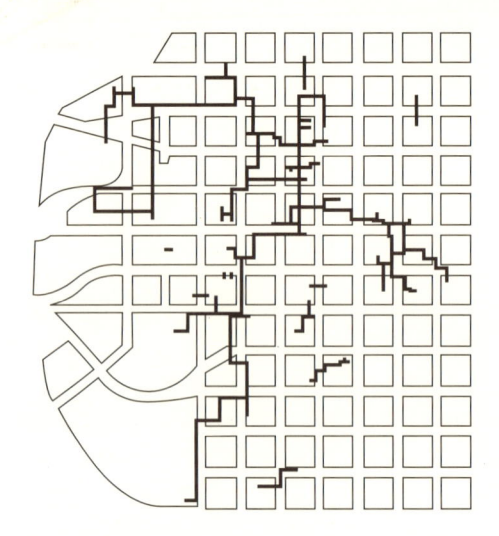

3.3 Downtown Houston bridge and tunnel system.
6.2 miles of interblock spines connect 26,000,000 square feet of space.

sages directly link freeways and garages to vast corporate interiors consolidating them all into an autonomous centripetal network. In Houston, for example, 6.2 miles of mostly below-grade tunnels interconnect more than 26 million square feet of enclosed space. Against such a massive reorganization of urban activity — the effect of turning the city outside in — the centrifugal fabric of streets and sidewalks implodes. With the elimination traditional pedestrian activity, an alternative, centripetal city emerges as the closed, exclusive reorganization of the urban sphere. No longer a presentation to and representation of the city in the world, the center of Houston is scarcely relevant to the surrounding city. Failing to constitute the open locus of civic identity — what used to be called civic pride — the imploded core has been reorganized into an elaborate, publicly subsidized office park for the region's many banking interests and oil and gas companies.

While the logic of centripetal development that ties the freeway to tunnels and bridges is relentless, many cities have developed expedient measures designed to contain the effects of freeway intervention and preserve, for the moment, the illusion of an open, centrifugal metropolitan core. Louis Kahn's 1953 plan for midtown Philadelphia is established on this basis. His massive cylindrical spirals — "Roman"-scaled parking garages directly adjacent to freeway exits — unabashedly fortify an embattled city against the onslaught of centripetal reorganization. These structures which combine regional parking and traditional urban activities were an attempt to initiate a productive relation between the centripetal intervention and the residue of the centrifugal grid. They served to terminate the centripetal order of the freeway and bolster the integrity of the existing street grid. Unable to extend beyond parking and reconfigure the basic cellular structure of urban buildings themselves, the centripetal reorganization of the city was prevented from overwriting the entire urban grid. The strategic positioning of Kahn's massive spirals "around the city center would present a logical image of protection against the destruction of the city by the motor car. In a sense, the problem of the car and the city is war"(Kahn, 1991, p.120).

Stopping centripetal reorganization at the parked car leaves the sidewalk and the street grid intact. Between garages the grid can reassert itself, linking buildings in an open field of connections within the larger scale of the freeway. This state of equilibrium between grid and ladder remains for the

115 INUNDATION OF SPACE

3.4 Louis Kahn, Plan for Midtown Philadelphia, 1953.

moment the basic morphology in many contemporary urban cores. While grid erosion can be contained, however, the overall implosion of the surrounding urban field is not effected. The preserved grid and its building stock are no longer linked to a larger metropolitan continuum, but are enveloped within the boundaries of a closed spatial field. As the spatial continuity of the centrifugal city is compromised, urban centers lose their connection to open, generative urban processes and become historic theme parks for sightseers, festival marketeers, urban theorists and other tourists. Kahn's plan, beautiful as it is, would not have saved the city from closure. It merely supplied the infrastructure for the artificial preservation of its qualities. The urban core is for the moment stable, but — festival marketplaces notwithstanding — it is unclear whether the cores have already been destroyed in the effort to preserve them.

While there are limits to the centripetal reorganization of the urban core, these limits only serve as stop-gap measures. While fragments of grids are preserved, they cannot withstand the effects of closure. In the absence of an organized defense of the historical grid, the extension of the order initiated by the freeway proceeds in the centripetal development of bridges and tunnels directly connecting parking sites into the tunnels and cores of a reconfigured urban architecture.

THE ELLIPSIS

The postwar metropolitan core displays the unique conditions of contemporary spatial production. Imploded urban space often seems more the by-product of some urban chain reaction than the result of a conscious act of design and planning. As a residual effect rather than a prescribed quality, imploded space is impossible to identify and categorize in conventional terms. Its irregularity and vast extent often preempt isolation, identification and traditional classification. In this regard, the association of imploded space with designed or constructed space (a category inclusive of the great urban places of the world) seems unlikely. The imploded space of the contemporary city is without effective taxonomy, so much so that it is impossible to construct a critical language commensurate with the urban phenomenon. Moreover, it is impossible to recognize that a taxonomy of contemporary urban space is even missing. It is for this reason that its qualities remain everywhere apparent yet subsequently unthought and unseen.

It is this lack of a conceptual armature which accounts for what is perhaps the primary characteristic of imploded space: its inability to function as the traditional focus of urban identity. As the residue of highly organized forms, it is always perceived as a disorganized effect, completely lacking in qualities. The preemption of centrality — its inability to hierarchically "gather" urban form and thus urban meaning — is what most distinguishes the imploded space of the contemporary city from traditional urban space. Being an unformed, non-figurative and disorganized entity, it fails to become the traditional locus of civic enfranchisement, yet it exists in abundance in the representative core. Imploded space becomes the most unique of urban spaces, paradoxically internal to the city yet external to its working life. As the locus of economic, political or cultural enfranchisement becomes increasingly concentrated into the closed centripetal figure, its spatial residuum disappears, often remaining visible only to those who share its disenfranchised state (Solà-Morales, 1995).

For the purposes of distinguishing the characteristics of imploded space and bringing it into a dialectical relation with contemporary urban form, imploded space will be referred to as an "ellipsis." An ellipsis is the characteristic type of contemporary urban space produced by implosion and is the inevitable result of centripetal development. It stands in contrast to the open continuous field of centrifugal expansion as it exists "outside" exclusive urban development. In other words, the ellipsis only exists in inverse relation to the form of the centripetal figure or ladder. The ellipsis is, by definition, neither designable nor programmable. Nor can it be a hierarchical, centralized urban feature. It is not a case of delayed or uneven development or the result of fluctuations in the land market, and it does not inherently constitute an incomplete or subordinate state. These spaces, which figure so decisively into the character of the contemporary city, are systematic phenomena subject to the quantifiable processes of centripetal production. As such they are subject to the same rigor of analysis undertaken on more coherent and deliberate types of urban space.

FREE SPACE

The centripetal reorganization of the prewar city has resulted in its division into two separate and non-intersecting worlds. These worlds are the result of a division of the continuous centrifugal field into a closed centripetal form and its spatial residuum. While the historical center has always functioned as a palimpsest recording the traces of urban transformations, this form of organizational schizophrenia seems to be unprecedented. In contrast to the familiar qualities of traditional "urban space," the emergent qualities of the ellipsis are perceived as alienating and hostile. The elaborate skywalks or tunnel systems interconnecting increasingly defensive urban structures constitute a new centripetal labyrinth which, like a self-fulfilling prophecy, fuels a fear of the outside and the excluded. These armatures and the spaces they connect produce a virtual second city over and below the implosion of contemporary urban space.

The modernist paradox described above —the pursuit of a city of open space which results in closed and exclusive urban form — finds its ultimate expression in the reorganization of the inner city. Here a city founded upon the primacy of space is pursued in full denial of its debilitating material consequences. Glass towers, massive freeway systems, colossal enclosed atriums, skybridges and millions of automobiles — the manifest explosion of space in the postwar city — attest to a desire for space. This constitutes a marked spatial bias which is neither incidental, unduly coerced, nor artificially contrived. Its effects stem from what Fredric Jameson has referred to as a "cultural dominant."

It is especially in the "inner city" that the dream of space, such as a high-speed urban expressway, produces a landscape of perceived dread, such as the South Bronx. It is here that dreams of space turn into prisons only to generate more dreams and more prisons. In a spiral of increasing exclusion — a virtual militarization of the environment which seems to end only in absolute closure — the ultimate corporate ghetto is under construction. And the world that has been consigned to the "outside" of the urban fortifications is restless.

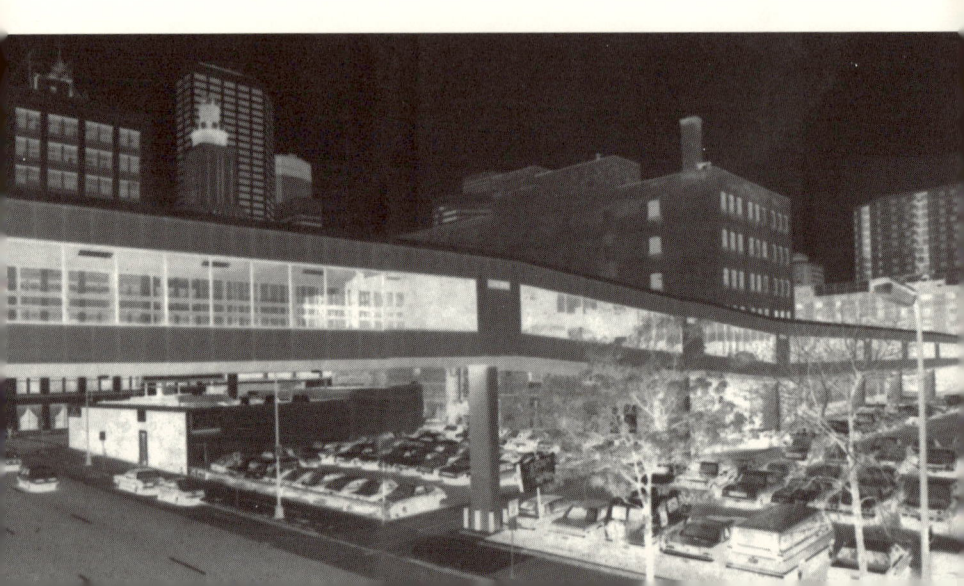

There are many morality plays, some of them ancient, about the coexistence of two separate and unequal societies. A contemporary version is manifest in the struggle between the ladder structure of a corporate *gesamtkunstwerk* and the other "fallen" city of pedestrian fragments and spatial inundation. This division into two opposing cities — what Mike Davis calls "spatial apartheid" (1993, p.14) — might be a subject of debate. While it is necessary and important to evoke the specter of exclusion by class and race, it does little to address the foundation of contemporary urban development. The story of social outrage is as easy to construct since it remains patently true. But it does not identify, let alone help answer, the treacherous paradox outlined above: we all remain in some sense prisoner to a "cultural dominant" of space — an incessant utopia of space which is pursued in full denial of its material consequences. This paradox accompanies all of our present urban production, and is rooted in a set of complex desires which are impenetrable by moral argument.

Perhaps a solution lies not in the process of impeding development, of prohibiting or infilling the production of contemporary urban space. Who, then, should be the first to give up their fast cars, their generous views, their private open space, their privileged secession from the life of the metropolis? The point may not be the elimination of contemporary urban space, but a vigorous and renewed production — a full if not final playing out of the persistent dream of space in dialectical relation to the armature of contemporary urban production.

As the remapping of the city center continues, the grid implodes and collapses into space. Simultaneously two cities rise out of a traditional urban

3.5 "Skywalk," Minneapolis, Minnesota, 1983.
Photograph by Walker Art Center.

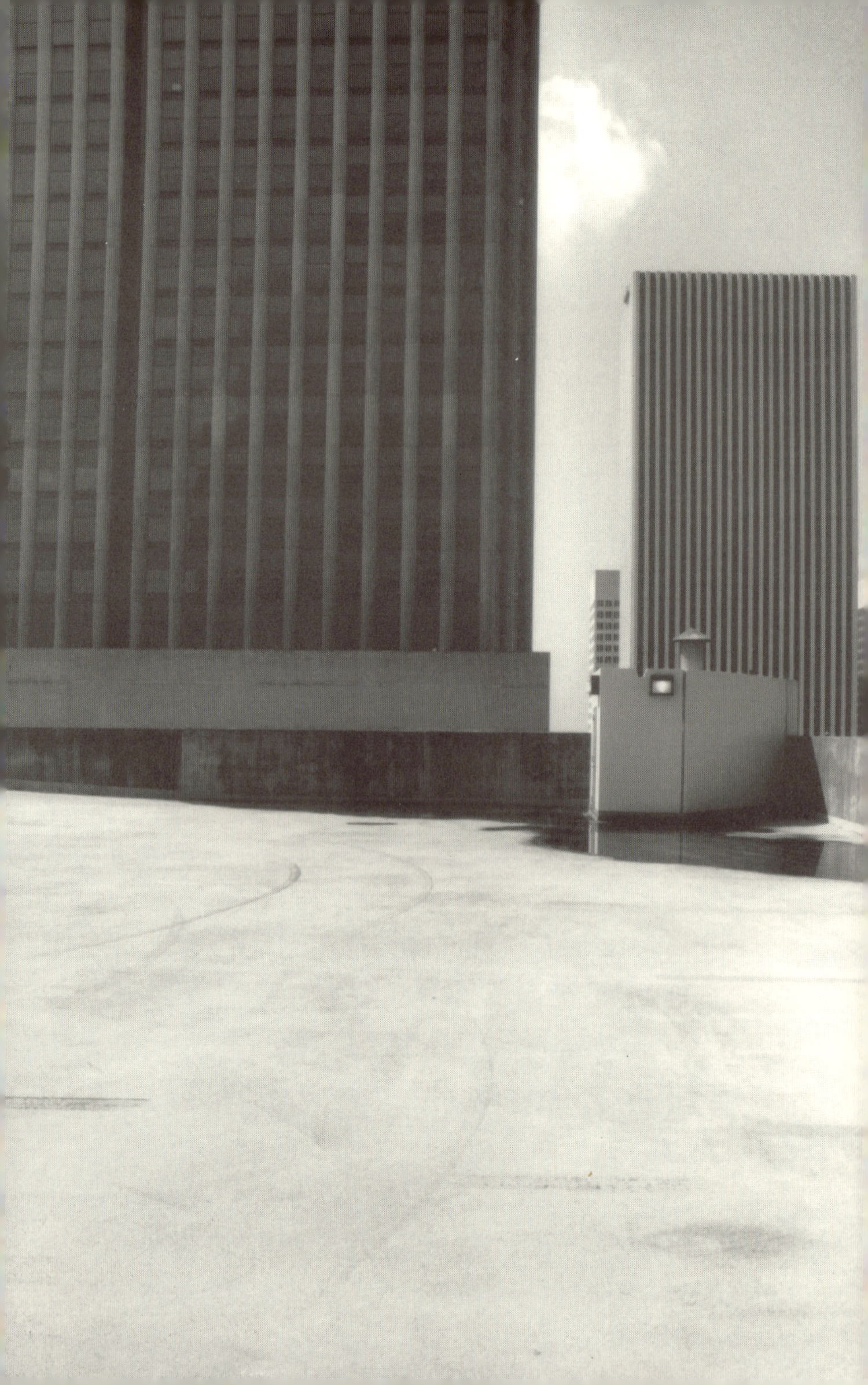

ground, an inside and an outside, a ladder and an ellipsis, locked in a paralyzing opposition. Alongside the city ordered by the ladder, an anti-city emerges, the demobilized scene of mass absence. It is a familiar despotic world commonly known as the "inner city." It is the lapse of the welfare state, the final space that, after countless bureaucratic "wars" (on Poverty, on Crime, on Drugs, on Homelessness), power is completely unable to grasp, and ultimately knows it cannot control. It is free space.

URBAN ARCHITECTURE

With the reorganization of automobiles and pedestrians, the transformation of the open city is nearly complete. From freeway to garage to skywalk, the final effect is in the reorganization of urban buildings themselves. In the ubiquitous cores and plates of high-rise construction, centripetal development generates an architecture uniquely related to its own organizational qualities.

The grid of the 19th-century city produced its own building morphology which has been characterized as an "Alphabetical City" (Holl, 1978). Fifty years ago, this grid typology was decisive in the construction of the open centrifugal city. It was flexible in aggregation and subdivision, it accommodated a remarkably broad range of program types, it was successful in forming public space and, at the same time, it was infinitely reproducible, resisting the closed vocabulary of traditional urban forms. The street walls and light wells of C,U,E,O,H, or F-shaped buildings were shaped not only by the prewar light and air codes but more generally by the logic of the centrifugal urban development. Many gridiron buildings were sympathetic to the extensive spatial field, and not only through a typological response. Louis Sullivan's urban facades, for example, or the exotic massing strategies of Raymond Hood are both architectures inextricably bound to the continuities of the centrifugal spatial field.

3.6 Houston Parking Deck, 1995.
Photograph by Karin Taylor.

The Alphabetical City was perhaps the last architecture responsive to the open city of centrifugal urban development. Since its decline as an active building morphology — at precisely the moment the grid began to implode — its buildings have become urban relics, surprisingly indifferent to the qualities of centripetal reorganization. Their ability to resist the reorganization often makes it possible to imagine that the drastic mid-century implosion of the urban field ever occurred. Urban backdrops in films and books, television interviews with the "man on the street," the travel industry, political rallies all take place in the vestiges of an open 19th-century context. In many cities one can still exist within these vestiges of the centrifugal urban order and be completely oblivious to its passing. Aside from the appearance of large groups of tourists and an inordinate number of specialty shops, signs of the radical inversion can in some rare locations be completely ignored. Yet, the fragments which survived the reorganization have already been thrust into the inverted spatial field created by the implosion. Once connected to greater continuities, they now negotiate the new binary field, finding themselves either "inside" a zone of historical preservation and stasis, or "outside" in a world of rapid obsolescence and decline. These buildings cannot, or cannot much longer, effectively continue to sustain our concepts of urbanity or the basic social well-being implicit in open urban forms. In the imploded space of the ellipsis, these relics of another city persist truly out of space and time. Either fetishized or reviled, dressed up as period pieces, or abandoned to decline, they are survivors of an unprecedented mutation of space.

Since the decline of the centrifugal grid and its associated building typology, the closed centripetal grid has itself generated an urban architecture which, like the Alphabetical City, grows out of the premises established by the larger spatial field. The buildings of the open grid often generated multiple sidewalk entrances and multiple means of vertical access and egress. In contrast, the core of the centripetal high-rise generates a singular hierarchical route/root, like the trunk of a tree or the spine of the freeway from which it is fed. Unlike prewar urban construction, the core and plate organization of the postwar slab and tower is, in its section, a literal ladder formation. Like the spinal configurations which precede it, the bank of elevators in a high-rise core restricts movement into a single hierarchical circuit. In this way new linkages can undermine multiple street access points and instead connect directly from the freeway to garages, to bridges and tunnels, through atriums, directly into the high-rise core. It is in the consolidation of the core that the new centripetal order generates an urban architecture directly connected to its larger spatial field.

Tying the circulation of the urban building directly into the regional scale of the freeway completes or totalizes the centripetal reorganization of the city down to its cellular structure (which is also imploded by "open office" planning). This is the manner in which the circuit is finally closed, in which the most intimate scale of the city is brought into line with the regional organization of space. It is no coincidence that all of the circuits of the reorganization are centripetal figures. In restructuring the inner city into one seamless corporate *gesamtkunstwerk*, the ladder is ubiquitous in its employment and in its effect.

INSIDE

Centripetal redevelopment is often associated with the novelty of its most conspicuous spatial feature. The inner city "atrium," calculated to impress as much as any palace or cathedral, performs both a representational and an organizational role in centripetal development. At key intersections between skybridges and high-rise cores, strategic nodes emerge which frequently flourish into dramatic spatial spectacles. Atriums often act as the significant control points of centripetal development — the spatial fulcrum for millions of square feet that centripetal linkages serve to connect. Given the exclusive qualities of centripetal form, atriums exist to focus an already refined level of organization and control. Operating, often literally, as the panoptic eye of the corporate enclosure, they make a system of excessive exclusion and control that much more apparent. The atrium is as banal and coercive in its organizational sense as it is spectacular in its architectural sense.

One cannot go far in an assessment of postwar atriums and their role in the transformation of urban morphology without referring to their prime innovator, the architect John Portman. Having built in many major American cities, Portman is the architect of inner city reorganization. All of the rhetoric of centripetal urban organization — the garish celebration of its interiorization and closure never imagined by earlier generations of modern architects — is provided by Portman in his inner city atriums. Yet his contribution to the contemporary city should be understood not only in the design of lavish, upscale hotels, but in the consequential irruption of contemporary urban space that his developments produced in their wake. His massive enclosed atriums are only by coincidence known as hotel lobbies as it is understood that their greatest impact is in the implosion of the surrounding spatial field. It is necessary to reconsider the inner city atrium as a critical function within the centripetal reorganization of the urban core. In this effort it is important to look, not only at Peachtree Plaza, but the almost single-handed reorganization of the core of Atlanta, not only the Renaissance Center, but of the continued depletion of downtown Detroit, not only the Bonaventure Hotel, but the fortress development on Bunker Hill and the rest of urban Los Angeles it aggressively excludes.

An early Portman development of particular diagrammatic clarity is his redevelopment of the Embarcadero area of San Francisco. The project initially responded to the grid implosion initiated by the adjacent Embarcadero Freeway and the imminent inundation of the adjacent pedestrian grid. A group of relatively innocuous buildings connects five city blocks along their central axis, forming a superblock terminated by a colossal atrium node. Reconfigured as a single building, these blocks internalize pedestrian activity about a central axis, which is elevated twenty feet above the street. The scenario is familiar. Double-loaded corridors become new "streets," interior partitions become "storefronts" which lead into a hotel lobby swollen to the proportions of a "plaza." The investment of centripetal reorganization with a common urban language is the crucial operation. Like his other atriums, the Embarcadero Center is the outside inside, or the inside for which there is no acknowledged outside. The "outside" formed by the imminent implosion of the grid is aggressively denied by preempting its content. Complete with its own climate, internal management, hours of operation, and rented police force, this urban landscape presumes the status of native urban space, which it attempts to supersede but can ultimately only simulate. Nevertheless, the development is an early manifestation of a freeway, garage, bridge, atrium, tower configuration.

Unlike Atlanta or Detroit, the Embarcadero area did not collapse under the pressures of Portman's reorganization. The reassertion of the pedestrian grid did not reverse the greater effects of spatial implosion. Grid erosion can be artificially halted, as it was in Kahn's proposal for Philadelphia, but the effect of the implosion on the surrounding spatial field remains unaffected. No longer integrated into the spatial continuities of centrifugal development, the "Embarcadero" has predictably turned into a theme park for sightseers, aggressive suburban shoppers and other tourists. Which is precisely the audience the space of the atriums anticipated. Those who continue to be awed and

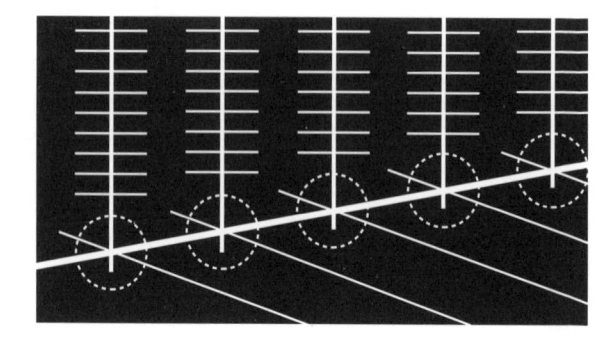

diagram 3.3
The Atrium Node

At key intersections between skybridges and high-rise cores, strategic nodes emerge which frequently flourish into dramatic spatial spectacles. Atriums often act as the significant control points of centripetal development — the spatial fulcrum for millions of square feet that centripetal linkages serve to connect. Given the exclusive qualities of centripetal form, atriums exist to emphasize or focus an already refined level of organization and control. Operating, often literally, as the panoptic eye of the corporate enclosure, they make a system of excessive exclusion and control that much more apparent. The atrium is as banal in its organizational sense as it is spectacular in its architectural sense.

impressed by the inner city atrium, at the expense of native urban space, are the real citizens of the Centripetal City. From the "street person" who willingly accepts the architecturally coded terms of his or her exclusion, to architectural critics who interpret it as an hermetic *tour de force*, the fantastic manipulative space of the atrium does nothing more than re-present and thus parody the primacy of space. In other words, while it attempts to be nothing if not a celebration of space — some sort of cathedral to the unique spatial biases of contemporary urban production — the inner city atrium is ultimately only a simulated world which is compromised from the outset, unable to acknowledge the far more consequential space its construction has brought into being

IMPLODED NODE

In the 1970s, Portman refined his hotel designs, specifically accommodating the atrium's role as a link connecting proliferating bridge and tunnel systems with new urban construction. In his preceding designs, which were inefficient O-shaped perimeter blocks, the atrium filled the center as a large courtyard surrounded by single-loaded accommodation of rooms. In a new, imploded version of the atrium, the rooms are no longer arranged around the perimeter, as in a traditional courtyard block, but instead are arranged in pure core and plate organization of the postwar speculative high-rise. The atrium thus becomes, not a stylized version of a traditional courtyard, but something entirely different where, at the intersection of the remapped pedestrian system and the high-rise elevator core, a significant hollowing out occurs. This hollow space emanating from the core is the realization of the imploded node, the archetype of which is the Peachtree Plaza Hotel in Atlanta of 1976. Here, the precise intersection of the tunnels/bridges and the core/plates is voided out as the core plunges down around a surrounding windowless shell. This top-lit blind box is the distinguishing feature of the imploded atrium, set onto the former grid organization in what Mike Davis calls a "fascist obliteration of street frontage"(1990, p.229). Acknowledging the internalization of monumental expression, the elevation is conceived, again, as if an urban exterior did not exist. On the interior, the floors are stepped back in section around

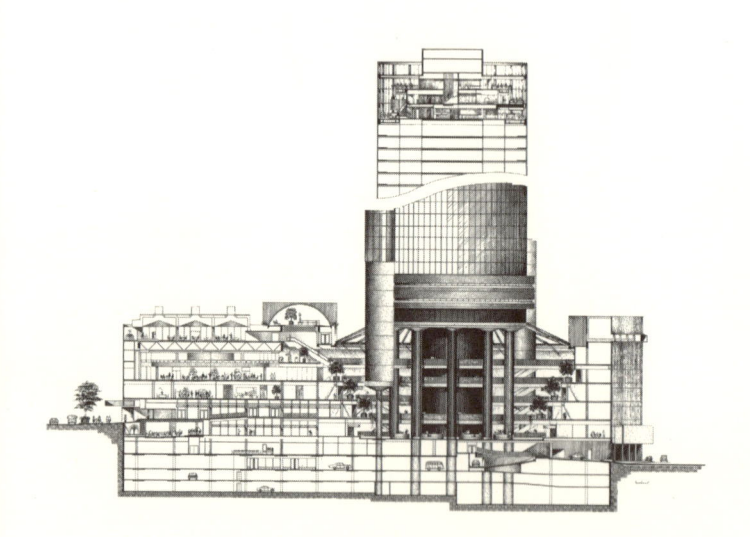

3.7 John Portman, Westin Peachtree Plaza, Atlanta, 1976, section.

the central "column" of elevators banks forming the final linkage in the chain, providing access to private rooms.

Besides being a good backdrop for high budget films, the Peachtree became the model for new Portman hotels built throughout the 1970s, the most infamous of which is the Los Angeles Bonaventure. The Bonaventure itself became a kind of backdrop in the 1980s to a seminal argument by Fredric Jameson concerning the emergence of a postmodern spatial sensibility. In his argument, space becomes a "cultural dominant" in a way that supports observations made above concerning the primacy of space in the contemporary city. For it is in the Centripetal City, specifically the imploded node of the Portman atrium, that Jameson makes his case for a culturally pervasive spatial bias. It is a compelling analysis of contemporary urban space that has yet to evoke a sufficient response.

A SPATIAL DOMINANT

First published in 1984, Jameson's "Postmodernism, or, The Cultural Logic of Late Capitalism" delivered a reading of postmodernism totally at odds with the then prevailing definition of the term, which had come to stand for nothing more than a promiscuous form of eclecticism. "Postmodern architecture" could not be further removed from Jameson's critical use of the term as it emerged from an analysis of a variety of academic disciplines, each enduring significant "epistemological ruptures" in their respective modernist practices. What made Jameson's approach unique was his application of a materialist link — between an economic substructure and cultural superstructure — to what had previously been considered as only a "revolution" in style. The postmodern was defined by Jameson not as another style, but as the cultural manifestation of a new phase of economic development identified by the economist Ernest Mandel as Late Capitalism. In binding the superstructure to the infrastructure, Jameson challenged the understanding of postmodernism as a novel aesthetic option in an essentially pluralist field. Postmodernism was a "cultural dominant" (1991, p.4) exclusively driven by the economic conditions which produced it.

Beyond the critique of eclecticism and of style, Jameson suggested that this cultural dominant distinguished itself from the preceding culture of high

3.8 "Plaza of the Americas Skywalk." Dallas, Texas, 1984.
Photograph by Evans Caglage.

modernism in a shift of emphasis from the temporal to the spatial as a direct response to what he perceived to be a "crisis in historicity." Jameson defines the postmodern as a collapse of the temporal, or an "attempt to think the present historically in an age that has forgotten how to think historically in the first place." The collapse of the temporal has been brought about by a number of events, chief among them being the completion of the process of modernization. Jameson insists that the modernist imagination was fueled by a dialectic between the modern and the pre-modern, where the juxtaposition of the two always provided a temporal fix between a recent premodern past and an emerging modern future. The transition to the postmodern occurs when modernization succeeds in eliminating all of the vestiges of the premodern organization, and the dialectic between the modern and the premodern collapses. Where only the modern exists, we are already in the state of the postmodern, "since what we call modern is the consequence of incomplete modernization and must necessarily define itself against a nonmodern residuality that no longer obtains in postmodernity. . . " (Jameson, 1994. p.20).

For Jameson, this absence of a modern/premodern dialectic results in profound temporal confusion and a shift in emphasis toward the spatial as characteristic of all postmodern production. To take an obvious example, the radical intervention, in 1958, of Mies van der Rohe's Seagram Building into the masonry fabric of Park Avenue was a revolutionary intervention in the architecture of the city. The remarkable photographs of the beaming glass prism lit up against the dark enclosure of the existing masonry buildings was a realization of Mies' photomontages of the 1920s celebrating a historical rupture between the old city and the new. This rupture was a revolution made manifest in a potent juxtaposition of form. It attempted nothing less than the presentation of a historical moment — an ambition it shares with a great many modernist interventions, from Mendelsohn's department stores, to the Centre Pompideau, to Coop Himmelblau's rooftop conversions.

This temporal rupture of 1958 stands in contrast to our contemporary "postmodern" view of the Seagram Building. What is now significant is a spatial rather than a temporal reading — where the present appearance of the building is virtually absorbed into the deep spatial continuity of the completely glass-walled corporate landscape. The postwar redevelopment of Park Avenue (a significant seat of global capital in its own right) profoundly altered the significance of the Seagram Building. It is by now difficult to distinguish Mies' building from the many curtainwall buildings which it subsequently inspired. While the appearance of the building has not been altered since 1958, the physical and cultural context against in which it is viewed has completely changed. The Seagram Building has lost its temporal fix. Instead of being the mark of a revolutionary urban transformation, an historical watershed made manifest, the object has been cut loose in the postmodern world — set spatially adrift in a landscape of transparency and reflection.

Following the success of Mies' intervention, the dialectical brick/glass, premodern/modern landscape of Park Avenue began an immediate renovation, quickly rebuilding its masonry fabric. As the modernization of the street approached completion, the dialectic between the premodern masonry fabric and modern glass-walled space collapsed into a homogeneous, mono-semantic world which, in its ultimate abstraction, remains divested of its temporal coordinates.

A POSTMODERN SUBLIME

For Jameson, this temporal confusion and subsequent shift in emphasis toward the spatial is connected to a number of events — the accelerated pace of electronic reproduction and high-speed transportation, demographic explosions, massive economies of scale, unlimited access to world markets, the aggressive development and deployment of technologies — a by now predictable litany of contemporary upheaval which nevertheless comes together for Jameson in what he called a "postmodern sublime," the "bewildering new space of late or multinational capital." In speaking of cultural production in the most general terms, Jameson claimed that "beyond all thematics or content" the best postmodern work offers us "some glimpse into a postmodern or technological sublime, whose power or authenticity is documented by the success of such works in evoking a whole new postmodern space in emergence around us." Defined in this way, the cultural dominant of postmodernism was to be manifest in architecture as the "privileged aesthetic language" of space.

What makes all of this a point of departure for the present investigation of contemporary urban space was Jameson's identification of his postmodern sublime with an existing urban space. This identification turned on his analysis of a "full-blown postmodern building," the atrium lobby of John Portman's Bonaventure Hotel in Los Angeles. In choosing a building that received little if any attention from the proponents of a postmodern architecture, Jameson went out on a limb proclaiming the emergence or irruption within the city of an unprecedented type of urban space:

> . . . this latest mutation of space — postmodern hyperspace — has finally succeeded in transcending the capacities of the individual human body to locate itself, to organize its immediate surroundings perceptually, and cognitively to map its position in a mappable external world. It may now be suggested that this alarming disjunction point between the body and its built environment . . . can itself stand as the symbol and analogon of that even sharper dilemma which is the incapacity of our minds, at least at present, to map the great global multinational and decentered communicational network in which we find ourselves caught as individual subjects. (Jameson, 1991, p.44)

3.9 John Portman, Westin Bonaventure, Los Angeles, interior.
From: Jameson, *Postmodernism, The Cultural Logic Of Late Capitalism.*

Even in 1984, Jameson's analysis may have seemed like late news, but it nevertheless remains uncontested in revealing a unique type of contemporary urban space which is both mirror and reflection of the advancing processes of contemporary economic development. Jameson describes the atrium space of the Bonaventure as a kind of "rift" in the mappable grid of downtown Los Angeles, appearing as the forecast of a new cultural dominant of space. This rift is like an erasure of the urban known into which a local, premodern gridded city finally collapses under the demands of a volatile global economy.

Jameson's descriptions of these spatial ruptures are based on a set of precise contradictions. He essentially describes the space of Portman's atrium as being vast and unknowable. Yet, at the same time he describes it as a "total space, a complete world, a kind of miniature city." It is a complete, closed and totalizing space, a discrete episode in the larger city; yet it is at the same time beyond our ability to actually perceive something that "we do not yet possess the perceptual equipment to match." This paradox, a sort of discretely formed abyss, presents a spatial problem. In the context of the existing city, postmodern hyperspace is described as a kind of urban "black hole," something very much like the imploded urban spaces of centripetal reorganization. By Jameson's definition, it is the emergence of an unmappable space in the still mappable remains of a conventional centrifugal grid. This marks the full development of the space of late capitalism as unknowable space in the vernacular world of the American urban grid.

Jameson's analysis of an unprecedented type of contemporary urban space suggests a gap or hiatus within the conventional fabric of the urban known, and anticipates the full emergence of another kind of city more properly belonging to the present mode of production. While the actual analysis of Portman's atrium was not extraordinary (it sounds a lot like Scully on the Carceri, actually), its implications were. Jameson was arguing that this spatial

3.10 John Portman, Westin Bonaventure, Los Angeles, aerial view.

implosion — the realization of a new global network of late capital — was already manifest as a unique form of urban space. The concrete nexus of the emergent spatial/cultural dominant of postmodernism would not be found in some newly synthesized global medium, but in the city itself. It would be predicated on an altogether unprecedented type of space whose specific anatomy was already revealed through analysis of contemporary urban production.

THE CLOSURE OF LATE CAPITAL

Jameson's description of "postmodern hyperspace" in the atrium of Portman's Bonaventure Hotel does not coincide with the analysis of centripetal development presented here. The preceding urban evaluation — the erasure of the grid, the intervention of the freeway, the implosion of urban space, the extension of the ladder into tunnels, skywalks and cores, and the development of its atrium intersections — all lead to what may be understood as an attempt to map that specific postmodern sublime identified by Jameson. But the spatial qualities evoked by Jameson are not necessarily the organizational qualities associated with the centripetal coordinates of the atrium — which is after all nothing more than the homogenous space of a large corporate interior.

One could argue that far from being the manifestation of an unmappable sublime — the effect of our inability to "map the great global multinational and decentered communicational network" — the Bonaventure atrium is all too mappable as a functioning coordinate of the exclusive centripetal network. As the most interesting variation on the Peachtree Plaza model, the Bonaventure multiplies the number of centers symmetrically around a dominant core. This reiteration of centers serves to enforce a centralized, hierarchically closed diagram. Indeed, the exotic spatial effects that Jameson described seem from this vantage to be calculated to obscure its role of coordination and control, which is clearly revealed in the plan geometry. What from an involuted view may appear an unfathomable sublime may from a larger perspective be nothing more than corporate eyewash, obscuring the claustrophobic enclosure of an exclusive centripetal network.

But holding Jameson to his example would only ignore the larger substance of his analysis concerning the development of contemporary urban space. His claim that our present culture has developed a marked spatial bias in response to an "historical deafness," and that this bias is not only limited to specific cultural products, but effects a much broader social sensibility — a cultural logic — seems to override the specific analysis of Portman's atrium. This cultural sensibility identified by Jameson is a more precise definition of the contemporary urban "primacy of space" from which this analysis was started and which was identified as instrumental to centripetal reorganization. "Postmodern hyperspace" ties these considerations to both the infrastructure of late capital and to the concrete urban/architectural phenomenon which has already been described.

It should not be difficult to assert that some version of a postmodern sublime (in the absence of Nature and God, Jameson referred to it as an "hysterical sublime") does exist, but probably not in the reactionary closure of Portman's atrium. If it does exist, the sublime is not likely to be located inside the armature of corporate development, but outside in the spatial residuum of the inner city ellipsis. In a condition as polarized as the inner city, it is the inherent disorganization of its residue which offers the greatest opportunity for aesthetic expression — an expression unmediated by the preemptive organization of capital.

The collapse of the 19th-century urban core, like the collapse of the masonry fabric of Park Avenue surrounding the Seagram Building, signals the collapse of the modernist (premodern/modern) dialectic, and the arrival of a postmodern condition. For Jameson, postmodernism marks the initiation of a homogenous non-dialectical space where only the modern exists. Yet, while late capital is indeed responsible for the production of contemporary urban space, it is not the primary goal of its construction. As discussed, contemporary urban space is the byproduct of late capitalist construction which, in its paranoid refusal of an exterior condition, cannot acknowledge and therefore must suffer the consequences of its own production.

In 1992 Jameson updated and extended his position with regard to the spatial production of late capital. The distinction he originally described in the Bonaventure atrium — between a corporate infrastructure and the mappable space of the existing city — remains in the revision, but there is now an attempt to scramble the terms. In what he refers to as the "Blade Runner syndrome" he purposefully confuses the distinction between the inside and the outside, albeit with dramatic effect:

> ...the interfusion of crowds of people among a high technological bazaar with its multitudinous nodal points, all of it sealed in an inside without an outside, which thereby intensifies the formerly urban to the point of becoming the unmappable system of late capitalism itself. Now it is the abstract system and its interrelations that are the outside: the former dome, the former city, beyond which no subject position is available, *so that it cannot be inspected as a thing in its own right, although it is certainly a totality*.(Jameson, 1994, p.157, emphasis added)

The description is alarming if not altogether nihilistic. By refusing a subject position external to his "high tech bazaar," Jameson is apparently resolving the duality inherent in contemporary urban development into a single homogenous space. To restate the argument: the overlay of the ladder onto the mappable centrifugal fabric causes the grid to implode and the space of an inner-urban ellipsis to emerge. The ladder constitutes the corporate inside

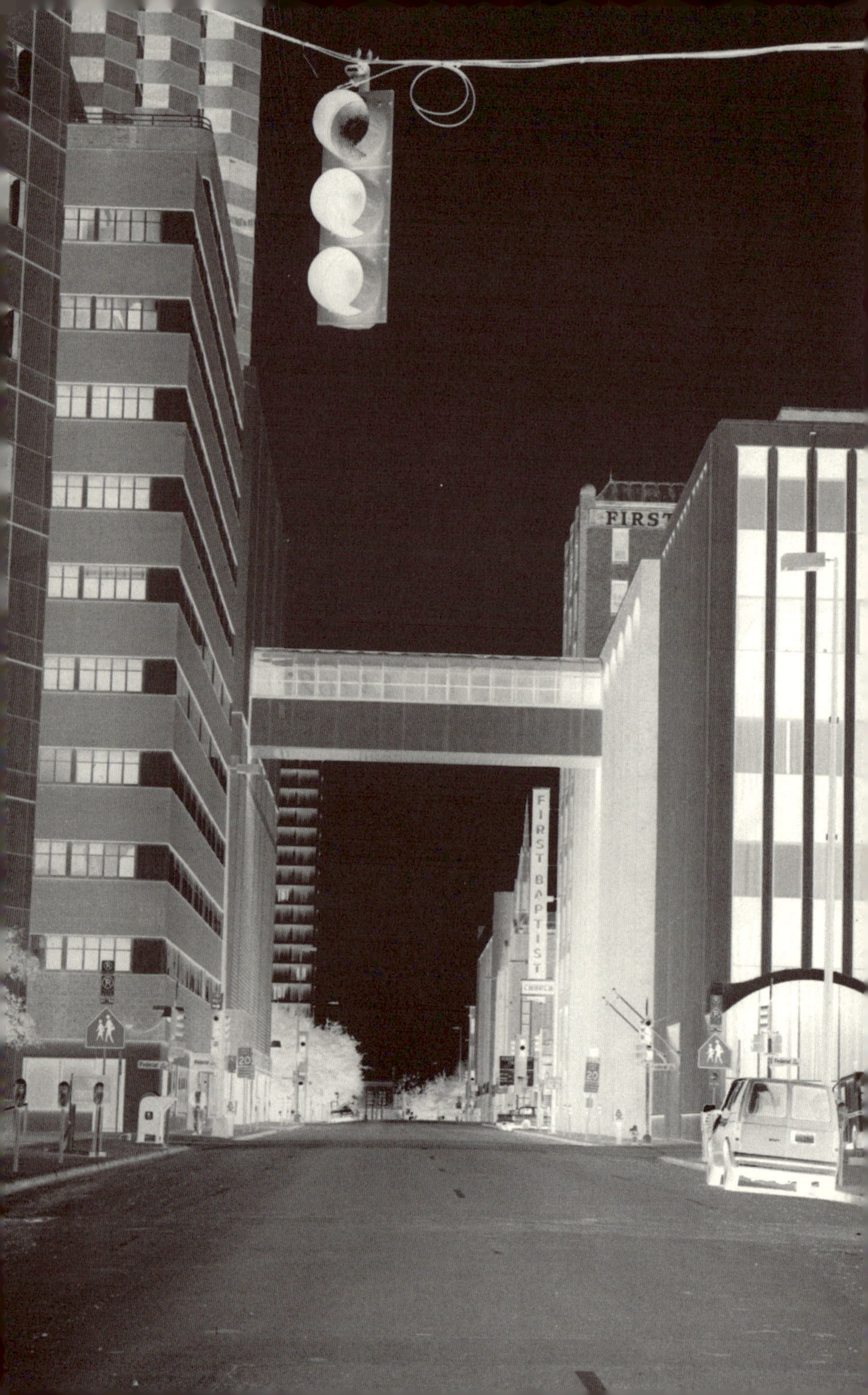
FIRST
FIRST BAPTIST
CHURCH

of centripetal development — an interjection of boundaries into the city. The imploded urban space of the ellipsis is by definition outside of the centripetal organization which produced it, yet they both remain potentially interrelated. Jameson's postmodern hyperspace is a paradoxical space where an unmappable gap in the mappable fabric — a hiatus or ellipsis — is contained within the mappable space of the city. By now, it should be apparent how mappable the centripetal reorganization of the city is. In its elimination of choice and its consolidation of activity, in its absolute homogeneity, it is eminently more mappable than the conventional city. What is unknowable, however, is the residue of its production. The inner-urban ellipsis must finally be defined here as all that is left of an "outside" or open urban world. The atrium is not the unmappable within the mappable context of the contemporary city. Rather, the situation may well be the inverse; the atrium and ladder system is what is mappable, and imploded urban space is what is ultimately unmappable, extensive, and perhaps may pass for some sort of sublime expression.

What remains difficult in Jameson's Blade Runner model is the ultimate collapse of the outside, the "inside without an outside. . . . the former city, beyond which no subject position is available." While there may be some merit in the denial of an external totalizing perspective, this would ultimately only advantage capital itself. It is clear that Late Capital wants to marginalize if not eradicate what is "outside" its control, and it is this effort that Jameson may ultimately accommodate in his scrambling of the terms. One can admire the rhetorical tension Jameson sustains here between inside and outside. His attempt to avoid the closure of the binary opposition and instead reinstate the play between the two terms is a beautiful kind of literary demonstration of

3.11 Dallas Streetscape, 1995.
Photograph by Karin Taylor.

precisely the space which is needed. But the entrenched inside/outside polarity of corporate development — a "stalled dialectic" — will unfortunately not fall before the force of its suggestion. It must be understood that Jameson is responding to the passing of modernism and, with the collapse of all remaining premodern enclaves, the inevitable emergence of late capital closure. The homogenous space of the corporate environment may indeed mark the triumph of a fully modernized late capitalist state, but the increasingly potent residuum of its production should not be underestimated.

3.12 Buckminster Fuller, project for a geodesic dome over 22nd through 64th streets, Manhattan, 1962.
Midtown Manhattan as a colossal corporate atrium.

Which is to say that the homogenous space of late capital is fatally compromised by the absence of a dialectic, and this is of course a surprise to no one. The paradox has been a recurrent preoccupation in both science fiction and Modern Architecture. The most recent merger being the incredibly banal "Biosphere 2" project in Arizona which, like the legacy of Buckminster Fuller it extends, is nothing if not a reactionary celebration of closed systems.

NATIVE URBAN SPACE

Urban theorists are by now indifferent, if not numb, to the popular associations made between contemporary urban space and intractable social pathologies. The so-called "inner city" is an absolute dystopia, the master dystopia, and its pervasive medium is contemporary urban space.

Yet, flying in the face of bureaucratic fear, the explosion of space in the old urban centers has spun a mythology which Ludwig Hilberseimer would be stunned to perceive. The space of the Ellipsis has many predecessors and many analogous configurations: Pynchon's Zone, Koolhaas' Post Architectural Void, Deleuze's Smooth Space, Jameson's Hyperspace, Solà-Morales' *Terrain Vague*, the brutal ambiance of nearly every story J.G. Ballard has written, the list could easily expand. What they have in common is a desire to cultivate the unmappable "outside" of an encroaching world system that is prefigured by the seamless or absolute closure of the corporate *gesamtkunstwerk*, a closure made possible by the centripetal organization of the ladder.

The attempt to locate what remains of native urban space, of open, unmappable urban space, to seize the possibility of habitation which might exist off the corporate map is the point of these dystopian nightmares, which seem to be on the verge of becoming the grotesque celebrations of a new reality. The need to make available a "subject position" within the implosion of grid space, outside the world system, is a tentative objective of these fantasies, as it is indeed for the present work. Urban architecture, not to mention architectural culture (not to mention political culture), will only exist "outside" of a closed system. It can only unfold in native urban space.

Through the remapping of the city and the implosion of the grid, two cities emerge out of a traditional urban ground, an inside and an outside, ladder and ellipsis, an elect and a preterit, a World System and the Zone. As everyone suspects, the possibility for real invention lies within the Zone, in navigating the treacherous, dangerous, degraded world of contemporary urban space, which has been associated with the formation of the "inner city." About all it has going for it at the present moment is its inaccessibility to both corporate and bureaucratic power.

Despite an often frantic need for an alternative closure, one must be cautious in simply asserting the possibility of an ideal "subject position" in native urban space. In such speculation, several problems emerge which deny such quick and easy solutions. The first and most obvious problem is that any direct design intervention would expose native urban space to immediate colonization. While it is important to seize contemporary urban space as an alternative to closure, it is much more important to retain its qualities of an alternative. When a particular kind of "absence" such as native urban space becomes the object of design, it loses its distinguishing qualities and becomes "presence" — a presence long anticipated and quickly exploited by capital. An alternative to colonization has already been suggested in the relatively disorganized residual qualities of contemporary urban space itself. As will be seen, these qualities constitute a powerful antidote to the excessive organization of closed urban form.

A second more difficult problem with directly constructing an alternative subject position is that we ourselves are the product of closed systems — we are bound to the interior of the economic, political and cultural system that simultaneously sustains and impoverishes us. It would be absolutely naive to imagine it possible to simply travel into an alternative environmental state, that some kind of Archimedean point could fundamentally change our acquired values, reorganize our economies, germinate an alternative politics, and otherwise alter our destiny. The problem here is that any point outside or beyond the position which one occupies already accepts the boundary established by closed systems. To insist that one may occupy the "outside" is to be limited by the inside/outside parameters that reinforce and establish the urban conditions for which an alternative is sought. In the next chapter it will be precisely demonstrated how closure produces the most exclusive and restrictive of "subject positions." The idea of escaping such forms of inscription would be as much about the production of alternative subject positions as about alternative or native urban sites.

FOUR:
THE CENTRIPETAL CITY

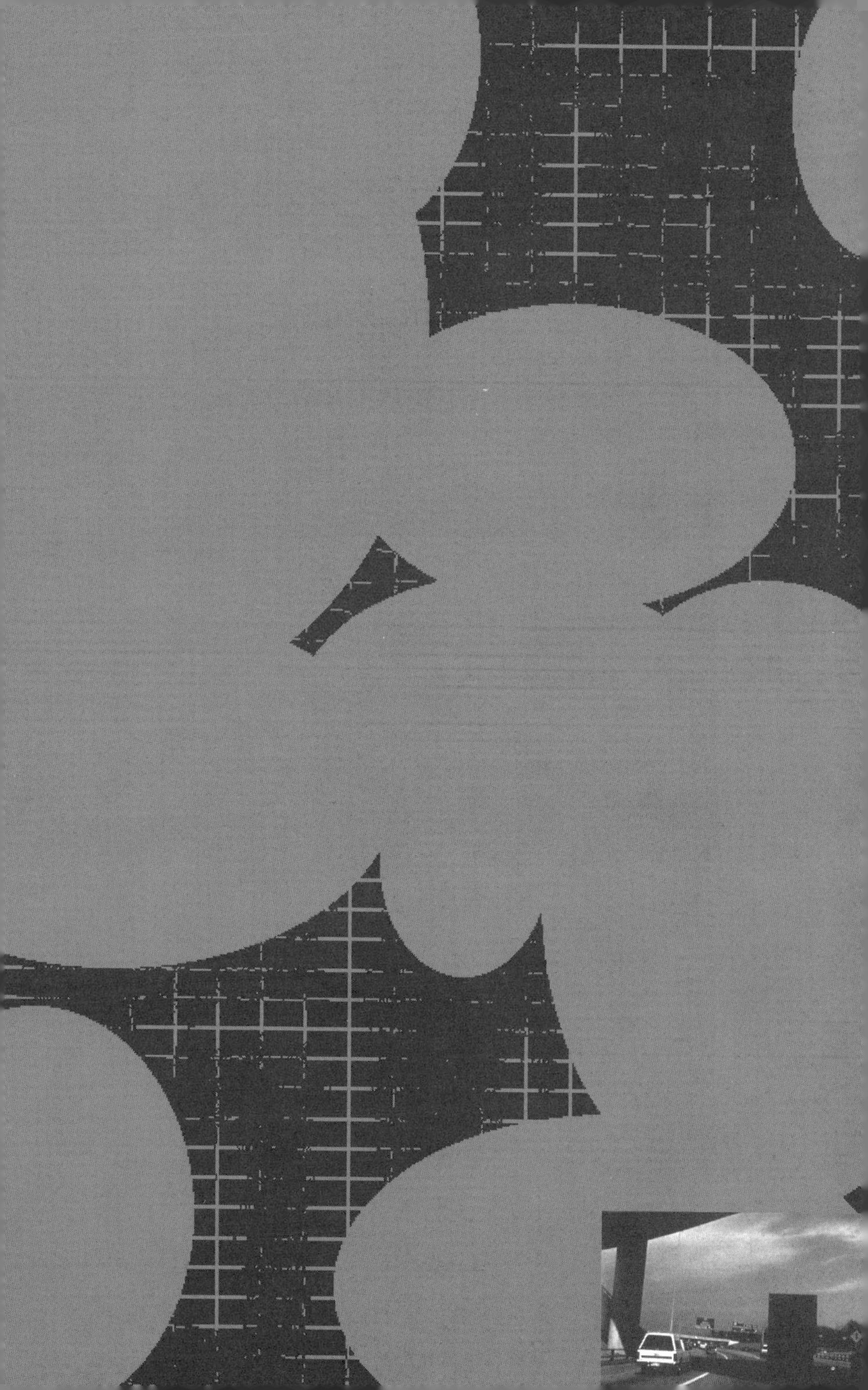

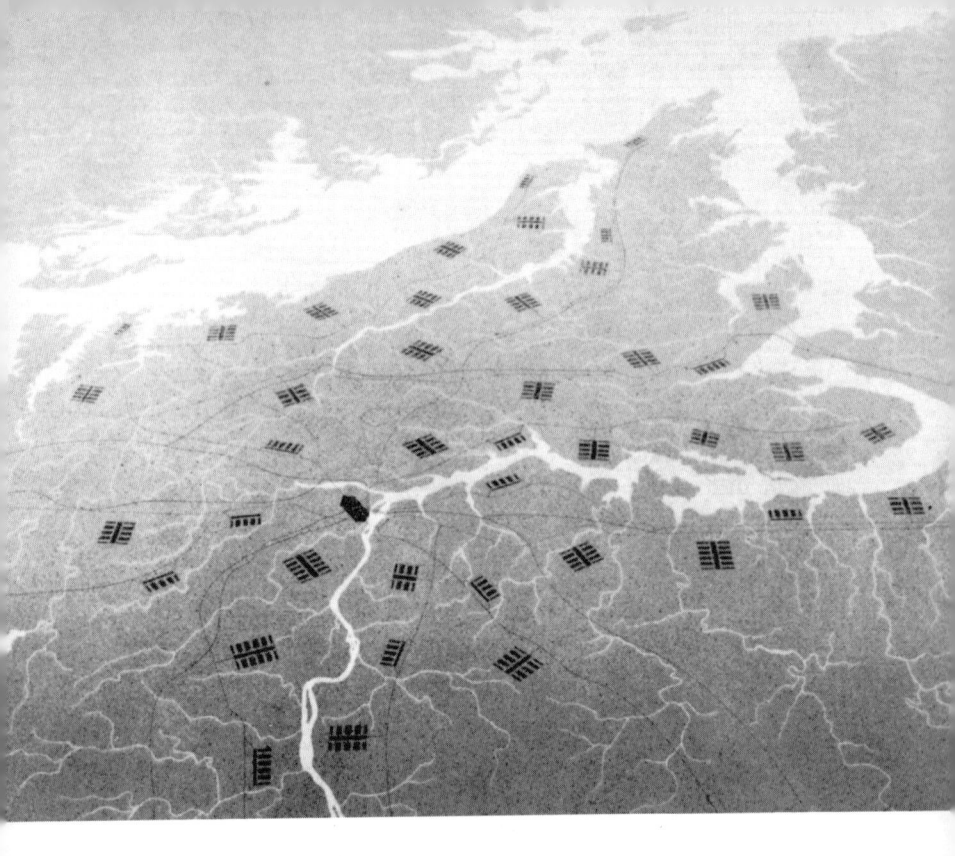

4.1 Ludwig Hilberseimer, Washington D.C. replanned.
From: Hilberseimer, *The Nature of Cities*.

THE CENTRIPETAL CITY

Chapter four addresses centripetal expansion as it emerges on the urban periphery. The characteristics of postwar development are related to what will be defined as weak metropolitan form where obligations to the urban whole are drastically qualified if not altogether dismissed. Weak metropolitan form emerges from the decline of the model of metropolitan growth referred to as Centralized Polynuclear Expansion. This model — first advocated at the beginning of the century and ultimately implemented in the postwar period — is both innovative and traditional in its effect. It is innovative in the sense that it produces a unique binary or polynuclear urban field, and it is traditional in the sense that it sustains a centralized urban hierarchy. With the weakening of the model, the inherent conflict between its traditional and innovative qualities has thrown the contemporary city into a kind of interregnum — or inability to evolve — where traditional urban strategies cannot die and new urban strategies cannot emerge. This interregnum is the key to a series of urban mutations unique to contemporary production.

    Chief among these mutations is the manner in which weak metropolitan form gives rise to excessively strong nuclei of development defined as the closed centripetal figure or ladder. In the absence of a strong metropolitan center, the binary field of centripetal production has evolved in increasing degrees of exclusion, division, and polarization. These strong local nuclei will be characterized as closed urban systems, or more specifically as corporate enclaves, set against the chaos and disorganization of a declining metropolitan order. As the centralized metropolis becomes more diffuse and disorganized, the corporate enclave moves toward more extreme degrees of closure, which in turn increases the disorganization of its residuum. What thus emerges in the contemporary city is a radically dispersed polynuclear order which, while never interlocking in (metropolitan) space, ultimately gives rise to a discontinuous or distributed unity of urban form.

As new nuclei of development approach absolute closure, their spatial residuum approach complete disorganization. The force of this disorganization is measured in the concept of entropy. As entropy increases, the residuum emerges, not as a metropolitan "Void" or vacuum, but as a persuasive economic, political and cultural site. As these sites become recognizable, the closed enclave will be increasingly confronted not with absence, but with a potent entropic counterforce.

BINARY STRUCTURES

The binary structure of this analysis has attempted to set up a dialectical argument as opposed to a single, directed line of investigation. It has often been suggested that such binary methods tend to digress from an active interaction between a pair of opposing terms into an exclusive and reductive polarity. The line dividing open dialectic and closed polarity has perhaps been glossed over in this analysis, crossed and recrossed as if the dialectic could never really stall, that it might ultimately prevail against closure. The text itself is rife with such would-be dialectical pairings — centric/linear, field/figure, time/space, lattice/tree, hierarchical/evanescent, center/periphery, inside/outside, ladder/ellipsis, form/space, open/closed, sidewalk/tunnel, explosion/implosion, apparatus/icon, order/complexity, strong/weak, centrifugal/centripetal, historical/abstract, figure/residuum, native/corporate, local/global — each an attempt to formally structure a contemporary urban analysis. One should not fail to notice the irony of an analysis structured on the premises so catastrophically lacking in its object. There is perhaps no better example of a reductive, undialectical polarity than the inner city division between closed corporate form and its excluded residual space. As it turns out, the dialectical field generated by centripetal expansion is not dialectical at all. Rather, the resulting polynuclear field has degenerated into an irreversible opposition between a privileged urban interior and a lapsed residuum. This polarity constitutes the familiar embattled landscape where an urban exterior is exploited to construct the most excessive of closed systems. On the postwar periphery, as in the reorganized urban core, these closed systems are set against a notorious condition that their own production has brought into existence.

Before capitulating to what may seem inevitable urban forces, it is important to understand the exact formal process of centripetal expansion and seek a more promising bottom line. The most significant characteristic of centripetal expansion is not its relative flexibility or the reductive pattern of its use, but the generation of a dialectical spatial field, an "inside" and "outside" condition that was virtually non-existent in prewar urban development. In theory, the 19th-century city would have generated a limitless and unbroken field of urban expansion. Each coordinate of that field would index a totalizing spatial order and suggest the existence of a universal continuum — singular, homogenous and uniform. By contrast, centripetal development produces a pattern of closed figures and a significant spatial exterior. The replacement of the singular universal continuum of the 19th-century grid with an interrupted spatial field — the binary inside/outside of centripetal development — is the crucial innovation of contemporary urban development.

While reductive polarization arises from the inside/outside binary field of centripetal production, this urban field could equally well sponsor, not polarization and closure, but a dialectical relation unique to contemporary urban development. Despite the difficulty in citing examples to the contrary, the polarization of the polynuclear field is not an inevitable urban process. The direct analysis of centripetal form reveals a latent potential in the residuum altogether missing from contemporary practice. While it is easy to condemn the contemporary city as a closed, exclusive, reactionary, and ultimately self-defeating environment, this does not constitute a definitive critique of its underlying form. The forces and effects of centripetal production supersede the circumstances that have brought them into existence. Considered as a formal process, a negative or inverse polarity is just as likely to occur as the positive polarity which is prevalent today. What is significant about this bottom line is that closed urban systems are not seen to be the inevitable effects of a binary spatial field.

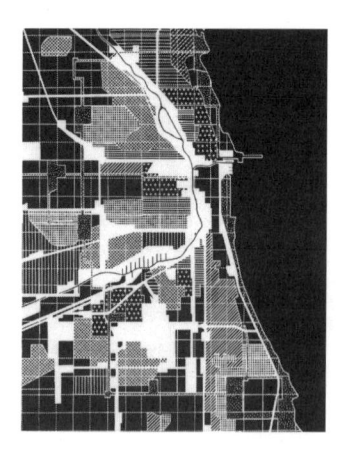

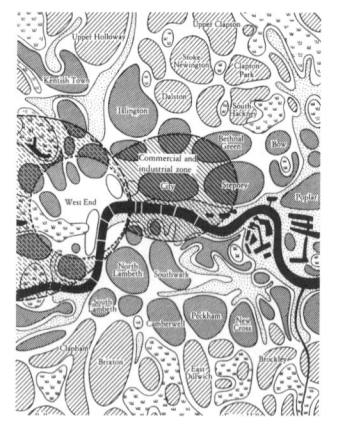

4.2 Universal urban field. Analysis of prewar Chicago.

4.3 Binary urban field. Analysis of postwar London.

LOCAL/METROPOLITAN

The perception of so-called urban "sprawl" as an unorganized and chaotic field is very much at odds with the experience of the contemporary enclave as a restrictive, overstructured urban environment. This conflicted reading coincides with two distinct scales of contemporary urban construction: the local and the metropolitan. In the initial stages of postwar development, a relatively erratic polynuclear field emerged with the aggregation of countless isolated subdivisions. Absent a mediating, metropolitan grid, these subdivisions were crudely linked to each other through their residual space giving the impression of a confused, disordered urban environment — a sprawl. The relation between postwar sprawl and the closed exurban enclave subsequently emerged as the operative dynamic of contemporary urban development. The perception of a chaotic sprawl creates the demand for a reductive, overstructured environment which in turn increases the apparent disorganization of the residuum as sprawl. On the whole, contemporary construction is neither restrictive nor chaotic, rather it is both depending on the relative scale of perception. At the local scale the Centripetal City is highly organized and restrictive, while at a metropolitan scale it is highly disorganized and chaotic.

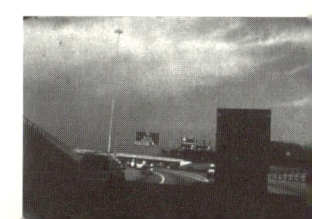

The specific relation between the local and the metropolitan scale of organization is critical to understanding contemporary urban form. A comparison between the 19th-century city and the postwar Centripetal City is again instructive. In the 19th-century city, metropolitan order and metropolitan identity were very strong. This strength was established by a single, hierarchical urban core and a precise edge or urban frontier formed by the limit of its block structure. In contrast, the local order of 19th-century urban district is relatively weak. For example, within the Commissioner's Plan itself, Midtown, the Upper West Side, Chelsea, and Harlem are acknowledged districts which nevertheless lack significant inflections of the larger gridded infrastructure. In contrast to the well defined metropolitan whole, local district boundaries within the grid are arbitrary and indistinct.

With regard to the centripetal organization of the contemporary city, the relation between the local and metropolitan levels of organization is inverted. In the postwar city metropolitan form is weak, and local districting is very strong. Against the chaos of metropolitan sprawl, nothing could be more structured than the closed centripetal figure of the corporate enclave. The postwar inversion of relatively strong and weak form is the corollary to the inversion/implosion of the urban spatial field.

The polarization of the contemporary urban spatial field is thus organized around two discrete scales, each diverging into equal and opposing degrees of order and chaos. The Centripetal City is characterized by strong pockets of isolated development surrounded by what will be called "weak" metropolitan form. Weak metropolitan form is not difficult to characterize. Throughout the postwar years massive zones of construction have emerged which stand beyond conventional means of urban representation. Somewhere between the scale of a single comprehensible ladder (such as a commercial mall interior or single subdivision street) and the scale of a regional road map, an unmeasurable urban realm has come to establish the space of routine existence. It is this apparent collapse of metropolitan identity into sprawl which propels the characteristic mutations of contemporary urban production.

CENTRALIZED POLYNUCLEAR EXPANSION

In order to understand the weak metropolis, it is necessary to briefly trace the last appearance of a relatively strong metropolitan form. What has been referred to as Centralized Polynuclear Expansion was first invented by Ebenezer Howard nearly a century ago. Centralized Polynuclear Expansion presumes a hierarchical urban core around which new autonomous nuclei gather in a dispersed but centralized pattern. As opposed to 19th-century urban extension, Centralized Polynuclear Expansion assumes growth to take place, not along a continuous urban perimeter, but as the outward projection of a series of spatially autonomous nuclei which together form a polynuclear field.

While the model was widely championed by architects and planners as a form of suburban extension throughout the first half of the century, it did not begin to supplant traditional patterns of open, centrifugal growth until after the Second World War. In many cases, postwar construction does not seem to comply with the idealized form of Centralized Polynuclear Expansion presented by its early advocates, yet the urban organization which emerged was strategically identical: spatially autonomous enclaves surrounding a dominant metropolitan center. While clearly autonomous, these postwar nuclei — including housing tracts, "new towns," commercial malls, office parks, industrial complexes, university campuses — most often defer in their placement to the historical urban core.

At this stage, Centralized Polynuclear Expansion appears to be the last coherent model of urban development produced in this century. However weakened it may have become over the fifty years of its widespread existence, the model remains the operative idea of contemporary metropolitan organization. It is, for example, the model which supports the idea of "sub" urban tracts despite the fact that there is little left for contemporary development to be subordinate to. It is also the model which continues to support the idea (and the necessary reconstruction) of declining metropolitan centers. No matter how spatially autonomous the new nuclei ultimately become, they continue to be located relative to traditional urban centers. In this regard, Centralized Polynuclear Expansion remains the dominant, if weakened, model of metropolitan urban organization.

Most everyone exposed to the popular press is aware that a city defined by a fixed hierarchical center and subsidiary periphery is out of synch with present and emerging urban realities. New exurban "centers" such as European "New Towns" or American "Edge Cities" have multiplied at an astonishing rate and, by the 1980's, established the daily experience of the majority of urban dwellers. An exclusive polycentric mode of development is by now so widely accepted that it scarcely becomes the occasion for comment. Historians, planners and theorists long ago pronounced the death of cen-

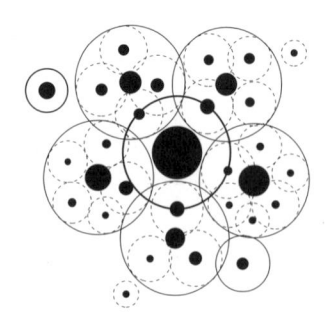

4.4 Patrick Abercrombie, Centralized Polynuclear Expansion.

ter/periphery schema and regard new exurban nuclei as the inevitable outcomes of forces identified and analyzed nearly a century ago. In spite of such professional acquiescence, these new exurban nuclei have failed to subvert the dominant metropolitan center. The apparent hegemony of the new exurban nuclei — their now established economic and political power over a besieged "inner city" — has never fully undermined the center. This paradox of a powerful polynuclear field unable to overcome the vestiges of a traditional, centralized, hierarchical model is the legacy of Centralized Polynuclear Expansion now in the process of playing itself out. The enduring significance of the center — idea and image of the greater urban whole — is the result of an inability to identify an alternative metropolitan model that is coherent or "strong" enough to replace it.

THE EMERGENCE OF THE POLYNUCLEAR FIELD

In order to analyze Centralized Polynuclear Expansion and understand how it sustains the present "weakened" state of metropolitan form, it is necessary to briefly retrace its historical trajectory. It is important to restate that polynuclear expansion did not emerge with suburbanization. With the exception of a small number of upper-class enclaves, early suburbs were rarely able to break with the spatial continuity of the open centrifugal grid. In the United States, the prewar stages of suburbanization — the 19th-century "Mainline" or railroad suburb, the turn-of-the-century "streetcar" suburb, or the early automobile subdivisions of the 1920s and 1930s — typically offered a sparser, greener version of the continuous grid from which they otherwise sought to distinguish themselves. While many of these suburbs were established beyond the leading edge of metropolitan growth, they invariably anticipated its arrival with their open gridded infrastructures. Once the city reached their

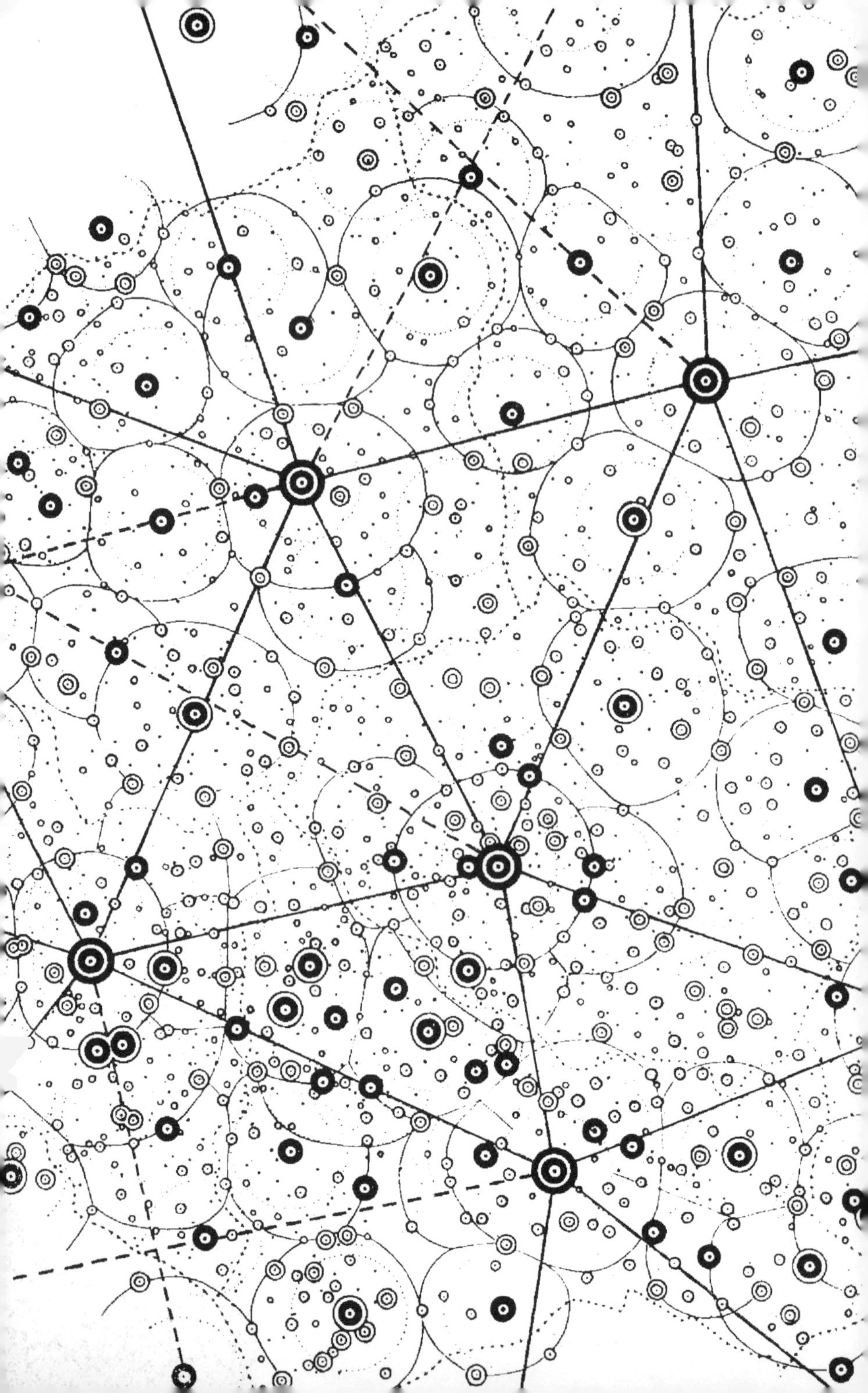

boundaries, these gridded developments were quickly tied into the gr metropolitan field. A cursory analysis of early suburban planning indicates that, even in the cases where there was a significant spatial discontinuity — such as the curvilinear street layouts of upper class "country club" subdivision — these developments did little to alter the dominant patterns of continuous gridded expansion. The majority of American suburbs laid out before the war were not closed, exclusive tracts but outbound extensions of existing gridded developments rendered less dense, more green, some with curves and minor interruptions, yet ultimately interconnected with a greater urban continuity.

Perhaps the most obvious example of open centrifugal suburbanization is the prewar gridding of the entire Los Angeles basin and San Fernando Valley in Southern California. This massive expanse of grid was the result of a supergrid established by survey lines (Rowe, 1991, p.198) and subdivided by a virtual real-estate monopoly spearheaded by Henry Huntington's Pacific Electric Railway Company (Jackson, 1985, p.180). This enormous open gridded infrastructure makes Los Angeles today, not the celebrated paradigm of postwar urbanism, but an anachronistic mutation of 19th-century expansion. This point is made clear by a comparison between the gridded prewar continuities of Los Angeles County and the laddered postwar discontinuities of Orange County immediately to its south. As a radically decentralized polynuclear field, the twenty-six nuclei or "cities" of Orange County (population: 2.6 million) represents the discontinuous closed organization of postwar centripetal expansion. Nothing could be farther from the street environment created by the great east-west Boulevards of Los Angeles — Pico, Olympic, Santa Monica or Wilshire — than the exclusive malls, office parks, and gated enclaves of the former Irvine Ranch. The contrast between the two counties reveals that the

4.5 Walter Christaller, Distribution of towns as central places in Southern Germany.

unique qualities of postwar urbanization are not found in the gridded continuities of automobiles and "sprawl" for which Los Angeles is known, but the radically discontinuous enclaves and closed urban systems represented by Orange County. While the emergence of the polynuclear field is often thought to coincide with suburban development, these examples show that this is not the case. There are both open centrifugal suburbs and closed centripetal suburbs and the distinction between them is crucial.

Centralized Polynuclear Expansion promised a radical leap out beyond the urban periphery to form a spatially segregated polynuclear field. Inasmuch as prewar centrifugal economies could never afford the significant vacancies of a "greenbelt," significant ellipses in the grid typically failed to materialize. One could conclude that this leap into polynuclear development was made meaningless by cultural and economic constraints. One could, at the same time, attribute to the early generations of Garden City planners great powers of prophecy (Hall, 1988, p.169). It was not until in the early 1950s that the polynuclear field exploded and radical spatial discontinuities can be observed in response to, among other things, the mass ownership of automobiles, government insurance of home loans, and a vast national freeway network. Whether in response to a professional advocacy of "greenbelts" in Europe, or in response to the speculative practice of "leapfrogging" in the United States (Rowe, 1991, p.27), postwar suburbs began to break, not only from the programmatic continuities of the traditional city — they were no longer simply bedroom communities — but, more significantly, from its spatial continuities. With the rejection of the open gridded infrastructure, there was to be no ultimate reconciliation with the continuities of the greater urban field. It was thus a deliberate spatial disruption which signaled a transformation in the mode of urban expansion and the emergence of the polynuclear field.

As the gridded extensions of prewar development were superseded by the closed figures and spatial reservoirs typical of postwar development, Howard's diagram came to serve as the implicit model, not only for the reconstruction plans of larger cities, but also for new unplanned cities. The real and lasting legacy of the Garden City is not that it made the city greener, or that it established a context for the detached dwelling, or that it took "x" number of children off the street by eliminating dangerous through traffic. Its primary significance was that it altered the premise of urban expansion. The city would no longer grow by gridded extension, but instead leap over the existing urban limit and initiate spatially autonomous centripetal figures segregated by discrete spatial reservoirs. With the initiation of a polynuclear field, Centralized Polynuclear Expansion ultimately supplanted gridded centrifugal extension. It remains the metropolitan model under whose steadily weakening or vestigial form the contemporary city continues to operate today.

The effect of bureaucratic intervention in the formation of the postwar city has been documented profusely, but its role in the propagation of closed urban systems has not been emphasized. Two key pieces of New Deal legislation, the Federal-Aid Highway Act of 1938, and the National Housing Act of 1934 set into motion the organizational forces that subsequently flourished after the war. Later augmented by the 1956 Federal Highway Act and the GI Bill respectively, the bureaucratic standardization of roads, residential construction, and subdivision standards set the parameters of the postwar urban construction. The role of the government in the construction of 41,000 miles of interstate and metropolitan freeways is direct and its effect on the reorganization of the urban core and the establishment of the postwar polynuclear field is decisive. The role of the FHA and VA is less direct. The FHA was set up in 1934 to revive the construction industry which had remained virtually dormant since the 1929 stock market crash. By insuring fully amortized, long term, low interest loans with little down payment, the FHA and later VA loans made mass ownership of housing possible. In order to qualify for the insured loans, however, the property had to meet prescribed guidelines. Government redlining of uninsurable neighborhoods ultimately enforced the economic segregation and subsequent homogeneity of existing subdivisions (Jackson, 1985, p.203), while the setting of specific subdivision standards explicitly required the reorganization of the urban open grid. Following patterns established by the early Garden City planners, FHA bureaucrats published a diagram in the late 1930's showing the preferred renovation of a traditional gridiron subdivision into an isolated development, of curved streets, parks, and a single entrance off a by-pass (Rowe, 1991, p.202). In other words, the plans produced by the picturesque tradition for the upper classes were routinized into func-

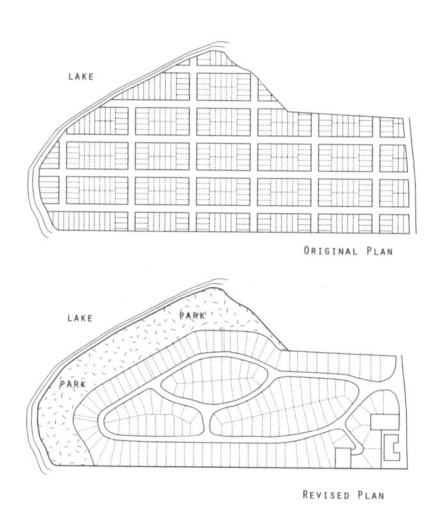

ORIGINAL PLAN

REVISED PLAN

4.6 U.S. Federal Housing Authority, Subdivision Guidelines. Suggested revisions for a hypothetical lakeside subdivision.

tional diagrams of closure dedicated to the ultimate protection of government investment in mass urban construction. Given that there is no better example of a closed system than a government bureaucracy, it is not surprising that the FHA would reproduce its own internal organization in the vast urban environments it administered.

GRID, LINE AND CENTER

The implosion of the hierarchical urban center and the rapid proliferation of new exurban nuclei have more recently obscured the logic of Centralized Polynuclear Expansion. As the hierarchical center collapses under the weight of its "subsidiary" mode of development, the idea of the city as a totality shifts from a centralized metropolitan figure to a labyrinthine field or topology of sprawl. This transformation has already been defined as the movement from a sub-urban to a super-urban stage where new centripetal development overwhelms the prewar metropolitan core. At the threshold of the superurban stage, the metropolitan core is dramatically weakened, yet it remains a decisive force in contemporary urban aggregation.

The apparent transformation of a centralized polynuclear metropolis into a disorganized field of postwar "sprawl" can be understood in relation to a significant deviation from the model. As described, Centralized Polynuclear Expansion is a mode of urban expansion that overreaches existing city limits and establishes spatially autonomous nuclei of growth. As initially proposed, the model assumed a precise number of figural sub-centers which were of a predetermined size and discrete shape. For example, Howard's "Social City" projected six autonomous settlements, and Patrick Abercrombie's Plan for Greater London proposed fourteen "New Towns," each being discrete nuclei of development. In practice the surrounding sub-centers often failed to form

COUNTY
COUNTY
Spring
Bender Lake
SPRING CREEK
SCIAACA
HARDY TOLLROAD
RIVER VALLEY
SCHULTZ
BRIAR CREEK
TREE HOUSE
HIRSCHFIELD
TITLEIST
Mercer Park
ALDINE WESTFIELD
Creek
Cypress
TREASCHWIG
Horseshoe Lake
Eternity Park Cemetery
St Mathew Cem
Mueschke Cem
WESTFIELD
HUMBLE
WESTFIELD LP
61
HUMBLE WESTFIELD
THEISS
RAYFORD
BAUMGARTNER
ESSMAN
H AND R
HARDY
HOUSTON
CITY
Turkey
FARREL
RICHEY
TURKEY
North Harris
WOODED PINE
EAGLECREST
CANDLERIDGE
CARRIAGE POINT
PARK
MILLSTONE
FOUR OAKS
OLD WOODS
WOODCREEK
TRAVICK
BIRCH PARK
BARBUDA
GAYMAN
ARUBA
GRENADA
TOBAGO
MIDWAY PLAZA
IBIS
CARSBROOK
SHELDONHAM
COUNTRYSIDE
BANQUO
LAKEWAY
COW
GULCH
GOODFELLOW
WILD
WOODS
BIRNAM
CYPRESSWOOD
M P RR

coherent entities, if for no other reason than the modest scale of bo⸺ and public investment could rarely match the ambitious scale of the tneo⸺ Instead of coherent town-sized nuclei, what frequently emerged were a countless number of small, discretely formed tracts which came together into an evanescent urban field. As the center began to collapse under reorganization and as new development failed to configure large, coherent nuclei, this field was transformed into a zone of discontinuous centripetal figures mediated by a new type of residual urban space.

These new tracts and residual spaces are not, however, the only ingredients of sprawl. In its weakened state, the historical urban core continues to influence the organization of the contemporary polynuclear field. This influence, however negligable, operates in radical conflict with the inherently non-hierarchical field of autonomous suburban nuclei. The conflict between a residual, hierarchical centralization and an emergent non-hierarchical dispersion is decisive with regard to the understanding of sprawl. Inherent to the idea of Centralized Polynuclear Expansion, this conflict is based on a conflict between traditional and innovative modes of urban organization. The traditional mode establishes a definitive urban hierarchy associated with a primary urban center and a subordinate urban (and natural) periphery. The innovative mode establishes a binary or polynuclear urban field characteristic of contemporary centripetal production. A metropolitan model that promotes the emergence of a unique polynuclear field and simultaneously sustains an archaic central/peripheral morphology establishes a complex antagonism between tradition and innovation — field and center — which goes a long way towards accounting for the present stasis in contemporary urban evolution.

**4.7 The Polynuclear City. Houston Subdivisions,
Farm to Maket Road 1960, Street Map, Detail.**

Caught between the hierarchical city that was, and the polynuclear urban field which is to be, "these suburbs," according to Hilberseimer, "can neither stay alive nor die" (Pommer, 1988, p.108).

In the early decades of the 20th-century, the archaic or retrograde character of a centralized hierarchical city was recognized by modern architects and planners, and a number of metropolitan alternatives to it were proposed. What typically emerged from these proposals were *non-centralized* polynuclear models. The modernist strategies consistently rejected the centralization and hierarchies of the Garden City while retaining its innovation of the polynuclear field. Two general categories of non-centralized polynuclear models emerged: the linear models of Milutin and Hilberseimer and the supergrid and superblock model developed most extensively by Frank Lloyd Wright. While these metropolitan models never achieved the widespread acceptance of Centralized Polynuclear Expansion, they are relevant precisely because contemporary development has grown to resemble them. While the linear and supergridded cities were proposed as antidotes to centralized planning, they have subsequently emerged within its presently weakened form, both vying to replace its increasingly irrelevant organization. These non-centralized metropolitan patterns provide a convenient template for the reading of contemporary urban environments.

Linear "cities" formed around interurban freeways are ubiquitous in contemporary urban development and hardly need description. On the periphery, where freeway construction often precedes urbanization, its role in generating new urban growth is decisive. An interstate or national highway gives way to a primary urban freeway. This freeway is supplemented by opposing one-way "feeder" roads on which large scale commercial and administrative services are located —shopping malls, discount megastores, and isolated office buildings — and replace, at a much larger scale, what used to be called a "strip." At freeway over- and underpasses, the feeder road intersects with secondary roads or "collectors" which receive the primary axes of private development. These primary axes (analogous to the spine of the settlement unit) are typically marked by gated entries and serve to organize discretely planned local developments. Off these axes, a succession of spines overlap, the number and complexity of which depends on the size of the development. In many instances, the transition from the metropolitan linear structure of the freeway to the local linear structure of the centripetal street spine is seamless. As a reiteration of form, a complete if not comprehensible unity of local and metropolitan levels of urban organization is established.

A similar description could be made of the second predominate non-centralized polynuclear model, the supergrid. As a hybrid of closed centripetal development at the local scale and open centrifugal development at the metropolitan scale, the supergrid provides a compelling analytical tool. The theoretical model can be characterized by a non-hierarchical grid laid over an undeveloped landscape. This open metropolitan gridding is not reiterated by further gridding at a local scale as seen, for example, in Los Angeles and other prewar centrifugal suburbs, but is infilled by an imploded series of disconnected centripetal figures which produce sizable amounts of residual space. As related to actual sites, isolated office parks or housing tracts are organized by strictly discontinuous *cul-de-sac* developments which fall within a larger gridded network typically derived from survey lines or a pre-existing pattern of rural roads. The obvious and most radical theoretical context for the supergrid is Frank Lloyd Wright's development of Broadacre City. The master plans of Chandigarh and, more recently, of Milton Keynes are also clear examples.

The simultaneous overlay of both linear and gridded polynuclear patterns onto the vestiges of a centralized city accounts for weak metropolitan

diagram 4.1
The Superblock

The superblock strategy supports closed centripetal development at the local scale and open centrifugal development at the metropolitan scale. The model is defined by a non-hierarchical grid typically laid over an undeveloped landscape. This supergridding is not reiterated by further gridding at a local scale but is infilled by a series of disconnected centripetal figures which produce sizable amounts of residual space. As related to actual sites, isolated office parks or housing tracts are organized by strictly discontinuous cul-de-sac developments which fall within a larger gridded network typically derived from survey lines or a pre-existing pattern of rural roads. The obvious and most radical theoretical context for the superblock is Frank Lloyd Wright's development of Broadacre City. The master plans of Chandigarh and, more recently, of Milton Keynes are also clear examples.

form or "sprawl." As noted, the effect of sprawl is the result of a conflict between a residual hierarchical figure and an emerging topological field. Attempts to trace an aggregate order out of a condition of peripheral sprawl yields the simultaneous existence of 1) linear patterns established by primary transportation arteries, 2) an urban field established by a large scale supergrid, and 3) a vestigial centralized pattern which has not yet collapsed under the dominance of new polynuclear construction. In an overlay of the three systemns the linear models become the "spokes" radiating out of the vestigial center and the supergrid spans the field in-between these spokes. In this way the modern linear and field models become subsumed within the vestiges of traditional centralized form.

While further analysis of urban sprawl could be undertaken, it is clear that it is not simply a field of residual effects, but a powerful array of conflicting urban armatures. Given such conflict, there is little wonder why a legible metropolitan order has yet to find its way into the popular urban imagination. The complexity of overlaid linear, gridded, and radial organizational patterns ultimately falls short of producing a coherent alternative to the waning effects of Centralized Polynuclear Expansion.

THE INDETERMINATE CENTER

Frank Lloyd Wright was not joking when he stated that Broadacre City "will be a city so greatly different from the ancient city, or from any city of today that we will probably fail to recognize its coming as the city at all" (quoted in Frampton, 1980, p.190). The radical nature of Wright's decentralized proposals have been historically underestimated. No other modern architect sought to overthrow the centralizing and hierarchical motifs of traditional urbanism as thoroughly as Wright. Despite his interest in a linear industrial city, Le

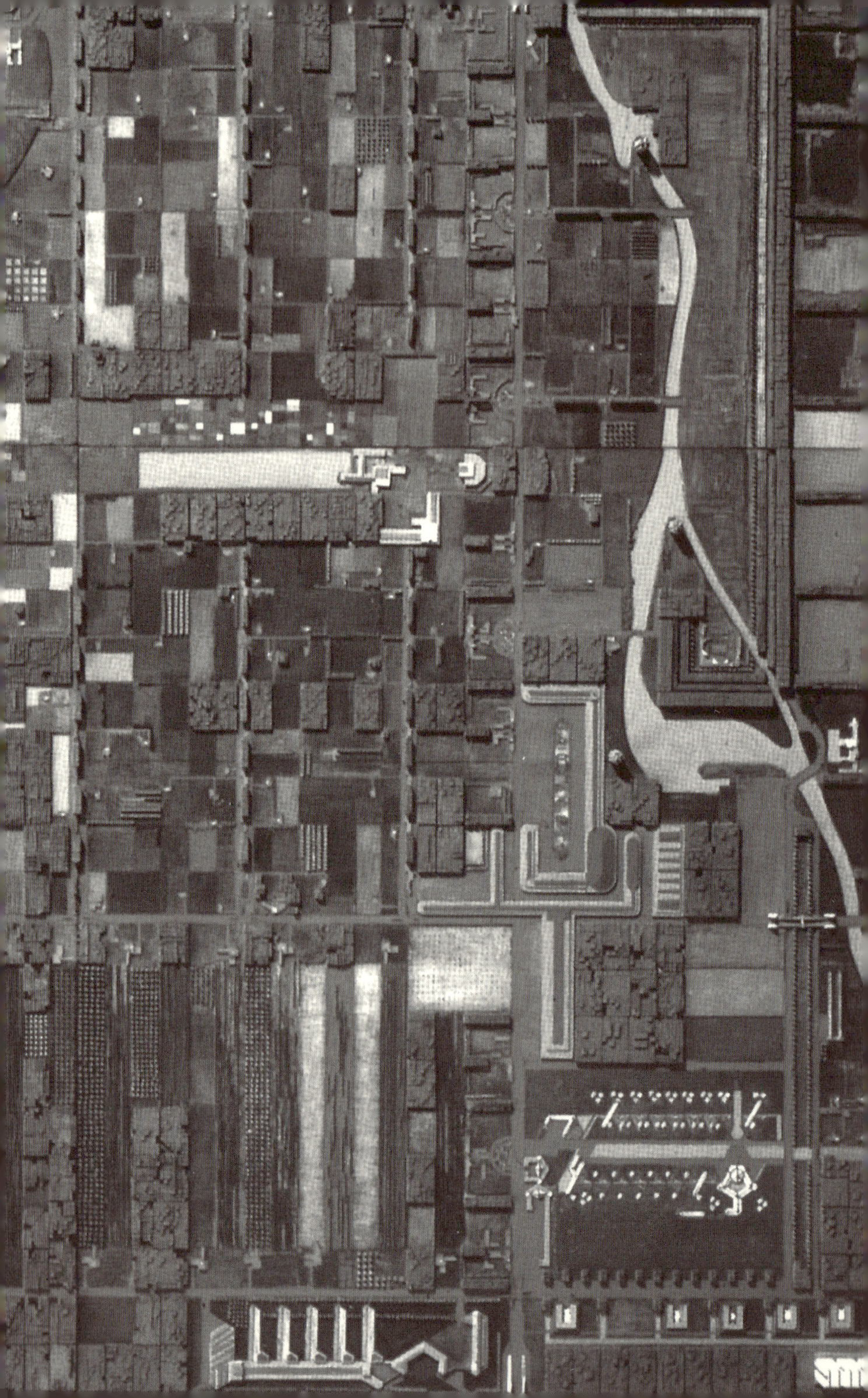

Corbusier, for example, consistently sought to reinforce centralized urban hierarchies. His monumental 1946 proposal for the reconstruction of St.-Die' is both a nostalgic reconstruction of a representational core and an analogue of its implosion. Wright's conception of a fully decentralized polynuclear urban field remains as foreign to the urban imagination today as it did when he first articulated it in 1936. And he may well be proven correct: that we fail to recognize a centerless city as a city at all.

The characteristics of the contemporary metropolis continue to be set by the indeterminate status of the urban center. Centralizing metropolitan patterns inexplicably persist without market support and beyond all social and political probability. Yet, while they persist, they do so in a highly qualified state, remaining only as traces or displacements of a former hierarchy, operating on the edge of complete irrelevance. Despite the massive implosion and reorganization of the urban core, Centralized Polynuclear Expansion has continued to inscribe decisive hierarchies onto the form of the contemporary city. Countless urban redevelopment schemes, special bond issues, "Renaissance" centers, new hotels, museums, sports stadia, opera houses, libraries, convention centers, and corporate high-rises, not to mention the ceaseless activities of the Rouse Company or the reconstruction of the Potsdammer Platz, even the flourishing of "downtown" Los Angeles, attest to the persistence of a prominent urban center and its continuing ability to proffer not only a greater metropolitan identity, but a subordinate "peripheral" status upon all that surrounds it.

The structuring relation between center and periphery remains a deep-seated model of organization motivated as much by unstated spiritual and

4.8 Frank Lloyd Wright, Broadacre City (model detail).

aesthetic prejudice as by the momentum of new urban construction. Given the mounting built evidence, it is not difficult to argue that Centralized Polynuclear Expansion has continued to configure what can be called the psychological space — the political, juridical, and cultural space — of contemporary urban development. In this space it remains possible to imagine great cities which possess active, symbolic centers of civic importance: the sacred seats of economic, political, cultural, spiritual, and historical life. It may be argued that contemporary urban life continues to be ruled by such unacknowledged and unscrutinized symbolic centers which institution and practice have yet to fully erode. However weakened or marginalized its effect, a city lacking a substantial center may be unimaginable, if not socially and politically intolerable.

This ongoing persistence of the center evokes two opposing responses. A first response would claim that the vestigial center embodies a spiritual and aesthetic resistance — the victory of an eternal cultural will set against the disintegrative forces of advanced capital. In this regard, the resilience of the center has been connected to a displacement of the sacred by Bachelard and the phenomenolgists, as well as by religious scholars including Mircea Eliade. As it tends to sustain an ancient urban code — an *axis mundi* — the vestigial center represents the promise of greater earthly and cosmic unity from which the idea of a metropolis derives. Against such a claim, however, one could argue an opposing view: that the endurance of the center is not the manifestation of a cultural resistance, but the manifestation of a regressive cultural pathology. In this regard the persistence of archaic hierarchical patterns constitutes an obstacle to the emergence of fully autonomous nuclei of development and their attendant spatial residuum. Remaining sub-urban or subsidiary to an archaic metropolitan core prevents the new exurban nuclei from claiming the greater social, economic, and political status they might otherwise acquire. It can be argued that the old hierarchies continue to cast a large part of both the urban and (perhaps most important) the natural world into a secondary position. Out of deference to a greater urban unity which ultimately cannot be sustained, these worlds may relinquish their own local responsibilities not to mention their own enormous potential. The present debate surrounding the desire of so many suburbs to secede from any greater metropolitan responsibilities reflects the ongoing antagonism between these two responses to vestigial centralization.

The legacy of Centralized Polynuclear Expansion has resulted in a rift between a contemporary urban imagination which subscribes to a dominant center and economic and political practices which often refuse to support it. An urban imaginary devoted to centralizing hierarchical motifs is incapable of accounting for the recent appearance of powerful exurban nuclei of development, the attendant Balkanization of societies along the lines of class and race, the reorganization of the urban core, and a necesary repositioning of the relation between the urban and the natural world. Likewise, contemporary polynuclear development is incapable of positioning private lives into any sort of meaningful inclusive context. This rift between center and field, tradition and innovation, figure and field, may be understood as a real obstacle to our present urban evolution. The inability of the center to either assert its hegemony or die off throws the metropolis into an interminable confusion.

THE METROPOLITAN ENDGAME

The characteristics associated with sprawl — peripheral dispersion, the discontinuous polynuclear field, the disorganized residuum of centripetal production, the overlay of centralized and topological patterns — all contribute to a definition of weak metropolitan form. The functional relation between the strong local form of the ladder and the weak metropolitan form of sprawl constitutes the fundamental structure of contemporary urban development. As local order continues to strengthen and metropolitan form moves toward complete disorganization, the possibility of a relevant and popular metropolitan imaginary grows ever more problematic.

The present crisis of metropolitan representation is related to an arrested stage of development where old models ineffectively persist and new models fail to emerge. Centralized Polynuclear Expansion has sustained urban production over the past half century, yet it has only recently become clear that it is a strictly transitional model, presently in the process of playing itself out. Following Fredric Jameson's assertion that the modernist imagination was motivated by a dialectic between the modern and the premodern, the transition to a "postmodern" urban condition will occur when modernization succeeds in eliminating all vestiges of premodern organization. In the present stage of urban development, this translates into the final elimination of the premodern urban core through its implosion, reorganization, and ultimate closure. The urban dialectic between the premodern urban core and the modern suburban periphery fails when the core is reorganized and its hierarchy collapses into an amorphous field of competing urban nuclei. Analogous to the Seagram Building in its masonry context, the Modern City loses its temporal bearing with the collapse of the historical core. With the end of traditional urban hierarchies the citizen of a postmodern city is set spatially adrift in an amorphous polynuclear field.

This reading of contemporary urban transformation positions the centralized polynuclear city as synonymous with the Modern City. This is significant, for it verifies what Christopher Alexander suggested thirty years ago: the polemical urban positions developed by the modernist avant-gardes are equivalent to the closed cities of contemporary urban production. Despite the early attempts to adopt non-centralized polynuclear models, modernists ultimately embraced Centralized Polynuclear Expansion as the metropolitan vehicle for their innovative experiments in architectural form. If there is anything to be learned from the Degree Zero Urbanism practiced by Hilberseimer, it is that the Modern City is more than an image of peripheral slab cities, more than a reversal of the urban figure/ground, and more than the specter of low income housing complexes based on the model of the *Ville Radieuse*. At the level of urban form, both the *Ville Radieuse* and the Garden City are the consequences of the larger idea of centripetal organization and expansion. While the Modern City has rarely been overtly associated with Centralized Polynuclear Expansion, such an association coincides with the definitions applied here. However weak it has ultimately become, the Modern City did have a coherent metropolitan form, a form that was defined around the hierarchical pairing of central and peripheral, historical and contemporary, premodern and modern, open and closed, pedestrian and vehicular, public and private. As centripetal forms come to reorganize the urban core and dominate the periphery, these structural dichotomies of Centralized Polynuclear Expansion become destabilized.

If the Modern City did have a coherent metropolitan form, it is not apparent that the centripetally reorganized city which succeeds it ever will. Being presently trapped between these two possibilities, it is impractical to speculate. Beyond the final collapse of traditional urban hierarchies, what may ultimately remain of metropolitan form is a featureless polynuclear field of endlessly repeated and relatively innocuous global corporate franchises. Each of these "Generic Cities" (Koolhaas, 1995, p.1248) — including the American "Edge City" and the European or Asian "New Town" — lack characteristic distinction, with each successive nuclei of development possessing no greater qualities than the next. Structured by a strict typology of inter-

...ble forms, the emerging Centripetal City may well be the sublime space of late capital prophesied by Jameson.

At the threshold of a postmodern or superurban stage of development, contemporary conditions are clear. As the polarization of the binary field continues, the local level of urban organization grows ever stronger, finally preempting the emergence of coherent metropolitan form, strong or weak. Released from all political, social, and economic metropolitan responsibilities, the city is set for the Balkanization of absolute closure set against the vulgar unity of global capital. The metropolis now vanishes as a subject of investigation to be replaced by the strictly local struggles of competing global franchises.

CLOSURE

With the decline of metropolitan centralization, the relation between new nuclei of development and their spatial residuum becomes highly polarized. As the boundaries of exurban nuclei have become more absolute, their residuum become more the subject of denial and disorganization. Large corporate enclaves now dominate new urban construction. In Houston, which is in an advanced stage of centripetal development, over fifty percent of all new housing starts are occurring in one of four large master-planned communities each controlled by national and international corporations (Ingersoll, 1994, p.10). The population of each of these isolated developments are approaching the 40,000 mark — the size of a small city. With the emergence of city-scaled nuclei, the urban field has transformed the complex organization of sprawl into discrete corporate franchises euphemistically marketed as "towns."

This coarsening of the fabric of sprawl by the emergence of new city-size corporate nuclei must be put into the larger context of centripetal development. Despite their urban scale, Edge Cities and corporate hometowns are not open cities or towns. They are not diversified by ethnicity, class, age group, or political affiliation, nor are they complete in the sense of providing real economic productivity or a consolidated civic realm. Edge Cities and corporate hometowns are not diverse organisms open to unexpected growth and change, but closed enclaves which are explicitly conceived to preempt unexpected growth and change. It is necessary to examine both the architectural and political consequences of these corporate entities before considering their effect upon metropolitan development.

The architectural consequences of closed urban production have already been suggested. Historically, the closed enclave was built against an open, unbounded centrifugal city. This relation between closed and open development supported the meaning of alternative, introverted worlds since at least the 18th-century. Monasteries, prisons, asylums, boarding schools, hospitals, what Michel Foucault called "heterotopias," defined the terms of their existence *apart* from the social and political mainstream. [Heterotopias are "countersites" where "arrangements that can be found within society are at one and the same time represented, challenged, and overturned: a sort of place that lies outside of all places and yet is actually localizable" (Foucault, 1993, p.422).] With the postwar decline of the open urban center, the possibility of a heterotopia or countersite, that may have once existed in the exclusive suburban enclave or the gated asylum, has diminished. In the absence of open cities, closed developments no longer function as countersites which are both a reflection of and a retreat from the greater urban world. Rather they are now themselves obliged to be the greater world that was heretofore represented by the city and the metropolis. To state the obvious, when everything is a countersite, there are no countersites, or no alternatives to the predominate social arrangements represented by the principal mode of urbanization. The massive postwar

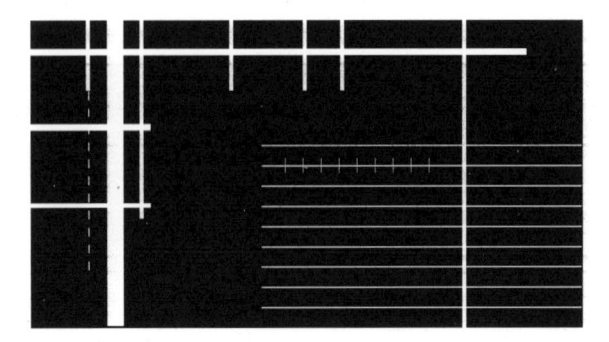

diagram 4.2
Centripetal Figure: Subdivision

The centripetal figure or ladder functions as the primary organizational element of the polynuclear urban field. Far from being a chaotic "sprawl," the polynuclear field supports a wide array of centripetal figures which are dispersed or distributed throughout the field as an organizational datum. Residential subdivisions, office parks, inter-urban freeways, commercial malls and university campuses are some of the common forms of contemporary urban development which are commonly structured by the centripetal figure. As the instantly legible components of what would otherwise seem a discontinuous labyrinthian field, the centripetal figure is emblematic of contemporary urban development.

retreat from the metropolis has been no retreat at all. When the retreats, there has been no escape, only a displacement of the previous social arrangements and their principal modes of urbanization.

No matter how deep their investment or how shrewd their simulation, closed corporate developments can never duplicate the qualities of the open city. Neither can they duplicate the qualities of the historical enclave. As noted above, the enclave built against the open city must be fundamentally different from the enclave built against other closed enclaves. Architectural language does not transcend a transformation of the larger spatial field. If architectural and planning conventions do not respond to this transformation, then those conventions are ultimately trivialized. If, for example, the architecture of new resorts, housing subdivisions or universities trades on the language of the traditional prewar city or the traditional prewar enclave, then they ultimately devalue the authenticity of those languages by neglecting the profound transformation of the urban spatial field. The recent decline of the open city and the transition to a superurban stage present a change in the rules of architecture that cannot be understated.

While the architectural consequences of closed urban production may be apparent, it is ultimately impossible to separate them from the political consequences which are driven in part by the evolution of form. The closure of the polycentric urban field involves the production of substantial interurban spatial barriers. These barriers aggressively separate and exclude urban development from the greater urban continuity. The largest of Houston's corporate nuclei, the Woodlands, is the single surviving development of HUD's Title VII new town program which was active in the 1970's (Fox, 1990, p.285). Its singular success is no doubt related to the fact that the Woodlands was built thirty miles from the center of Houston, to which it was subsequently connected by a toll road. The effects of such enormous spatial buffers are apparent in the

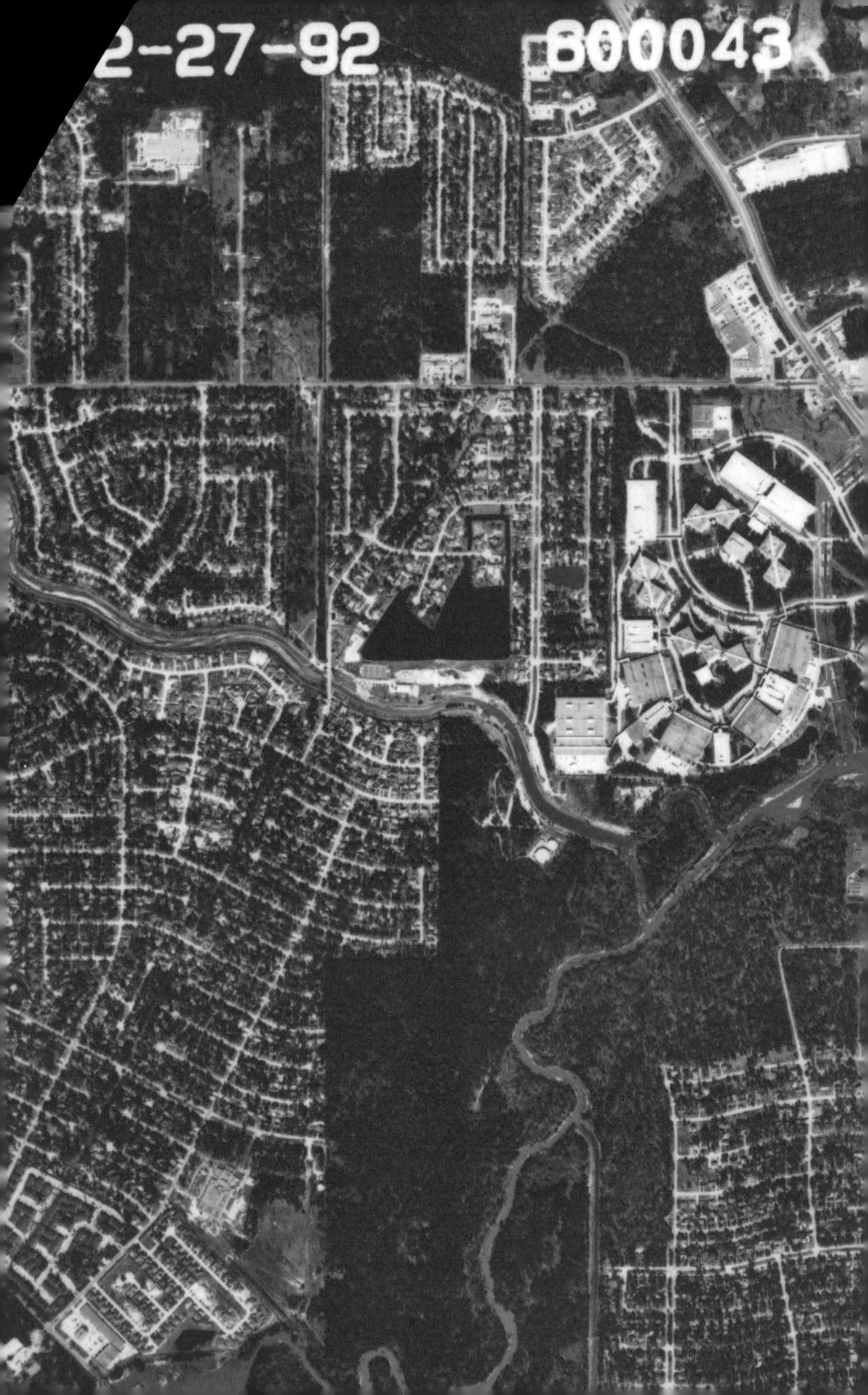
2-27-92
600043

disruption of any cultural and political interdependence between development and the city. Such government sponsored disruptions are now routine marketing strategies driven by aggressive competitive practices, all fashioned to increase market share. As urban isolation and exclusion have become exaggerated, a huge and successful industry has grown up around the virtual militarization of the domestic, commercial, industrial, and administrative enclave. These enclaves are on the verge of closing the circle where a media enervated population has reduced contact with the greater urban world down to the frenetic but agreeable traffic of an electronic feed.

The Common Interest Development, or CID, is the legal entity now established by corporate developers through a set of provisions written into sales contracts known as Covenants, Conditions and Restrictions, or CC&Rs. These restrictions, enforced by homeowner's associations, amount to the privatization of local government services and a complete, or near complete, secession from the social, political and economic organization of the city. These private regulations determine what you can plant, what you can paint, what you can park, what you can fence in, and how much you must pay for the maintenance of the "common area." They typically impose steep fines and immediate lawsuits for excessive noise, speeding, late fees, unkempt lawns and the presence of young children or pets. These regulations are conceived, not by the community itself, but by corporate initiative, and are thus strictly dedicated to the preservation of property values as the highest possible civic objective. As they are instated by developers, the courts uphold the CID as a business entity rather than a form of government, and it remains unregulated. The growth of the CID has exploded over the past two decades (McKenzie,

4.9 Compaq Computer Corporate Campus and adjacent urban environment, Aerial View, Houston Texas, 1992.

183 THE CENTRIPETAL CITY

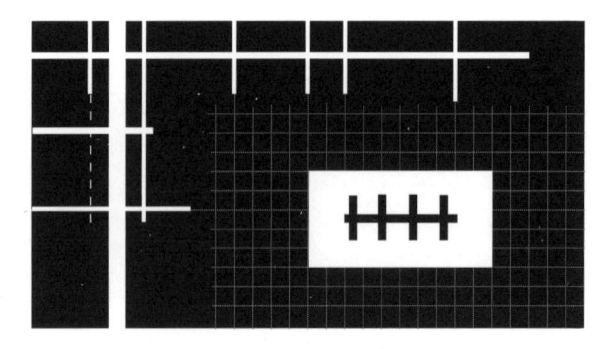

diagram 4.3
Centripetal Figure: Commercial Mall

The appearance of the centripetal figure in the postwar urban field is perhaps too obvious or too graphic to dwell on for long. Like the freeways, tunnels, skybridges, cores and plates of the inner city reorganization, these figures form a consistent pattern of centripetal organization. This apparent unity of form is extraordinary given the present conception of contemporary urban development as so much chaotic and disorganized growth. The critical elements of contemporary urban development all share a common structure across a broad range of urban scales suggesting a totality which is seemingly indecipherable to an urban imagination that can only see sprawl.

1994, p.11). In 1970 there were fewer than 10,000 homeowner's associations. By 1980 that figure had increased to 50,000, by 1992 there were 150,000 associations privately governing an estimated 32 million Americans. By 2000 it is projected that there will be 225,000 homeowner's associations forming another nation, now seceded, within the nation.

Architectural and political critiques of the popular secession from the life of the metropolis are now everywhere to be found (Reich, Lind, Kunstler, Garreau) and need not be repeated. It is important to note, however, that the point of such critiques must not be to disparage those who wish to secede. There are good reasons why the people who can afford it choose the security of closed corporate development over the greater freedom and choices of the declining open city. What ought to be disparaged is, of course, the fact that one must make the choice between security and freedom at all. The recent history of urban form tells us that such a compromise is not necessary, that cities have typically provided both. Despite the fact that we cannot return to historical urban forms, we must ultimately insist on cities that do not demand the surrender of either security or freedom. And this is where the interrelation between urban form and politics is undeniable. The stark alternatives between security and freedom are both engendered and reflected in the radically polarized state of the polynuclear urban field.[6]

It remains to be demonstrated exactly how much personal security or personal freedom is surrendered to the present urban dispensation. It should, however, be clear that the negative effects of metropolitan secession are not limited to those left behind.

THE SPIRAL

Following the decline of open centrifugal expansion, the construction of conspicuous metropolitan blocks, streets, and monuments was reduced nearly to zero. It is interesting to speculate what metropolitan representation would now represent had it not been weakened and diffused by centripetal expansion. While the greater New York region, for example, has endured a postwar demographic explosion, its apparent metropolitan form continues to suggest a city of prewar dimension. In other words, despite the dramatic increases in population, New York continues to be represented by the architecture of the five boroughs. Apart from the inadvertent view out the airplane window or the exponentially increasing size of telephone directories, the rapid rate of metropolitan growth remains obscured, nurturing middle class fantasies of sustainable growth immune to Third World vulgarities of overpopulation and scarcity. Through the seclusion and exclusion of exurban nuclei, postwar urban growth disappears at the limit of the prewar city. Traditional, cognitive forms of metropolitan representation have been frozen, so to speak, at prewar levels.

In effect, the absence of concrete metropolitan representation has concealed the postwar population explosion. By the end of the Second World War, mass politics and the resulting mass warfare had exhausted the desire to express the greater metropolitan "body." In the immediate postwar period, the representation of the metropolitan masses became so apparently problematic, so socially and politically dangerous, that it could no longer take on concrete urban form. In retrospect, the prewar metropolis was understood to have reached a terminal, hypertrophied stage, beyond which open and manifest expansion was no longer possible. The war was evidence that the metropolis — metropolitan politics, metropolitan culture, and the metropolitan economy — had indeed exceeded its limit. In the postwar period, the city would continue to grow, yet it would not take on the concrete forms of prewar metropolitan expression. This was accomplished by the new mechanics of urban growth. Ultimately the greatest consequence of centripetal expansion may be that it affected the disappearance of an immense, if ultimately troublesome, metropolitan crowd.

This aversion to the metropolitan crowd was reflected in the strategies of modern planners and architects. The association of 19th-century economic practices with the industrial conscription of so many faceless urban souls was essential to the ideology of urban reform. The industrial city was the dehumanizing apparatus by which the brutal routines of industrial production ground the urban subject down into a mindless, soulless anonymity. In response, the Modern City was based on nothing if not the historical elevation of this pitiable urban subject to a privileged or "elect" status. The Modern City sought to diffuse and disperse the anonymous metropolitan mass and promote the emergence of the discrete ego out of its faceless ranks. In so doing, it systematically traded off public life and communal representation in a strict observance of the privileged and private. As plazas, streets and monumental construction were traded off for private open space, detached housing, and the transportation infrastructure necessary to access them, metropolitan representation quickly disappeared.

It is not difficult to argue that the emergence of an "elect" urban subject out of the "preterit" masses of the industrial city drove the agendas of modern urban reform. This movement from the anonymous industrial wage slave to privileged corporate citizen is repeatedly demonstrated in the projects of Hilberseimer, Le Corbusier, and Frank Lloyd Wright. In a characteristic statement, Wright proclaimed, "we come, now, to the most important unit in Broadacres, the true center and the only centralization allowable: the individual home" (1969, p.167). While Wright's statement is echoed in many similar statements ("the problem of the house is a problem of the epoch"), the urban preconditions for the displacement from the anonymous metropolitan crowd to the privileged individual subject are rarely disclosed. This unique

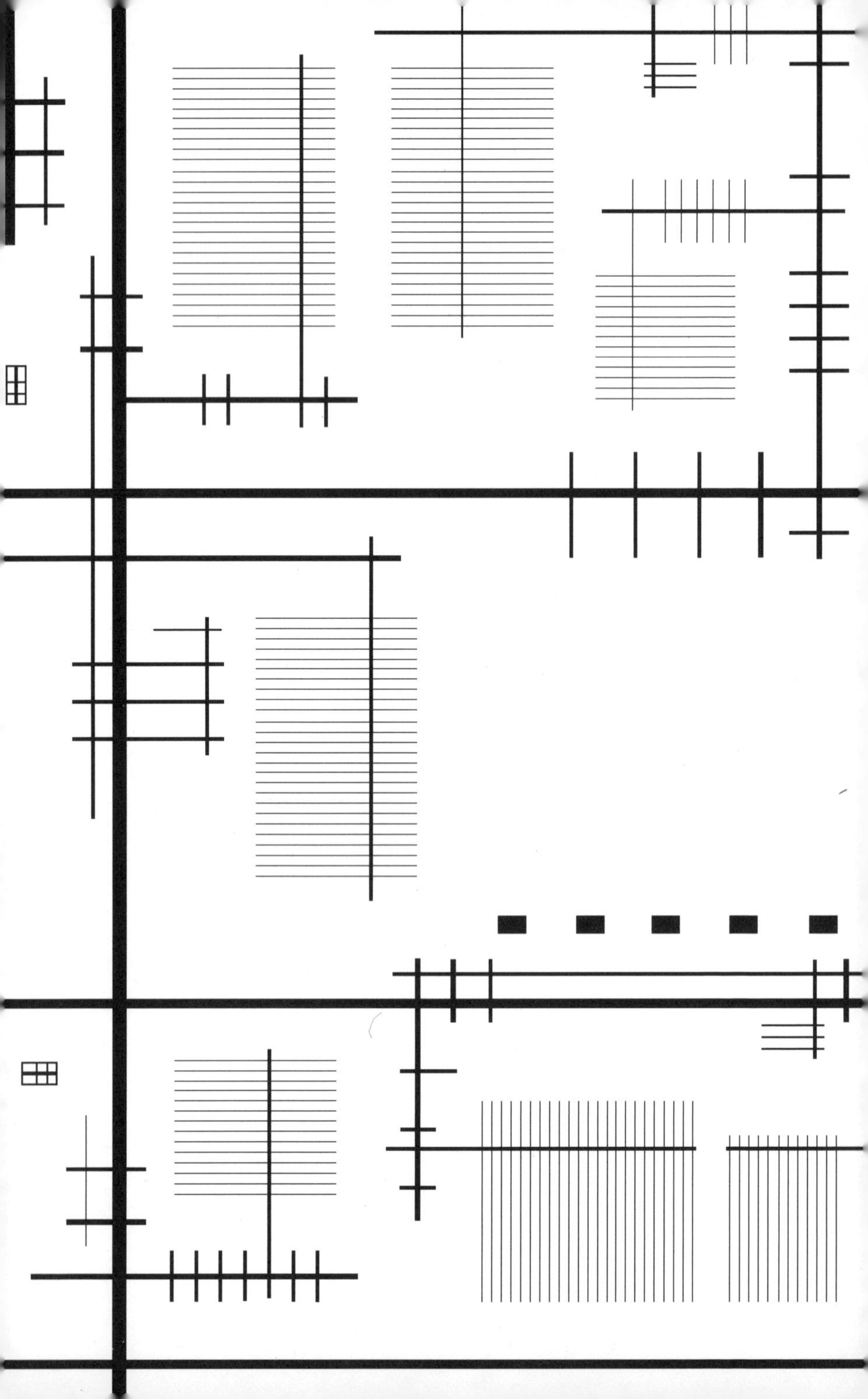

centering of the ego, "the only centralization allowable," is of ͻ effective in a weak metropolis. For the individual subject to emerge aͻ ultimate object of urbanization, collective representation must be disrupted and displaced. There is a vital connection between the decline of contemporary metropolis and the emergence of an ego-centric urban subject freed from existence within or obligation to the greater metropolitan body. This displacement of the "center" toward the private, the intimate, the constituent monad of a postpolitical consumer society, literally depends on the entropies of a waning metropolitan field.

The inscription of a privileged urban citizen into the metropolitan field can be observed in a pattern of movement through space leading directly toward Wright's individual "center." This pattern traces the figure of a discrete SPIRAL through a succession of overlaid urban armatures. As it typically appears in the postwar urban field, this spiral begins with a primary urban freeway and turns successively inward toward a singular origin or center. The imploded spiraling path — from freeway to feeder to collector to development spine to driveway — forms the trajectory of a closed urban system. Turning inward upon itself, the path configures a series of discrete segments. Each segment devolves into the next smaller stage of development, forming a pattern of increasing exclusion.

This path to closure — which always terminates in an exclusive destination or endpoint — stands in direct contrast to a path traced on a traditional urban gridiron. The path of the open grid is theoretically infinite in both directions. Unlike the closed figure of the spiral, it can never establish an endpoint, or "end of the road." As opposed to the *cul-de-sac's* termination of movement, the grid offers only a series of arbitrary stopping points, each a temporary respite from its relentless continuity. In contrast to this infinite extent, the spiral is closed and singular. This singularity is inherent in the form itself.

4.10 The polynuclear field: Spirals of exclusion.

Everyone now lives, not on an anonymous grid coordinate, but at the end of a particular path, on the last driveway, on the last *cul-de-sac*, in the last development of a city whose overall form is unknowable and irrelevant. In the Centripetal City we are right where we have always wanted to be, at the very origin of the spiral, each of our delicate egos safely seated at the base of a headlong downward implosion.

Through the labyrinths of sprawl, and along the path of a spiral, one by one, the privileged subject of the contemporary city is constructed. Inscribed in an inside for which no outside exists, this is precisely the exclusive contemporary subject position for which an alternative is sought.

PLANNED DISAPPEARANCE

The imploded spiraling path describes the subject position of centripetal development. This path, which routinely displaces the collective metropolitan body toward the privileged and the private, is the ultimate agent of absolute closure. It is a path driven by a powerful existential movement across an unknowable urban field. For the inhabitant, the city literally takes shape around the path. Through these spiraling vectors, the bewildering complexity of sprawl is directly connected to the intimate center of countless private lives. Closure thus has a form, or at least a mechanism to achieve exclusion. The spiral drives the ego-centric vision of the Modern City to its ultimate end, the inscription of a singular, universal urban subject.

This form of universal inscription reflects the good intentions of modern architects and planners. The elevation of the common urban citizen out of an anonymous preterition and into a privileged state heretofore reserved for an urban elite is an achievement that is difficult to criticize. Yet, it is never-theless true that much has been surrendered in the flight from the metropolitan condition. The direct relation between the formation of a distinct urban ego and centripetal development would be a surprise to many, including its greatest advocates. It is clear, for example, that the contemporary city has succeeded in dispersing the urban mass in countless directions toward Wright's "true center." Yet it is also clear that the heroic, self-reliant residents of "Usonia" or Broadacre City would scarcely recognize the good corporate citizenry now surrounding the master's compound at Taliesen West. Here, in the desert suburbs of Phoenix, the universal subject of the Modern City and the good corporate citizen of postwar development collide in a disturbing revelation; the Modern City is, and has always been, virtually synonymous with closed urban development. Analysis which positions the Modern City equal to centripetal production must conclude that the two terms are virtually interchangeable. In other words, "planning," in today's accepted sense of the word, is not capable of producing open urban systems and one is again left to wonder whether the myth of an open modern city of space only served as a cover for the emergence of urban closure.

Manfredo Tafuri certainly did not entertain any illusions of a new urban elect as he cynically sought to sum up the agenda of what he called "universal planning." In so doing, he wrote a peculiar pre-history of the postwar implosion of the city. As he understood it, the problem of the Modern City was "to plan the disappearance of the subject, to cancel the anguish caused by the pathetic (or ridiculous) resistance of the individual to the structures of domination that close in upon him, to indicate the voluntary and docile submission to those structures of domination as the promised land of universal planning" (1976, p.73). For Tafuri there would be little distinction between the utopia of a modern, open city and the reality of closed corporate development. The planned "disappearance of the subject" was thus no escape or retreat from the evil of the industrial city; it had nothing to do with repositioning the individ-

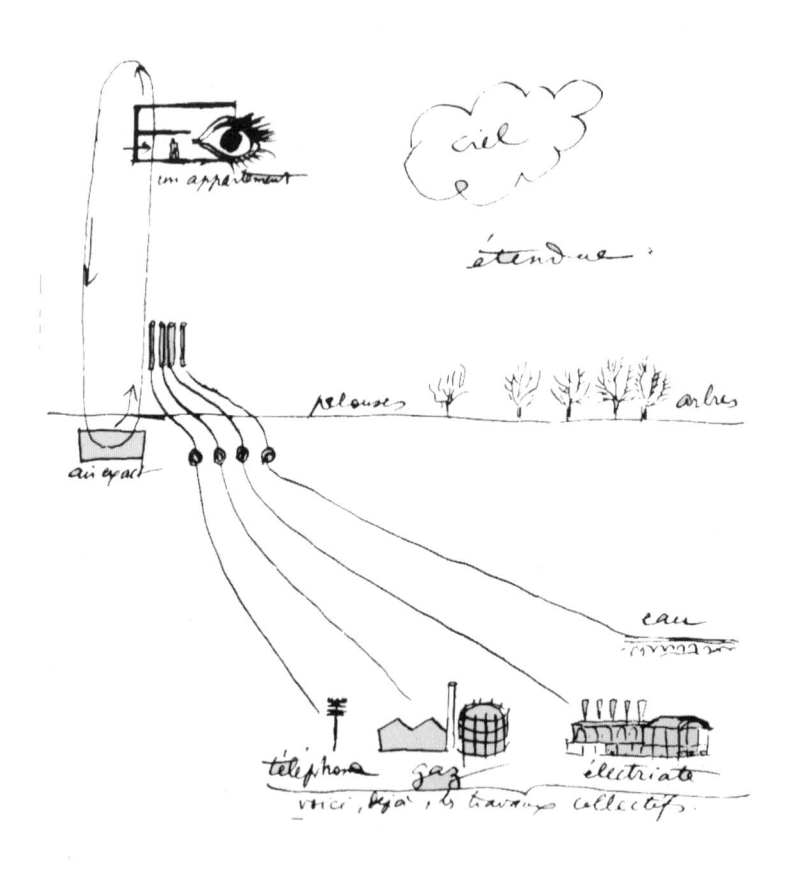

4.11 Le Corbusier, Unite' d' Habitation, Marseilles, 1946, sketch.
The Privileged Urban Subject.

ual or promoting individual agency. Rather, for Tafuri, the d'
the subject was the disappearance of the ego — of individu
choice. Universal planning was simply the means of easing
increasing demands of urban incorporation.

In a particularly trenchant remark in the *Death and Life of Great American Cities*, Jane Jacobs noted that planned garden communities "are really very nice . . . if you were docile and had no plans of your own and did not mind spending your life among others with no plans of their own" (1961, p.17). The statement was radical for the 1950's when it was written. Pitting the qualities of postwar housing tracts against the qualities of Greenwich Village must have seemed at the time more a cheap shot than a critical assessment of modern urban planning. Jacobs' implication was, however, that the vital and necessary contingencies supported by the open metropolitan grid provided an enabling network of opportunities that were usurped in a rigorously planned community. When everything is foreseen or planned, a vulgar routinization takes the place of independent initiative which is rendered ineffective if not actually pathetic by the absence of any apparent means of expression. Measured against the vigorous cultural and political energies of the open metropolis, the "life-world" of the good corporate citizen could only be seen as impoverished.

For the universal subjects of the ego-centric city, deliverance may only come as a mandate from a homeowner's association, but others do resist, even if the precise meaning of their struggle remains obscure. For those used to living in open urban environments, the rapidly diminishing choices of today's city are difficult to accept. In the meantime, prewar urban fabric and building stock continue to serve. It is clear, however, that within one or perhaps two generations, the open grid of many cities will be lost to the combined effects of dereliction and gentrification. Those who are aware of the ridiculous comnises demanded by the present dispensation must seek other options, and is no surprise that these options become apparent at the moment when real alternatives collapse. The need to forge an exterior point, to make available a subject position outside of the closed system, suggests a specific program for contemporary urban space. Architecture, as opposed to good corporate management, will only exist outside of a closed system. In that regard, a single, crucial question remains as to the ability of contemporary urban space to destabilize closed urban systems. Are the vortices of contemporary subject inscription now absolute, or are they instead, like the spirals of Babel, fated to incoherence and decline?

THE STRIP AND THE MEGASTRUCTURE

As the disorganization of the inner city residuum has come to be known as urban "blight," so the disorganization of the exurban residuum has come to be known as urban sprawl. Sprawl has been part of a distracted social consciousness since the late 1950s when centripetal production began to create a conspicuous and unprecedented "urban pollution." As good as any benchmark for its arrival is Peter Blake's *God's Own Junkyard*, which called attention to the brutal disorganization that, by 1964, had already transformed the often humane and modest dimensions of prewar American cities and towns. A remarkable image essay, Blake's book focused on the effects of mass advertising, mass construction, and mass consumption, all accumulating in an astonishing amount of mass refuse. The landscapes of car dumps, billboards, industrial pollution, utility poles, litter, the desolate space surrounding inner city housing projects, and the famous "Long Island Duckling" amounted to a catalogue of unsuspected and unwanted urban effects. The impact of the book was to notice the existence of this unique condition which had emerged so quickly and become so widespread that few had a conceptual framework capable of accounting for it. That a residual condition could appear within the matrices of a traditional urban continuity indicated a processes of development gone awry, producing an astonishing, uncontrollable remainder.

It can be argued that the idea of postwar "sprawl" was born at precisely the moment that new urban development achieved a degree of closure sufficient to exclude its effects. Once attained, this detachment turned sprawl into an irresistible object of analysis. Only a couple of years separates Blake's demonization of urban blight and "roadtown," and Venturi, Scott Brown, and Izenour's celebration of the "strip" in *Learning From Las Vegas*. Another remarkable image essay, *Learning From Las Vegas* analyzed the strip as the flashpoint in an overall phenomena which was known as urban sprawl or what the authors called "Sprawl City." The analysis was structured around a series of contradictory phenomena, the most striking of which was the relation between the interiors of the twelve major casinos and the exterior of the strip itself. On the strip, the experience was one of a barely controlled chaos of information, a garish ad-hoc environment of competing claims: a "vital mess," where buildings receded as inconsequential sheds, deferring to the primacy of fast-paced, frenetic activity. In the book, sectional diagrams and hundreds of photographs characterized the strip as an infinitely complex and animated environment which suggested an unprecedented form of postwar urbanization.

In contrast to the open flux and flow of the strip, the casinos were described as autonomous, internal worlds with low, dark, air-conditioned spaces, fully controlled by management. The gambling rooms established an antithesis to the street. As described in the text, the "combination of darkness and enclosure of the gambling room and its subspaces makes for privacy, protection, concentration, and control. The intricate maze under the low ceiling never connects with outside light or outside space. . . . One loses track of where one is and when it is. Time is limitless, because the light of noon and midnight are exactly the same" (Venturi, 1972, p.49).

The authors focused on a comparison between the casino interior with traditional monumental building sections, proclaiming for the casino interior a "new monumentality" (Venturi, 1972, p.55). It was, however, the polarity between the strip and the gambling rooms which came across as far more determinate in the analysis of the overall environment. With regard to the increasing polarization of the interior and the exterior found in most strip environments, the Las Vegas Strip establishes a clear model of the postwar polynuclear field where the casinos exist in isolated contradiction to the chaos of the sprawling automotive environment which surrounds them. If the

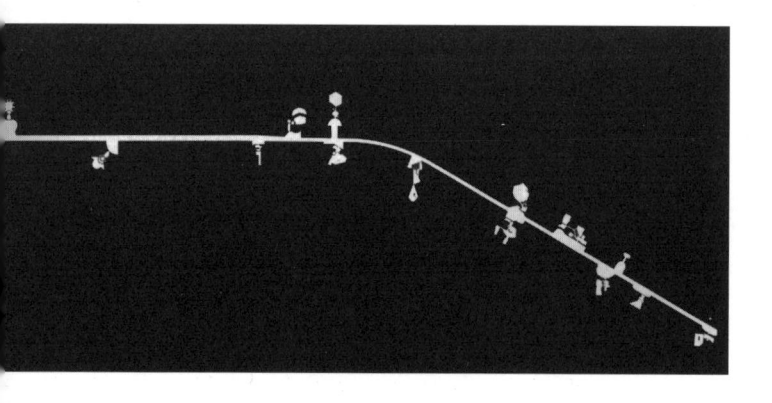

4.12 "Ceremonial Space," Las Vegas Strip
From: Venturi, Scott Brown, Izenour, *Learning From Las Vegas*.

strip was defined as open, inclusive and chaotic, then the gambling rooms are the epitome of closed, exclusive environments. In the casino, the ostensible activity is based on openness, chance, and genuine opportunity, but the reality is based on total control. As in all closed systems, the "games" are rigged from the start.

Learning From Las Vegas was a celebration of the "outside," of the vitality of the everyday environment that escapes the totalizing control of casino managers, willful avant-garde architects, and the "Strip Beautification Committee." These last two receive especially critical treatment in the book. Equating the tendencies of the 1960's megastructure craze with the activities of design review boards, they proclaim that "total Design comes to mean 'total control'" (Venturi, 1972, p.150). Against the architecture of megastructures, the authors propose an alternative, inclusive, heterogeneous urbanism born of sprawl. "We do not know if the time will come for serious architectural oceanographic urbanism, for example, as opposed to the present offshore posturing of the world futurist architectural visionaries" (Venturi, 1972, p.162).

In their analysis the authors of *Learning From Las Vegas* overlooked one particularly significant contradiction. The so-called oceanic urbanism of the Strip was itself structured on a relentless linear armature. In contrast to the original Las Vegas gridiron, and the pedestrian "strip" of Freemont Street, the organization of the upper strip was a discrete and reductive axis of development — a complete linear city. As revealed by the book's own map of "Nolli's Las Vegas," the Strip was itself a "mini-megastructure" in the making. Despite the messy vitality that attended the early stages of its development, the strip has evolved over the past twenty-five years as casino hotels of ever greater scale and degree of closure have filled in replacing their extravagant signs for various "ducks," lions, pyramids, and medieval fortresses. What was, in 1968, a chaotic polynuclear field has been unified around a single armature of corporate development. The recent appearance of atriums, skybridges and the massive "theme park casinos" make the case apparent. In its ongoing evolution, the Las Vegas Strip remains a powerful archetype as it is transformed from a vital polynuclear field into a seamless armature of corporate investment.

In the past twenty years, the idea of the strip has evolved in synch with the closure of urban form. Having given way to larger scales of corporate distribution, its substance has been literally absorbed into malls, discount warehouses and colossal theme park casinos. Through increasing scales of incorporation, the strip as "Sprawl City" has nearly vanished from the field of new construction leaving in its wake a residuum that is emptied out, abstract, and more purely spatial. It is this emptied space, not the present consolidation of the strip, which forms the emerging "oceanographic" field. It is in light of these more recent developments that the idea of sprawl becomes more simply defined as the residuum of exurban corporate nuclei. Sprawl, like inner city blight, is only a metaphor for the more general qualities found in the residuum of closed urban systems.

EXURBAN ELLIPSIS

As the chaos and vitality of the strip subsides into something more purely spatial or "empty," the exurban residuum becomes increasingly difficult to identify and analyze. The inability to grasp its qualities and characteristics is related to the apparent poverty of its content. While space at the periphery emerges by the same centripetal processes as it does in the inner city, the exurban ellipsis is ultimately more diffuse, less determined by preexisting conditions. By way of contrast, the voided space of the inner city continues to bear powerful traces of a prior, premodern occupation and, like a traditional urban palimpsest, possesses far more tangible urban qualities than exurban space. In that regard, vast suburban parking lots, the corporate "campus," the limitless expanse of the freeway, feeders, and strips are characterized by an unsettling lack of historical organization. It is, for example, the lack of historical organization — a temporal dimension — which accounts for the characterization of exurban space as empty or vacuous. In contrast to its inner city counterpart, the exurban ellipsis is distinguished by space and only space.

Analogues to inner city "free space" cited above — Pynchon's Zone, Koolhaas's Post Architectural Void, Jameson's Hyperspace, the fictional world of J.G. Ballard — were born out of a powerful historical substrate. What makes these examples potent is the striking juxtaposition between a prewar historical city and a postwar modern city — a temporal contrast which ultimately determines their effects. It is clear that such rich juxtapositions of space and time do not apply to the historical vacuums emerging at the periphery. The temporal dimension of the ellipsis has been jettisoned, and the resulting voids inherently lack the distinctive opposition that characterizes the inner city condition. It is precisely the absence of a dialectic that cripples the ability to imagine contemporary exurban space. The exurban ellipsis demands an alternative framework to understand what might otherwise be dismissed as its absence of qualities.

4.13 "Little White Oak Bayou and Downtown Houston," 1986.
Photograph by Geoff Winningham.

THE DISORGANIZATION OF SPACE

Given the ease with which critiques of the contemporary city are made, it is important to remember that these are critiques of its current practice, not the potential of its form. Analysis of form suggests that the polarization between the enclave and its residuum is not inevitable. There always remains a potential interrelation or dialectic between urban form and space whereby action in the enclave provokes an equal and opposing reaction in the residuum, and vice versa. In this regard, one could argue that an excessive degree of organization in the enclave triggers an equally excessive degree of disorganization in the residuum. This suggests the existence of a potent dialectic. It will be argued that as an equal and opposing force, the disorganization of space may be enlisted as a countersite or alternative to the excessive organization of form.

The exurban ellipsis is characterized by a specific type of disorganization which is best understood in contrast to the highly wrought organization of the enclave. It is a type of disorganization which emerges, not as the effect of forces surging out of control, but of forces lacking any structured organization whatsoever. While it is a form of chaos, it is the chaos of "sameness," a type of urban space where conceptual distinctions merge and combine and essential organizational dichotomies — between past and present, urban and natural, public and private, center and periphery — fuse into nothing. It is thus the space of an obscene randomness — an inherent incapacity to organize — as opposed to a robust upheaval normally associated with chaotic systems. It is implosive rather than explosive, freezing rather than burning, silence over noise, and stillness over action. In the postwar period, this type of disorganization has been associated with the second law of thermodynamics or entropy.

Entropy states that while it is theoretically possible for a closed system, such as an engine, to run at 100% efficiency, there is in practice always deterioration of the energy available to the system. This deterioration may be understood as an inevitable "disorganization" inherent to all closed systems. In a heat engine, for example, the difference in temperature between a hot region and a cooler region can be used to push a piston. The disorganization, or entropy, of the system comes from the tendency for the temperature to level out over time, going from distinct zones of hot and cold to one single warm zone. It is the organization or differentiation between the hot and the cold against the disorganization or "chaos" of a single uniform temperature which determines the capacity of a system to produce work. Entropy is the measure of disorganization inherent in any closed system.

Just after the Second World War, Norbert Wiener, founder and chief spokesman of the then emerging science of cybernetics, stated the implications of entropy in a manner that would drive the second law into the postwar world as a compelling cultural metaphor. Acknowledging as his source the work of Willard Gibbs, Wiener stated that "as entropy increases, the universe, and all closed systems in the universe, tend naturally to lose their distinctiveness, to move from the least to the most probable state, from the state of organization and differentiation in which distinctions and forms exist, to a state of chaos and sameness" (Wiener, 1954, p.12). The somewhat paradoxical phrasing of entropy as the movement from "organization and differentiation" to "chaos and sameness" transformed the second law into a general theory concerning the behavior of all isolated or closed systems. Wiener asserted that it was the difference or "non-equilibrium" of any system which enabled any sort of exchange to occur, be that temperature exchange, energy exchange, economic exchange, or especially, for Wiener, the exchange of information. Projecting the principle into "sets of outside worlds," he suggested that entropy was a pervasive phenomena in which all life would eventually gutter out into an undifferentiated soup:

. . . this non-equilibrium of the world about us is merely a stage in a downhill course which will ultimately lead to equilibrium. Sooner or later we shall die, and it is highly probable that the whole universe around us will die a heat-death, in which the world shall be reduced to one vast temperature equilibrium in which nothing really new ever happens. There will be nothing left but a drab uniformity out of which we can expect only minor and insignificant local fluctuations. (Wiener, 1954, p.31)

Among the many entropic processes apparent in the outside world, the postwar transformation of urban space must be among the most demonstrable. There is in exurban space a movement from organization and differentiation to chaos and sameness — "a drab uniformity" — where the relation between past/present, center/periphery, presence/absence breaks down into a condition which is simultaneously neither and both. In defiance of traditional categorization, the ellipsis is not urban space, nor can it be classified as natural. It is not of the past nor the present. It is not even a noun, but rather a verb, the index of a process — a sprawl now vanishing to the point that not even language can accommodate it. The orange helium vapor of nighttime parking lots, long abandoned agricultural fields draped over by power lines, immaculate corporate campuses maintained in silence save the splash of a "water feature," the brutal concrete and weeds of a freeway apron, the mind-numbing repetition of the ubiquitous suburban lawn: these are spaces which merge and blend, mocking discrete division and classification, and finally representing nothing outside of their own existence. Beyond the gates of the subdivision, the doors of the shopping mall, the exit of the parking garage, the windows of a high-rise, the uncounted acres of concrete, sod, asphalt and dirt that only by coincidence fall within legal urban boundaries, unknown and unknowable spaces fail to pass into structured consciousness. There may be, in a final analysis, nothing more than this lack of organization with which to characterize exurban space.

4.14 "Universal Studios Parking Lot." Universal City, California.
Photograph by Edward Ruscha.

But this lack of organization is not, or not only, a liability. Out of this near complete state of spatial disorganization new potentials emerge. To state it most simply, beyond the point where traditional categories break down, there exists the possibility of alternatives. New conceptions of urban space or new conceptions of the natural, for example, are not invented out of nothing, but emerge out of the transformation or in this case the "slurring" of traditional structures of form and thought. In the way the inner city ellipsis may produce something that may be called a new type of urban space which is not altogether urban, the exurban ellipsis may produce new type of natural space which is not altogether natural. Such new definitions of space and form which emerge in the ellipsis may ultimately "organize" real alternatives to the reductive closure of the exurban enclave.

If the inner urban ellipsis is characterized by the strong modernist dialectic between premodern and modern, prewar and postwar, the exurban ellipsis is characterized by the near collapse of any such dialectical organization. It is important to note that this condition of accelerated disorganization is not only a material disorganization but also a social and political disorganization. Unable to structure differences, the exurban ellipsis literally vanishes from the urban imagination, which is precisely why it is possible to state that the potential of contemporary urban space remains everywhere invisible and "unseen." That the potential of new urban space remains unseen is no accident, rather it is a critical component of the present urban economy. The caretakers of closed systems prefer an "inside without an outside," or an outside so disorganized as to form no viable alternative to corporate enfranchisement. Given an inherent hostility to either new inputs or reliable feedback, closed systems have a somewhat desperate stake in making all that is "outside" its limitations disappear.

In this regard, entropy can serve to structure a practice committed to defining and engaging the disorganization of the residuum. If the lack of conceptual differentiation has made certain urban potentials disappear, then an understanding of entropic processes may allow them to be thought again. This is understood to be the primary significance of an entropic definition of space. In its extreme degree of disorganization, exurban space may not seem to match its inner city counterpart. Yet what they both provide is a ground upon which to cultivate an alternative to absolute closure. This remains true whether that space emerges in the historical fabric of the city or is established on new ground.

POSTWAR REVERSAL

The emergence of entropy as a cultural metaphor coincided with the construction of closed systems throughout the period of postwar reorganization. Entropy can be considered in relation to these systems, not only as the means to identify their otherwise repressed residuum, but also as a concerted attempt to offer an alternative to closure, an alternative one is tempted to promote as a comprehensive economic, environmental and aesthetic position. Such positions have been in the making for the past fifty years, reaching a peak in the early seventies with the work of Thomas Pynchon and Robert Smithson, among others. It is necessary to briefly sketch these positions and locate them with regard to contemporary urban development.

In 1950, as the centripetal reorganization of the city was getting under way, Wiener wrote a popular account of the science of cybernetics in which he specifically described the postwar world which his science sought to address. In the context of this analysis, Wiener's description may seem more interesting for its spatial and geographic metaphors than for its outrageous and beautiful attempt to subvert the second law.

> *We are immersed in a life in which the world as a whole obeys the second law of thermodynamics: confusion increases and order decreases. Yet, as we have seen, the second law of thermodynamics, while it may be a valid statement about the whole of a closed system, is definitely not valid concerning a non-isolated part of it. There are local and temporary islands of decreasing entropy in a world in which the entropy as a whole tends to increase, and the existence of these islands enables some of us to assert the existence of progress. What can we say about the general direction of the battle between progress and increasing entropy in the world immediately around us? (Wiener, 1954, p.36)*

This was in effect a programmatic statement for what came to be called negative entropy. For Wiener, the "increasing entropy in the world immediately around us" was the experience of war, and in many ways his statement begins to account for the widespread emergence of closed corporate systems in the immediate postwar period. Entropy was, for Wiener, a sinister cosmic force against which it was necessary to construct isolated counter-entropic "islands" of progress. Skillfully mixing his physical and geographic metaphors, he projected the space of productive scientific and cultural work as a paradoxically "non-isolated" island. This strange, interconnected not-island was refuge and relief from what his science otherwise told him was the futility of engaging a universe in decline.

In the context of the present argument, Wiener's statement contains not only a description of postwar closure, but an uncanny premonition of postwar urban development itself. There is perhaps no more precise description of the postwar polynuclear field than a succession of "islands of decreasing entropy in a world in which the entropy as a whole tends to increase."

Ten years after this description was made, the idea of entropy would move out of the hard sciences to influence art and literature. The application of the idea to larger cultural forces would depart radically from that offered by Weiner. In effect, his "defense of progress" was completely reversed. In a short story which took the name of the second law, Thomas Pynchon displayed less concern about an ideological defense of progress than a description of its excesses. In the generation that separates these two writers, the idea of entropy was transformed from a defense of progress (fashioned against the military chaos of war) into an attack against it (fashioned against the corporate chaos of peace). Entropy as a broad social metaphor provided Pynchon with a scientifically sanctioned critique of closed systems and an antidote to a corporate order blind to its own destructive disorganization. Almost directly quoting Wiener, Pynchon commented on the leveling processes at work in the emerging postwar consumer culture:

> . . . he found in entropy or the measure of disorganization for a closed system an adequate metaphor to apply to certain phenomena in his own world. He saw, for example, the younger generation responding to Madison Avenue with the same spleen his own once had for Wall Street: and in American "consumerism" discovered a similar tendency from the least to the most probable, from ordered individuality to a kind of chaos. He found himself, in short, restating Gibbs' prediction in social terms, and envisioned a heat-death for his culture in which ideas, like heat energy, would no longer be transferred, since each point in it would ultimately have the same quantity of energy; and intellectual motion would, accordingly, cease. (Pynchon, 1984, p.88)

For Pynchon, who was part of a generation less effected by war than by the ensuing peace, scientific rationality and the postwar corporate world which it rapidly organized was itself the isolated system. Pynchon effectively defused Wiener's sleight of hand, positioning "progress" as a closed system and a temporary island, built upon nothing if not the denial of a surrounding sea of disorganization — a sea which was growing exponentially by the increasing insulation of new corporate nuclei. What Pynchon attempted was not only the identification but also the celebration of this sea of disorganization as an antidote to the debilitating effects of "progressive" corporate closure. Pynchon's outcast societies roaming the detritus of the military-industrial establishment, or Robert Smithson's "entropic landscapes" which engaged the actual sites and spaces of material disorganization, tap the residuum of closed systems and acknowledge a beautiful albeit fatal authenticity in their ultimate decline.

Wiener and others of his generation never considered that their islands of negative entropy would not only exclude, but dramatically accelerate the disorganization of the world outside the sanctums of progress. Nor did they consider that this accelerated disorganization would turn out to be aesthetically and politically potent, countersite. Translated into urban terms, Wiener's islands are the closed figures of centripetal production within the weak, disorganized universe of metropolitan decline. In an odd twist of his model, the contemporary urban landscape reflects these islands of apparently decreasing entropy, now made blind and indifferent to their own status as closed systems by the regressive simulation of openness. This reactionary closure is nevertheless bound to the surrounding sea of its own production, whose characteristics may yet serve a redemptive purpose.

COLLABORATING WITH ENTROPY

Wishing to neither praise the "marginal" nor condemn "God's own junkyard," it is only necessary to state the obvious: the residuum is not inert. Entropic forces do indeed run within the broad geographic spectrum that Wiener and Pynchon imagined. Increasing entropy is apparent in the energy crisis and in nuclear dumps; the greenhouse effect, the Balkan Wars, and the centralized economies of the former Soviet bloc, all exhibit entropic tendencies. There are, however, much narrower classifications of entropic phenomena relating to actual sites or landscapes, specifically landscapes associated with the residuum of closed systems. Mines, pits, quarries, toxic dumps, landfills, massive scenes

4.15 "After a Flash Flood," Rancho Mirage, California, 1979.
Photograph by Joel Sternfeld.

of deforestation form powerful scenes of dramatically increasing disorganization. As the shadow state of powerful, nearly autonomous modes of production, these "entropic landscapes" are characterized by a profound disorganization: the promiscuous intermingling of the natural and the man-made.

It is important to remember that this intermingling is not simply a juggling of abstractions, but constitutes the reorganization of existential constructs operating at the most basic levels of social organization. Anthropologists tell us that the distinctions between the natural and the artificial, the raw and the cooked, establish essential social molds upon which a basic working knowledge of the world is founded. Confusion between these distinct states compromises native abilities which allow both individuals and entire cultures to productively adapt to the organic materials and processes of their immediate environment. As such, these distinct states are consistently reproduced in the most basic of kinship structures across a broad range of societies. They are the basis of the universality routinely attributed to the binary structure of nature and culture. With regard to the city, this binary structure remains, even today, fully intact; its boundaries stubbornly refusing to be compromised.

Such boundaries are nowhere more evident than in the construction and maintenance of "nature" in the closed environments which comprise the postwar polynuclear field. In the world of the corporate development, markets are driven by a successful rendering of "softscape" as a benign complement to building commodities. So much of contemporary urban construction is merchandised as a class of natural "retreat" — the corporate "campus," "park," "meadow," "glen," "forest," "field" or "green" — where the grass is always green and cut, the parking lots are always swept, the trees always pruned, the water always clean if not dyed blue, and there are never any dead plants, patches of weeds or mud. Likewise, corporate enclaves never reveal signs of

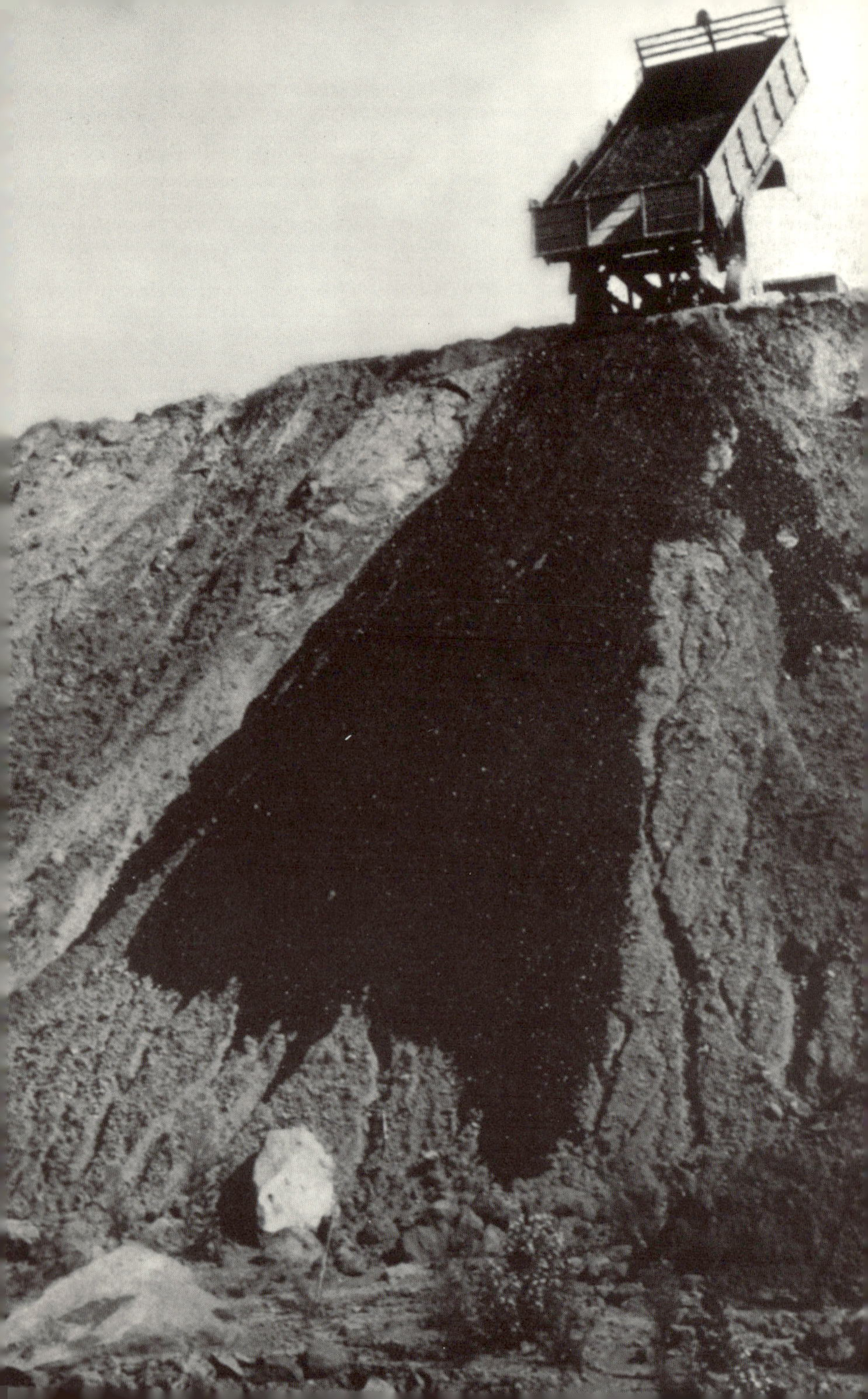

natural decay. Fresh paint, gleaming surfaces, transparency and reflection all convey the freshness of a "Now Leasing" sign advertising a brilliant investment opportunity. This precisely organized construction of the natural must be matched to the promiscuity of the entropic residuum. (In construction, for example, the organization of wood would suggest the disorganiztion of deforrestation, the organization of stone would suggest the disorganization of a quarry, the organization of metal would suggest the disorganization of a slag heap, the organization of asphalt, the disorganization an oil field, etcetera.) Corporate "nature" is closed and autonomous, immune to the ravages of time and the infinite extent of space. It is from actual nature existing in real space and time that the enclave must extract its resources, and it is for this reason that it must be occluded. The disorganization inherent in extraction produces a violence in the residuum which offends an already feeble social construction of reality, yet, it is only on the outside that nature is recuperated. It is in the profound intermingling of the natural and the man-made that the corporate clock is beaten — that time resumes, space extends and entropy is revealed as an intractable physical law.

The exurban residuum is clearly not urban space as it has been historically defined, nor does it qualify as a strictly "natural" condition. In a movement from urban to natural and back again — an ambivalence or confusion of opposites — both urban and natural space become unhinged from their conventional associations and new relations emerge. In an entropic landscape such as a quarry, a strip mine or a landfill, such a blurring of opposites becomes actual or material. As Smithson powerfully demonstrated in his reclamation projects, it is the site itself which challenges our ability to clearly see and classify the world. If it is impossible to extract the work of man from the work of nature, then it is ultimately impossible to privilege the work of man, simply because it cannot be located. Denying the privileged position of

4.16 Robert Smithson, "Asphalt Rundown," Rome 1969.
Photograph by Robert Smithson.
Estate of Robert Smithson, courtesy John Weber Gallery, New York

human actions is the crucial step in surmounting the powerful hegemony of closed systems. Smithson demonstrated twenty five years ago how an understanding of entropic processes can destabilize the increasingly naive positions of environmentalists. It is a crisis of classification — the inability to separate the man-made from the natural — which prevents the privileging our own actions and economies, and finally puts our presumptuous "stewardship" of the planet into a fresh perspective.

Such a dramatic realignment of the natural suggests the possibility of depolarizing other binary structures not the least of which is the polarized field of contemporary urban development. What is engaging about such realignments is that they not only reposition thought, but reposition the landscape itself. The entropic residuum surrounds us in the contemporary city and is growing more apparent, more palpable as all urban systems move toward absolute closure. While the world has always exceeded the concepts we employ to grasp it, this excess today establishes the frontier of our most intractable economic, political and cultural problems. It is perhaps our fortune to be routinely confronted with this excess — immersed in this excess — in the substance of contemporary urban space.

Smithson declared, "unlike Buckminster Fuller, I am interested in collaborating with entropy" (1979a, p.181). Against Fuller's reactionary advocacy of closed systems, Smithson's activities reveal the entropic qualities of the exurban residuum and engage these qualities as a powerful counterpoint to urban closure. It is clear that the disorganization of the residuum is not only a conceptual disorganization but a material disorganization. Lacking the capacity to structure differences, the exurban ellipsis has remained invisible for want of our ability to classify it. Strict classification is the purview of corporate managers who, like Fuller, ultimately prefer an "inside without an outside," or an outside so disorganized as to be palpably hostile as to form no real alternative to an otherwise comprehensive organization. As it turns out, the inherent disorganization of the residuum is not altogether inaccessible, and it is becoming more accessible every day.

SPRAWLING BABELS

The status of the city has been presented as it is found today, stalled at the threshold of a "superurban" stage. This threshold is characterized by a weak centralization and a powerful polynuclear field. No longer bound by traditional metropolitan responsibilities, exurban nuclei are free to move toward ever more exclusive or closed positions. These positions establish a regressive, oppositional space between the exurban nuclei and their spatial residuum.

In this oppositional space, exurban nuclei move toward ever stronger degrees of organization, while the residuum moves toward ever stronger degrees of disorganization. It has been suggested that a response to this condition is to recognize and promote the disorganization of contemporary urban space as an alternative to the effects of closure. Entropy as an idea, as an actual site, and as an aesthetic position is the means by which the disorganization of the residuum is recognized. It literally conducts the residuum into view and posits it as a field of potential engagement. The awakening of the residuum as a vital economic, aesthetic and political site ultimately disputes the authority of the enclave and disrupts the oppositional space of the polynuclear field. Entropy is thus instrumental, not only in revealing the residuum, but in ultimately depolarizing the binary urban field. In this regard, the entropic residuum is not to be embraced for its own sake (for the inherent value of the abandoned, the wasted, the decaying, the dispossessed, the marginal) but for its depolarizing effect upon closed urban systems.

The ignition of the residuum would instate a dialectic between closed

4.17 Deforestation, Brazil.
Landsat Aerial photgraph by NASA/U.S. Geological Survey.

urban form and open residual space. This dialectic has already been discussed, and it is clearly the driving force behind various projections of the Modern City. The centripetal strategies advanced by Howard, Unwin, Hilberseimer, Le Corbusier and Wright were meant to establish precisely this unique relation between form and space — seeking to invert their conventional relation and deliver, in the end, an unprecedented city of space. It has perhaps always been apparent that the radical non-centralized urban fields of points, spines and grids were imagined, not as the infrastructure of closed systems, but as the support of a new dialectic between urban form and space. As it turns out, these architects failed, yet they failed only to the extent that the transformations they imagined have yet to be implemented.

In the meantime, the polynuclear field has regressed into a reductive polarization preempting the dialectic which first drove its conception. By now, it has begun to appear that these closed systems are inevitable. Trapped in the inertia of current corporate practices, all things point toward an interminable exclusion, division, and stagnation. Yet the alternative trajectory of development imagined nearly a century ago suggests another set of possibilities that remain viable. Having moved from the single, hierarchical metropolitan center of "sub-urban" development, to the multiple closed centers of "super-urban" development, a platform is set for the breakdown of the structured center in what one should be cautious in calling a "post-urban" development. This trajectory toward a "post-urban" city of space remains, even today, the antidote to the imminent closure of urban form.

What would push this trajectory forward is the collapse of closed urban systems and the emergence of the dialectical interrelation between space and form. This is the crucial operation where the multiple centers of the polarized field begin to recede into a city that truly is dominated by space. What this new dialectic might be like has been already imagined and it comes as no surprise that its features may be deduced from the city that surrounds us:

Suburbia encompasses the large cities and dislocates the "country." Suburbia literally means a "city below;" it is a circular gulf between city and country — a place where buildings seem to sink away from one's vision — buildings fall back into sprawling babels or limbos. Every site glides away towards absence. An immense negative entity of formlessness displaces the center which is the city and swamps the country. From the worn down mountains of North New Jersey to postcard skylines of Manhattan, the prodigious variety of "housing projects" radiate into a vaporized world of cubes. The landscape is effaced into sidereal expanses and contractions. Los Angeles is all suburb, a pointless phenomenon which seems uninhabitable, and a place swarming with dematerialized distances. A pale copy of a bad movie. . . . Exterior space gives way to a total vacuity of time. Time as a concrete aspect of mind mixed with things is attenuated into ever greater distances, that leave one fixed in a certain spot. Reality dissolves into leaden and incessant lattices of solid diminution. An effacement of the country and city abolishes space, but establishes enormous mental distances. (Smithson, 1979b, p.76)

Beyond the irreconcilable opposition between corporate production and its residuum, it is already possible to conceive of a radical disorganization of the polarized polynuclear field. The result is an "effaced" landscape, a "circular gulf" which displaces the city and "swamps the country." As development progresses toward the eradication of polynuclear boundaries — the ultimate de-differentiation of the inside/outside into increasing disorganization — it specifies the reemergence of an encompassing metropolitan field. It is important to note that Smithson's description is not of a meaningless disorganization, nor does it advocate the revival of a coherent metropolitan condition. Rather it describes the effect of the metropolis displaced. Evoking the seemingly mundane qualities of contemporary urban construction, the workings of an inescapable urban whole are suggested. It is in the end an entropic whole which may be enlisted against the excessive (dis)organization of its parts. It is the vision of the long and desperately sought city of space.

THE RESIDUE IS NOT INERT

What if is there is no Vacuum? Or if there is — what if They're using *it on you? What if They find it convenient to preach an island of life surrounded by a void? Not just the Earth in space, but your own individual life in time? What if it's* in Their interest *to have you believing that?*
"He won't bother us for a while," They tell each other. "I just put him on the Dark Dream." (Pynchon, 1973, p.697)

Journalists, geographers, and social critics routinely evoke urban form as the ultimate evidence of the breakup of long-standing coalitions along the lines of class, race and nationality. In this regard, urban form is taken to be a reflection of economic, cultural and political forces already in play throughout the larger society. Mike Davis' declaration of "spatial apartheid" as consequent to a segregated "urban donut" (Davis, 1993, p.17) evokes an enduring metropolitan center/periphery organization. Alternately, Michael Lind suggests that the polarized polynuclear field is the reflection of intractable class divisions:

The real threat is not the Balkanization but the Brazilianization of America, not fragmentation along racial lines but fissioning along class lines. Brazilianization is symbolized by the increasing withdrawal of the white American overclass into its own barricaded nation-within-a-nation, a world of private neighborhoods, private schools, private police, private health care, and even private roads, walled off from the spreading squalor beyond. Like a Latin American oligarchy, the rich and well-connected members of the overclass can flourish in a decadent America with Third World levels of inequality and crime. (Lind, 1995 p.14)

In spite of such persuasive rhetoric, the repeated analogies between social trends and urban form are often naive, and betray a reluctance to acknowledge the obvious logic revealed in urban form. It is by now clear that centripetal form is not prejudicial with respect to race, class, or nationality.

4.18 Subdivision, Sugarland, Texas, 1995.
Photograph by Carmen Platero.

Withdrawal into suburban slums is now every bit as common as the withdrawal into well-heeled country club subdivisions. It is presumptuous, if not disingenuous, to infer that various social, political and economic institutions are suffering an irreconcilable fragmentation, as if urban form were the ultimate index of (dis)unification. While it is a truism to insist that print and electronic media have supplanted the unifying role previously fulfilled by the city, such insights are often lost on those who see the urban form as absolute. It is apparent that as the city moves toward division, dispersion, and dissemination, global capital, for example, appears to be moving in the opposite direction: toward an unprecedented and ambitious unity.

When capital expands beyond urban, regional and national powerbases, corporations merge, markets explode, and fundamental choices drop to their lowest common denominator. As we retreat into the not-so-privileged world of the *cul-de-sac*, we are increasingly absorbed into massive media markets, subjected to electronic surveillance, incorporated into centralized HMOs, tracked by sophisticated software and scrutinized in enormous bureaucratic databases. Coherent metropolitan order may be weak, but the agents of consolidation and incorporation abound, so much so that one suspects the fragmentation of the city may be nothing more than compensation for what we must otherwise surrender. In this regard, the suburb is no longer a "retreat." Far from blocking the effects of a pervasive conscription into global markets, weak metropolitan form facilitates the decline and collapse of all that exists between the individual and the multi-national. In other words, weak metropolitan form is the infrastructure of unification: not the unification of the city, but the unification of emerging global markets.

Looking beyond the apparent urban fragmentation, such a unity is not difficult to perceive. While ladders exist in isolation, they are apparently everywhere, structuring everything. As metropolitan unity weakens, local nuclei are strengthened, and the resulting urban field achieves, not random "sprawl," but a radical, discontinuous or distributed unity. It has been shown that residential subdivisions, office parks, commercial malls, airports, skywalks, high-rise sections and freeways all apparently issue from the same template. This apparent unity of form is extraordinary given the present conception of contemporary urban development as so much uncontrolled and disorganized "sprawl." That the majority of urban elements share a common order across a broad range of scales suggests a totality which remains completely obscure to popular perceptions of the city. The implications of such "transparent" forms of organization are, to say the least, socially and politically suspect.

Power presently flows in the vacuum that is the perception of contemporary urban space. It is this vacuum that creates the discontinuous unity of absolute closure. The maintenance of the vacuum as a vacuum is the priority of closed systems. Contemporary urban space must be sustained as an "outside" — a criminal landscape of drugs, gangland violence, and vigilante policemen; a lethal environment of the diminishing ozone, dangerous smog, and UV radiation; a depleted world of broken communities, broken homes, and broken lives — a self-fulfilling prophecy rehearsed each half-hour on corporate news broadcasts. It often seems unlikely that such a pervasive structure of exclusion could ever collapse, that the "outside" could ever be redeemed, and those that inhabit it could ever escape from what and who the mangers of closed systems require them to be.

If, however, through the observation of powerful entropic processes, the spatial residuum were to emerge from this oblivion, then the power flows of absolute closure would surely be destabilized. For the "outside" is no "vacuum," contemporary urban space is no "Void," metaphysical or otherwise. The residuum is not inert. As urban space emerges as an undeniable local force, it would be capable of obstructing, connecting or otherwise effectively controlling the mediation between discontinuous global franchises. In this way the entropic residuum could emerge as a countersite and directly intercede in the parameters of closure. This intercession precisely defines the new dialectic between urban space and form which triggers a " post-urban" breakup of closed and exclusive urban systems and the final and full arrival of the city of space.

It would be naive to suggest here that the depolarization of the polynuclear field will emerge by a direct and willful intervention. It has been proposed that the emergence of the residuum as a vital economic, cultural, and political site will occur, not as a singular act, but as the reciprocal effect of closure. As closed systems approach complete autonomy, their residuum will correspondingly approach a maximum level of disorganization or entropy, and they will no longer remain invisible and unimportant. This movement toward maximum organization and maximum disorganization is presumably charged with the inevitability of a physical law.

It is, however, irresponsible to suggest that such specific transformations of urban form are necessary and inevitable, and that we need do no more than sit back and watch it all happen. The danger in understanding the evolution of cities as a teleological process is that it ultimately undermines the designer's capacity as an active agent capable of meaningful intervention. The manner in which centripetal development has been presented here — as an autonomous logic relentlessly moving toward a city of space — has been saturated with a determinism that is by now nearly exhausted. Given the substandard urbanism this logic has already sponsored, one may wish to insist on a free hand, to demand the latitude necessary to recreate the urban world based on the full extent of our capacities to imagine it. Embracing the parameters of centripetal form laid out here would seem to compromise these efforts from the start. To promote the entropic disorganization of the city and the complete collapse of metropolitan representation could amount to nothing more than an enormous evasion of responsibility.

There exists in urban speculation a fine line between prognostication and creation which associates seemingly autonomous urban forces with the will of the designer to actively participate in their unfolding development. It is obvious that the centripetal reorganization of the city would have occurred in spite of Howard's or Hilberseimer's or Wright's impressive attempts to promote it. The question here is not one of invention, but of the ability of lucid planning to indicate the logic of these extensive urban processes and move that logic toward progressive ends. One might speculate that what has made these plans powerful is not their creative verve or their unabashed utopian component, but their ability to divulge a larger trajectory and elevate its potential as form beyond the gross compromises that invariably attend its realization. It is precisely here, I would submit, that the designer is engaged in meaningful urban intervention.

The countersites of contemporary urban space will continue to evolve towards an increasing awareness of their inherent potential irrespective of our "yes" or "no." Beyond simply waiting out an endless urban interregnum, a precise outline of a presently emerging form needs to be articulated and driven toward a positive outcome. The so-called Void of contemporary urban space is already full — charged with economic, political and cultural meaning. The vital and indispensible potential of such meaning can be suggested in a few concluding remarks.

CONCLUSION:
MASS ABSENCE

MASS ABSENCE

The well known photograph of a mass demonstration in front of Giuseppe Terragni's Casa del Fascio is one of the most fascinating and haunting images in the history of Modern Architecture. All that an architecture of modernism could be was simultaneously revealed and betrayed in the second of the shutter's collapse, marking for an instant a watershed in which an entirely different outcome can be glimpsed — the specter of a modernism of drastically different consequences.

The photograph is only reluctantly contained within the limits of orthodox modernism. A difficulty in reading it stems from a contradiction between the building's architectural autonomy and its apparent ability to represent a modern political state. Terragni's building is an architectural *tour de force*. It manifests, perhaps more than any other modernist work, the autonomy of the architectural artifact, the ability of the building to speak about the discipline from which it springs, and to reveal its in-built formal, technical, and cultural intentions. In this regard, the Casa del Fascio has few rivals in the history of modern architecture. In its rigorous proportioning systems, its reference to a traditional typology, its refined plastic syntax and its tectonic clarity the building is resolved, in and of itself, in all of its essential qualities.

What is then so disturbing about the photograph is how the building, being so elegantly hermetic, has come to function as an icon of the Fascist state. How can a self-referencing object, timeless in its fidelity to the art of its discipline, be capable of addressing a specific place, time, and political ideology? How can a modern building simultaneously represent a thoroughly contemporary political body and, at the same time, sustain an argument which transcends representation, voluntarily denying or suppressing its power to represent anything but itself?

This apparent paradox, which is represented nowhere more clearly than in the image of the Fascist demonstration, represents less a contradiction than a subtle and powerful artistic and ideological force which briefly flourished in modern architecture during the 1920s. The contradiction is of course not a contradiction at all. The history of architecture is written with buildings which manifest such contradictions. The ability to both reference autonomous form and support a powerful historical moment is, for many, key to the legitimacy of monumental construction. What is then unique about the Casa del Fascio is that it carries out this tradition within an overtly modernist idiom. As the subsequent histories of modern architecture were written, this was not supposed to happen. Modernism was nothing if not a historicist reaction to an autonomous culture of architecture. It was specific to the 20th-century, and the rejection of an overriding monumental culture drove its polemic. Thus, the image of the Fascist rally remains problematic because it represents the ability of modernism to sustain an ancient tradition: the uniting of autonomous form with historical contingency.

The outrageous plastic, technical, and material virtuosity of the Casa del Fascio is undeniable. What has always been more difficult to grasp is the building's participation in its political moment. One might say that the desire to represent a thoroughly contemporary political body is one of the chief ambitions of early modern architecture, one of the primary ways in which it made itself historically specific. While the precise identity of any political constituency is difficult to define, it is possible to argue that modernism sought to represent not a fading monarchy, or the power of the church, or even 19th-century bourgeois democracy, but the broader spectrum of an emerging, empowered majority. That majority might have been Communist or Socialist. For a short time in Italy, it was even possible to conceive of it as Fascist. The point is that this empowered majority became the collective political subject of modern architecture and urbanism.

Such claims have always presented difficulties for those who consider modernism to be only an autonomous discourse. It is the technical and material virtuosity of the Casa del Fascio which has been addressed by scholars; its politics have been dismissed as merely unfortunate. Such analyses correspond to the idea of modernism as it was rewritten since the Second World War: modernism as an autonomous, ideologically untainted discipline bound to the expressive devices of its own plastic and material existence.

Any overt ideological aspect of the modern project, any subtle dialectic between autonomy and representation, was eliminated with the rise of totalitarian regimes in the 1930s and the momentary victory of the "New Traditionalism" and Socialist Realism. As has been observed, but not precisely for these reasons, this was the historic moment in which the dialectic between representation and autonomy collapsed in on itself; or, one might say, the grace of the early modernists to sustain the dialectic was lost. The subsequent haste to fashion modernism as the antithesis of totalitarian realism led to abandoning the idea of modern architecture as the setting for an overt ideological inscription of mass society and opened the door for the presumably apolitical, ego-centric vision of the Modern City discussed above. In other words, it was more important for modernism to contradict the excesses of totalitarian ideology than to sustain its own collective project.

Following the war modernism shifted towards its autonomous artistic and technical tendencies, abandoning, if not discrediting as a whole, its ideological involvement. The Casa del Fascio's apparent contradiction between artistry and ideology, autonomy and representation, was "resolved" in its confrontation with totalitarian realism. From this point forward the subsequent history of modern architecture as an autonomous discourse, innocent of overt ideological intentions, was written. With little commentary on the fate of its overt social and political goals, Modernism succeeded through its opposition to the totalitarian state, but only at the cost of denying its own collective ambitions. Reyner Banham once remarked that the Second Word War was fought to make the world safe for modernism. The sentiment has always rung true inasmuch as it also prompted its inverse: that Modern Architecture was ultimately made "safe" for the postwar world.

IDEOLOGIES DANCE ABOUT IN THIS VOID

Modernism's denial of contemporary political space — the concrete representation of the collective metropolitan subject — returns in the photograph of the Casa del Fascio, and this is why it remains, even today, so poignant and so disturbingly alien to our own possibilities. The photograph suggests that, at least for one moment, the modern city was to be the anthropomorphically inscribed scene of contemporary political action, the manifest space of an unprecedented urban collectivity. Perhaps the image continues to disturb us not so much in recalling that particular day in Como, as in forcing a critical reflection on the architecture and urbanism which grew out of it. The arresting vision of modernism in support of an overtly popular political front haunts not just the culture of architecture but, more significantly, the built reality of the contemporary city. In its overt inscription of the masses, the Casa del Fascio is so remote from the recognizable reality of contemporary urbanism that, in spite of its modernity, it scarcely occurs to construct the obvious historical connection.

Perhaps, however, a connection between the revolutionary discourses of the 1920s and the contemporary urban environment is altogether beside the point. Rather than merely sustaining modern historiography, it would be more interesting to focus on the historical rupture or inversion represented by

Terragni's monument and its legacy. Its ostensible modernism aside, the building stands less as a progenitor of the contemporary urban environment than its direct antithesis. Terragni's built space of mass politics stands in direct opposition to contemporary urban space, the vast unoccupied and neglected residuum, presumably emptied of ideological intention. The parking lots, gutted central business districts, undeveloped/redeveloped land, corporate buffer zones, and endless carscapes are spaces which are hostile to physical occupation. Anthropomorphic inscription, the formally acknowledged presence of the human figure, the presence of the pedestrian and demonstrator alike, is violently preempted in the inner city and exurban ellipsis. Yet it has already been shown that these spaces are not simply empty, or certainly not empty of meaning. Tied into an interurban field, they are not neutral spaces, or spacings. They are instead to be understood as absences, vacancies, hiatuses or empty centers, as full of potential significance as the space of any urban environment.

In contrast to the space of Como, these spaces are characterized as where people are not, where the urban collective is profoundly marked or inscribed by its absence. The contemporary urban ellipsis seems in many ways to represent the disappearance of the urban citizen, the default of a political body, the impossibility of constructing out of the masses either an urban subject or an urban object, the index of a remarkable mass absence.

The resolution of the inherent dialectic within early modernism, the move toward a one-dimensional autonomy, the loss of the collective subject and the subsequent rise of an ego-centric urban pattern all establish a watershed which has not been adequately emphasized. Ranging far beyond the debate over appropriate style, the attempts by both the early avant-garde and the totalitarian state to inscribe the urban political masses continue to reverberate negatively in the spaces of the contemporary city. The politics of

Terragni's building clearly belong on the other side of the catastrophe which was the Second World War, in the receding tide of which our present cities continue to be constructed. In our postwar retreat from the city we are, in effect, still "demobilizing" from that catastrophe. The voids of the contemporary city, the gaps and lacunae that have come to characterize contemporary urban space, are not without meaning: they are the residue, the detritus deposited by that catastrophe. Modernism has delivered the city that, by the mid-1930s, we should have already been expecting. The cost of denying its collective project can ultimately be assessed in the broad and empty sweep of the contemporary urban ellipsis.

A CALCULATED WITHDRAWAL

It would be naive to leave standing an impression that the early modern dialectic between autonomy and representation was simply abandoned and that, by extension, it can now be reconstructed on the model provided by Terragni or others. The collapse of collective representation was never a matter of choice to accept or reject (nor subsequently to revive). The "crisis of representation" in architecture, then as now, is motivated by forces beyond the prerogatives of the discipline, and this is in spite of the many heroic attempts to circumvent its limitations architecturally.

It would also be naive to characterize the move of discourse away from ideological representation and toward disciplinary autonomy as preempting significant connections between modern buildings and the cities they ultimately construct. As was suggested in the discussions of the ellipsis, these connections persist. They did not simply disappear, however obscured or involuted their meanings may have become. While neglected by almost everyone, contemporary urban space persists, and it would be absurd to think that it does not effect the characteristics and qualities of the environment that it constitutes. In this regard it is important to track the motives and consequences of the entropic residuum. What does it mean, for example, to suggest that the inner city ellipsis has come to signify the collapse of modern political space — a mass absence? Beyond a certain dramatic interest, what could be gained from such an understanding of contemporary urban space? Why would anyone want to promote it?

To track these motives it is necessary to return to the so-called contradiction between autonomy and representation, artistry and ideology. The shift of modern architecture away from representation was not simply an abdication of the discipline's political role (and the author's political will). It was rather a calculated ideological choice. More than a denial of representation, the move toward autonomy can be understood, not as a retreat into the inner logic of the discipline, but as a specific ideological statement regarding the impossibility of contemporary political representation.

In spite of the heady utopian fervor of the early avant-garde, the potential for a mass political consensus has always been regarded with a lot of skepticism. If there was doubt as to the actual existence of a mass sentiment or will, there was still greater doubt about a coherent, unequivocal representation of that will in urban space. This apparent crisis in representation was evident within modernism from the beginning and forms its implicit counter-utopian project. From this perspective, modernism's move toward a strict autonomy and abstraction — its desire to transcend representation in favor of immanence and presence — can be understood to mask a more radical political will. In this regard abstraction is a calculated withdrawal from an impossible political moment, an overt refusal to participate in the social and political pathologies unfolding in the early 20th-century city and ultimately the undesirability of gratuitously constructing the masses into a collective urban subject.

At least since the polemic of Adolf Loos, the willfully muted object has represented a calculated strategy of refusal stubbornly lodged within the utopian project of mainstream modernism. Karl Kraus's admonition to step forward and be silent perhaps steeled Loos in his refusal to represent the social and political disaster that was *fin de sciecle* Vienna. A certain asceticism attends this refusal, implicit always in the mute interventions into the traditional city (not exactly like ripping out your tongue in the public square). Loos's strategy maintained the choice of refusal which was perhaps the only choice left to make. Aldo van Eyck's dilemma "if society has no form how can architects build the counterform?" (Smithson, 1968, p.13), is echoed by Aldo Rossi's remark "I am proud that I have not often built for people when I did not know where they were" (Rossi, 1981, p.48). These are all statements of a radical political will, not aesthetic evasion.

A NEGATIVE SOVEREIGNTY

Such may be the motivation for a calculated withdrawal from political activity and the subsequent implosion of the conventional channels of urban representation. It suggests not an absence of meaning but a potent silence, an abandoned forum, an involuted city square (Hedjuk, 1992, p.16). Accepting for a moment the plausibility of such a strategy — the emergence of a full blown postpolitical collectivity — what are its urban implications? How exactly would this refusal and subsequent silence be received and understood?

It may be best to answer this by postulating the alternative to silence. In a 1979 interview with Michel Foucault, the French philosopher Gilles Deleuze referred to Foucault's texts as revealing the ultimate "indignity of speaking for others"(Foucault, 1977, p.209). The phrase sums up the force of Foucault's reflections on the history of institutions and power. After the discourses of the "human sciences" have been dissected and analyzed, after their role as an alibi for power has been demolished and revealed in all of its historical specificity, there is a question that remains: in whose name is this discourse spoken, and who, precisely, is being spoken for? For those who presume to construct public discourse, a warning is issued concerning the ultimate "indignity of speaking for others" and, implicitly, the indignity of being spoken for. When urban designers, either at the beginning or the end of this century, propose the revival of "public space," for whom do they speak? What constituency has been located? What political, social and cultural field is being brought into play, and who will be its players? Beyond any essentialist notions of urban community (for example, Clarence Perry's Neighborhood Unit), in whose greater interests are such associations made? And exactly how and on what occasion may the politics of streets and squares be refused?

The subjects that the urban designer so eagerly seeks to construct into a universal community may not, or may no longer, be so amenable. They may intuitively suspect the motives of a gratuitous urban representation, and refuse to become its unwitting subjects. There are, in fact, all the signs that the attempts to define such a subject have more recently been preempted. Jean Baudrillard posed the question in terms of gratuitous representations in all media, and the effects of a subsequent and deafening silence.

. . . as for the silence of the masses in relation to the media . . . I (originally) gave this silence a pejorative and negative sense. Later on I turned this hypothesis around. . . . I proposed that this silence was a power, that it was a reply, that the silence was a massive reply through withdrawal, that the silence was a strategy. It is not just a passivity. It is precisely a means of putting an end to meaning, of putting an end to the grand systems of manipulation, political and informational. And at the moment, the masses, perhaps, instead of being manipulated by the media, actually utilize the media in order to disappear. It is a strategy of disappearance through the media. For the masses it is a way of neutralizing the

fields that one would like to impose on them. One wants to impose a political field, one wants to impose a social field, a cultural field: all of that comes from above: it comes through the media, and the masses reply to it all with silence; they block the process. And in that, it seems to me, they have a kind of negative sovereignty. But it is not like an alienation. At the moment it is not at all certain that the media are a strategy of power for controlling and manipulating the masses in order to force them into silence. Rather, it is perhaps a case of the strategy inverted, that it is the masses who hide themselves behind the media. That is they nullify meaning. And this is truly a power. On one side there is the political class, the cultural class, etc., who produce meaning. . . . And on the other side there are the masses of people who refuse this meaning which comes from above, or who block it all because there is too much meaning, too much information. (Baudrillard, 1993, p.88)

The collapse of public monuments, streets, and squares into a formless primacy of space is the fallout of this silence. And it is an arrogance, equal to the most strident of polemicists that presumes the inhabitants of the contemporary city must now be led back to the presumed sanity of a traditional urban community — the unwitting subject of a now universal inscription. Such may address the effective role of silence with regard to the contemporary public sphere and also suggest the specific political potency of the inner city and the exurban ellipsis.

CODA: THE PEOPLE ARE MISSING

In (early) American and Soviet cinema, the people are already there, real before being actual, ideal without being abstract. Hence the idea that the cinema, as of the masses, could be the supreme revolutionary and democratic art, which makes the masses a true subject. But many great factors were to compromise this belief: the rise of Hitler, which gave cinema as its object not the masses become subject but the masses subjected; Stalinism, which replaced the unanimism of peoples with the tyrannical unity of a party; the break-up of the American people, who could no longer believe themselves to be either the melting-pot of peoples past or the seed of a people to come. In short, the people no longer exist, or not yet... the people are missing.

... this acknowledgment of a people who are missing is not a renunciation of political cinema, but on the contrary the new basis on which it is founded.... Art, and especially cinematographic art, must take part in this task: not that of addressing a people which is presupposed already there, but of contributing to the invention of a people. (Deleuze, 1989, p.216)

The refusal to speak or build for people when you do not know where they are, and the subsequent mass absence of the contemporary urban ellipsis, is "not a renunciation of political (architecture), but on the contrary the new basis on which it is founded." The importance of not "addressing a people which is presupposed already there" is, at this moment, fundamental to the "invention of a people" we are at present unable to see.

For those who disparage the contemporary city as unlivable and unworkable, who read nihilism in the implosion of the public realm, the inversion of this realm suggests, however subtly, another possibility. Freed from the repression of an overarching or universal inscription of corporate collectivity, the urban ellipsis is not only a space of haunted absence, the inertia of bad faith, but may also contain the possibilities of a *tabula rasa*. It truly is "free space." Thinking back to the early modernist attack on traditional urban representation, the void that they savagely created in their abstractions was not politically nihilistic. The possibilities latent in Malevich's non-objective world were unlimited, yet these possibilities arose out of a condition similar to our own. Quoting from his Suprematist Manifesto, we may note evidence of a hidden political significance in the ultimate refusal of representation:

The ascent to the heights of non-objective art is arduous and painful . . . but it is nevertheless rewarding. The familiar recedes even further and further into the background. . . . The contours of the objective world fade more and more and so it goes, step by step, until finally the world —everything we loved and by which we have lived — becomes lost to sight. . . . No more "likeness of reality," no idealistic images — nothing but a desert! (Malevich, 1959, p.68)

It is better to suffer the void of abstraction than gratuitous representation, better to be lost than to languish in the "objective world" of closed urban development.

There has been an attempt to re-envision what remains of contemporary urban space, and to speculate on the possibility of habitation which may exist off the corporate map. The articulation of a "subject position" outside of the world system may be read into Malevich's manifesto, as indeed it may be read into the modern project as a whole. If Modernism did foresee and urge on the inevitable terms of modernization, it can also be seen to have accounted for its consequences. Simply stated, while modernism did not invent closed centripetal production, it did invent a language by which it could be overcome. Its greatest legacy lies not in the planning of closed urban communities, but in generating an effective legacy of space. Malevich ultimately suggests a powerful longing for the treacherous, dangerous, and potent world of contemporary urban space: "No more 'likeness of reality,' no idealistic images — nothing but a desert!"

6.1 Swallows Meadow, Houston, Texas.
Photograph by Bruce Webb.

POSTSCRIPT: LACUNAS, By Lars Lerup.

Connectedness is the spirit of the city. It will most probably remain so for all time with one important qualification: in an era of progressive virtuality, connectedness need not be physical.

Albert Pope's conceptual breakthrough is not primarily the recognition of the peculiar blips on the otherwise contiguous map of the city, but in the characteristics and future importance of this archipelago of voids. Robert Smithson set the agenda of the *kenofilia,* love of emptiness, (in opposition to *topofilia,* the love of place) in his succinct description of the radical difference between the built fabrics of Manhattan and Passaic, New Jersey, suggesting that the latter may have replaced Rome as a world city.

To others these holes may appear idiosyncratic at best but also invisible, mere jump-cuts in the ebb and flow to and from the city. However, with Pope's reflections, it is clear that the voids (in what I have previously called the *holey plane*) are systematic, essential and, as it may prove, fortuitous components of the comportment of the real estate machine. Leapfrogged, the voids are elastic blobs that allow the developer to hang on to his profit margins. The size and shape of the blob may in fact be a complex reflection of the dynamics of land costs, market forces, building practices, and peculiarities of local conditions. These voids may be the result of raising costs and the availability of cheaper land just beyond, or they actually may be the result of the autonomous evolution of the form Pope has called the ladder. Either way, these holes — a form of unintentional land-banking held in focus by Pope's analysis — are restored to a new potential. Are they the last frontier of the city?

The conventional argument would suggest that all we need to do is to fill in the holes and complete the destiny of a contiguous city, but Pope cautions that such knee-jerk reaction fails to understand the new city. Instead, he seems to say: *this galaxy of voids needs to fulfill its own destiny as discontinuity.*

This postscript is written longhand on one of the ninety thousand islands that dot the Baltic Sea between Stockholm and Helsinki. Here the tradition is simplicity: no running water, no sewage or septic tanks, no cars, and human occupation is limited to a couple of precious and exhilarating months during the summer when the sun barely goes to rest beyond the horizon. Surrounding *kobbarna och skären*, modernity in the form of boats — rowed, sailed, motorized and any combination thereof, slow or fast, well-sailed or aggressively pushed for peak-performance, large or small — criss-cross the waters reminding those on the islands that the City is not far away. Yet even the ear-shattering noise of a polluting two-stroke engine fades once the first autumn storm signals the return of Nature's rule. This cyclical occupation allows the islands the necessary respite to replenish the rainwater cisterns, to return human waste to dust, to let the micro-biological processes reform the pollutants, and to replace the drinking songs with nature's own ambiguous moans.

This self-imposed simplicity, standing in stark contrast to the life in the cities on the main land, may hint at the reverence with which one should regard Pope's archipelago, i.e., the domain of the voids may be best put in the hands of a custodian, or they may survive on their own. The nature of these voids, says Pope, is currently unclear, and he seems to suggest that they should remain so. Like animals (to paraphrase Luc Ferry, the French philosopher) these lacunas are the backside of the city — *the other* — whose very nature is deeply *ambiguous*. And it is the *custody of this ambiguity* that is one of the sources of our own humanity.

Finally, it is with great satisfaction that we look foward to the publication of *Ladders,* not just for the personal accomplishment of its author, but as an additional affirmation of Rice's search for the Open City.

Bergdalen 24, Gränö, June 1996

ILLUSTRATION AND PHOTOGRAPH CREDITS

Front cover

"Swallows Meadow." Subdivision, Houston, Texas, Photograph by Bruce Webb.

Establishing shots

Frame 1 (p. i), "Skybridge." Dallas, Texas, 1995. Photograph by Karin Taylor.

Frame 2 (p. ii), "Downtown Houston." Texas, c. 1970. Photograph by Alex S. MacLean / Landslides. From: Jaquelin T. Robertson (1983): *Modulus 16.*

Frame 3 (p. iv), "Parking Deck." Houston, Texas, 1995. Photograph by Karin Taylor.

Frame 4 (p. vi), "Truck-flip." Houston, Texas, 1994. Video frame by Dung Ngo.

Frame 5 (p. viii), "First Ward and Downtown Houston." Texas, 1986. Photograph by Geoff Winningham. From: Geoff Winningham (1986): *A Place of Dreams: Houston, An American City.*

Frame 6 (p. x), "Lyons Avenue." Houston, Texas, 1986. Photograph by Geoff Winningham. From Geoff Winningham (1986): *A Place of Dreams: Houston, An Americn City.*

Frame 7 (p. xii), "Truck-flip." Houston, Texas, 1994. Video frame by Dung Ngo.

Frame 8 (p. xiv), "Parking Lot off FM 1960." Houston, Texas, 1994. Photograph by Larry Albert.

Frame 9 (p. xvi), "Buffalo Bayou near Woodway at Loop 610." Houston, Texas, 1986. Photograph by Geoff Winningham. From: Geoff Winningham (1986): *A Place of Dreams: Houston, An American City.*

Frame 10 (p. xviii), "Wet Feeder." Houston, Texas, 1995. Photograph by Nicola Springer.

Frame 11 (p. xx), "Little White Oak Bayou and Downtown Houston." Texas, 1986. Photograph by Geoff Winningham. From: Geoff Winningham (1986): *A Place of Dreams: Houston, An American City.*

Frame 12 (p. xxii), "Sunbelt Subdivision." Sugarland, Texas, 1995. Photograph by Carmen Platero.

Frame 13 (p. xxiv), "Under Interstate 45, north of downtown." Houston, Texas, 1986. Photograph by Geoff Winningham. From: Geoff Winningham (1986): *A Place of Dreams: Houston, An American City*.

Frame 14 (p. xxvi), "Strip." Houston, Texas, 1994. Photograph by Haemin Lee.

Introduction

Frontispiece (p.0), "Louisiana Street." Houston, Texas, 1993. Photograph by Steve Traeger.

Figure 0.1 (p.4), Superstudio, "Live *with* objects and not *for* objects." Photocollage, 1972. From: Emilio Ambasz (1972): *Italy: The New Domestic Landscape Achievements and Problems of Italian Design*.

One: The open city

Frontispiece (p.14), "339th Avenue." Phoenix, Arizona, 1995. Photograph by Sze Tsung Leong.

Figure 1.1 (p.16), Urban grids. Redrawn from: *Lotus International—19* (June 1978).

Figure 1.2 (p.20), Go game played between Hoshino Toshi and Yanabe Toshiro, December 20, 1950. Redrawn from: Richard Bozulich (ed.) (1992): *The Go Almanac*.

Figure 1.3 (p.26), Ludwig Hilberseimer, Integrated Smoke-Producing Industries; Plan for Chicago, 1944. From: Ludwig Hilberseimer (1944): *The New City: Principles of Planning*.

Figure 1.4 (p.30), "Park Avenue." Looking north from Grand Central Station, Manhattan, New York, 1924. From: Henry Collins Brown (1924): *Fifth Avenue Old and New*.

Figure 1.5 (p.30), Centrifugal Growth of London, 1840-1929. From: Eliel Saarinen (1943): *The City: Its Growth, Its Decay, Its Future*.

Figure 1.6 (p.34), 1811 Commissioner's Plan of Manhattan, New York. From: Henry Collins Brown (1924): *Fifth Avenue Old and New*.

Figure 1.7 (p.38), "By-law Streets." London, 1890. From: Leonardo Benevolo (1971): *The Origins of Modern Town Planning*.

Figure 1.8 (p.42), Frederick Law Olmsted, Jr. and Grosvenor Atterbury, Forest Hills Garden, NewYork, 1908. Redrawn from: Richard Plunz (1990): *A History of Housing in New York City: Dwelling Type and Social Change in the American Metropolis*.

Figure 1.9 (p.46), "The Seven Ranges of Townships," surveyed in Ohio, 1796. From: John W. Reps (1965): *The Making of Urban America*.

Figure 1.10 (p.48), "Speculative Row Houses on West 133rd Street." Manhattan, New York, 1882. From: Nathan Silver (1967): *Lost New York*.

Figure 1.11 (p.50), "New Mexico, 1957." Photograph by Garry Winogrand. Courtesy of Fraenkel Gallery, San Francisco, and copyright The Estate of Garry Winogrand.

Two: Urban implosion

Frontispiece (p.54), "Truck-flip." Houston, Texas, 1993. Video frame by Dung Ngo.

Figure 2.1 (p.56), "Minneapolis - St. Paul, Minnesota." Aerial view at night, 1985. Photograph by Howard J. Sochurek. From: Vincent Scully (1988): *American Architecture and Urbanism*.

Figure 2.2, (p.60), "Linear City." Subdivision and Strip, Farm to Market Road 1960, Houston, Texas, 1992. From: City of Houston (1992).

Figure 2.3, (p.66), N.A. Milutin, Proposal for a Linear City on the Volga River, Russia, 1929. From: N.A. Milutin (1974): *Sotsgorod: The Problem of Social Building*.

Figure 2.4, (p.68), Ivan Leonidov, Competition design for Magnitogorsk, Russia, 1930. From: Selim O. Khan-Magomedov (1983): *Pioneers of Soviet Architecture*.

Figure 2.5, (p.70), Ludwig Hilberseimer, A New Settlement Unit, 1944. From: Ludwig Hilberseimer (1944): *The New City: Principles of Planning*.

Figure 2.6, (p.74), Ludwig Hilberseimer, Proposal for the Replanning of Chicago, Illinois, 1940. From: Ludwig Hilberseimer (1944): *The New City: Principles of Planning*.

Figure 2.7, (p.76), Ebenezer Howard, Diagram of the "Social City," 1898. Redrawn from: Ebenezer Howard (1898): *To-morrow: A Peaceful Path To Real Reform*.

Figure 2.8, (p.80), Ludwig Hilberseimer, Perspective view of the University of Berlin from the Heerstrasse, Competition, 1937. From: Richard Pommer (1988): *In the Shadow of Mies: Ludwig Hilberseimer, Architect, Educator and Urban Planner*.

Figure 2.9, (p.82), Ludwig Hilberseimer, Replanning of Marquette Park, Chicago, in three stages, 1950. Redrawn from: Ludwig Hilberseimer (1955): *The Nature of Cities: Origin, Growth, and Decline; Pattern and Form; Planning Problems*.

Figure 2.10, (p.84), Ludwig Hilberseimer, Replanning of Elkhorn, Wisconsin, in four stages, 1955. Redrawn from: Ludwig Hilberseimer (1955): *The Nature of Cities: Origin, Growth, and Decline; Pattern and Form; Planning Problems*.

Figure 2.11, (p.86), Ludwig Mies van der Rohe, Brick Country House project, 1923. Redrawn from: Kenneth Frampton (1980): *Modern Architecture: A Critical History*.

Figure 2.12 (p.90), Ludwig Mies van der Rohe, "Illinois Institute of Technology." Aerial photomontage, 1939-1941. Photograph by Hedrich Blessing. From: Ludwig Hilberseimer (1956): *Mies van der Rohe: Chicago 1956*.

Three: Inundation of space

Frontispiece (p.98), "Plaza of the Americas Skywalk." Dallas, Texas, 1984. Photograph by Evans Caglage, *The Dallas Morning News*. From: Mildred Friedman (ed.) (1985): *Design Quarterly 129: Skyways*.

Figure 3.1 (p.100), "Downtown Houston." Texas, c. 1970. Photograph by Alex S. MacLean. From: Jaquelin T. Robertson (1983): *Modulus 16*.

Figure 3.2 (p.106), "The Interurban Sprine." Centripetal reorganization, Boston, Massachusetts. From: Leonardo Benevolo (1971): *History of Modern Architecture*, Volume 2.

Figure 3.3 (p.114), Downtown tunnel and bridge system, Houston, Texas, 1994.

Redrawn from: *Houston, Harris County Atlas*.

Figure 3.4 (p.116), Louis Kahn, Toward a Plan for Midtown Philadelphia, Pennsylvania, 1953. From: Allesandra Latour (ed.) (1991): *Louis I. Kahn: Writings, Lectures, Interviews*.

Figure 3.5 (p.120), "Skywalk." Minneapolis, Minnesota, 1983. Photograph by Walker Art Center. From: Mildred Friedman (ed.) (1985): *Design Quarterly—129: Skyways*.

Figure 3.6 (p.122), "Houston Parking Deck." Houston, Texas, 1995. Photograph by Karin Taylor.

Figure 3.7, (p.130), John Portman, Westin Peachtree Plaza (section), Atlanta, Georgia, 1976. From: Paolo Riani (1990): *John Portman*.

Figure 3.8 (p.132), "Plaza of the Americas Skywalk." Dallas, Texas, 1984. Photograph by Evans Caglage, *The Dallas Morning News* From: Mildred Friedman (ed.) (1985): *Design Quarterly 129: Skyways*.

Figure 3.9 (p.136), John Portman, "Westin Bonaventure." Interior of lobby, Los Angeles, California, 1990. Photograph by Nakashima Tschoegl & Associates, Inc. From: Frederic Jameson (1991): *Postmodernism, or, The Cultural Logic of Late Capitalism*.

Figure 3.10 (p.138), John Portman, "Westin Bonaventure." Aerial view, Los Angeles, California, 1990. Photograph by Clyde May. From: Paolo Riani (1990): *John Portman*.

Figure 3.11 (p.142), "Dallas Streetscape." Dallas, Texas, 1995. Photograph by Karin Taylor.

Figure 3.12 (p.144), Buckminster Fuller, "A Dome over Midtown Manhattan." Aerial photocollage, 1962. From: Martin Pawley (1990): *Buckminster Fuller*.

Four: The Centripetal city

Frontispiece (p.146), "Buffalo Bayou, near Woodway at 610 Loop." Houston, Texas, 1986. Photograph by Geoff Winningham. From: Geoff Winningham (1986): *A Place of Dreams: Houston, An American City*.

Figure 4.1 (p.150), Ludwig Hilberseimer, Washington D.C. Decentralized, 1955. From: Ludwig Hilberseimer (1955): *The Nature of Cities: Origin, Growth, and Decline; Pattern and Form; Planning Problems*.

Figure 4.2 (p.154), The centrifugal urban field. Analysis of prewar Chicago. From: Aldo Rossi (1982): *The Architecture of the City*.

Figure 4.3 (p.154), The centripetal urban field. Analysis of postwar London. 1944. From: Leonardo Benevolo (1980): *The History of the City*.

Figure 4.4 (p.158), Patrick Abercrombie, Centralized Polynuclear Expansion. From: Sibyl Moholy-Nagy (1968): *The Matrix of Man: An Illustrated History of Urban Environment*.

Figure 4.5 (p.160), Walter Christaller, Distribution of towns as central places in Southern Germany, 1957. From: Walter Christaller (1966): *Central Places in Southern Germany*.

Figure 4.6 (p.164), U.S. Federal Housing Authority, Subdivision Guidelines, 1935. Redrawn from: Peter Rowe (1991): *Making a Middle Landscape*.

Figure 4.7 (p.166), The Polynuclear City. Subdivision street map detail, Farm to Market Road 1960, Houston, Texas, 1992, From: City of Houston.

Figure 4.8 (p.172), Frank Lloyd Wright, "Broadacre City," model detail, 1934-1958. From: Robert Fishman (1994): *Architectural Design — 64; 3/4*.

Figure 4.9 (p.182), "Compaq Computer Corporate Campus." Houston, Texas, 1992. From: City of Houston (1992).

Figure 4.10 (p.188), *Spirals of Exclusion*. Figure drawn by author.

Figure 4.11 (p.192), Le Corbusier, The Privileged Urban Subject.; Unitè de Habitation, Marseilles, France, 1946. From: Leonardo Benevolo (1971): *History of Modern Architecture,* Volume 2.

Figure 4.12 (p.196), Robert Venturi, "Ceremonial Space." From: Robert Venturi, Denise Scott Brown, Steve Izenour (1972): *Learning from Las Vegas*.

Figure 4.13 (p.200), "Little White Oak Bayou and Downtown Houston." Texas, 1986. Photograph by Geoff Winningham. From: Geoff Winningham (1986): *A Place of Dreams: Houston, An American City*.

Figure 4.14 (p.204), "Universal Studios Parking Lot." Universal City, California, 1967. Photograph by Edward Ruscha. From: Edward Ruscha (1967): *Thirty-Four Parking Lots in Los Angeles*. Copyright Edward Ruscha.

Figure 4.15 (p.210), "After a Flash Flood." Rancho Mirage, California, 1979. Photograph by Joel Sternfeld. Copyright Joel Sternfeld, courtesy Pace Wildenstein MacGill, New York.

Figure 4.16 (p.212), "Asphalt Rundown." Rome, Italy, 1969. Photograph by Robert Smithson. From: Robert Smithson (1979): *The Writings of Robert Smithson*.

Figure 4.17 (p.216), "Deforestation." Brazil, 1992. Landsat aerial photograph by NASA/U.S. Geological Survey. From: Payson R. Stevens and Kevin W. Kelley (1992): *Embracing the Earth: New Views of Our Changing Planet*.

Figure 4.18 (p.220), "Sunbelt Subdivision." Sugarland, Texas, 1995. Photograph by Carmen Platero.

Conclusion: Mass absence

Frontispiece (p.226), Guiseppe Terragni, "Casa del Fascio, Como, Italy." 1936. From: Thomas Schumacher L. (1991): *Surface and Symbol: Guiseppe Terragni and the Architecture of Italian Rationalism*.

postscript / references

Figure 6.1 (p.240), "Swallows Meadow." Subdivision, Houston, Texas, Photograph by Bruce Webb.

Figure 6.2 (p.252), Ludwig Hilberseimer, The Elements of City Planning, 1940. Redrawn from: Richard Pommer (1988): *In the Shadow of Mies: Ludwig Hilberseimer, Architect, Educator and Urban Planner*.

back cover

"Downtown." Aerial view, Houston, Texas, 1975. From: City of Houston (1975).

251 PHOTO CREDITS

ACKNOWLEDGMENTS

There are not a lot of debts out on this book, but they are all big ones. First is to William Sherman, Alan Plattus, Richard Ingersoll, Sanford Kwinter and Stephen Fox, who have read and challenged many parts of the book. In spite of its ultimate faults, which only I can claim, the book has been substantially shaped by these collaborations. Second, to Sze Tsung Leong, Sharon Steinberg, Karin Taylor, Dung Ngo and especially Lonnie Hoogeboom who made a difficult editing, design and production happen. Third, a really big one, to Lars Lerup who made the project possible. In Lars, many of us who neither write, nor build, nor design, nor criticize, nor draw, but attempt to do them all, find an important teacher and ally; we are greatly indebted to him for it. Finally, the biggest debt of all goes to the architect Kathrin Brunner who supported the long and ugly incubation of this work in such amazing ways that it ultimately takes real gall for me to put my name on it alone. It is finally an intellectual debt that I owe all of these people and, while I don't quite know why it should, I hope the result will pass as partial payment.

There is only one other debt which is owed to a past teacher who would otherwise be appalled to be associated with this effort, but who sketched (in reproach) the diagrams reproduced on page 62 and 64. This book aspires to the innate intelligence contained in those sketches.

REFERENCES

Alexander, Christopher (1965): "A City is Not a Tree." *The Architectural Forum.* Vol.162. (April) p.58-62; (May) p.58-61. Reprinted in Jonathan Crary, et al. (eds.) (1985): *Zone 1/2.* Baltimore: Johns Hopkins University Press. p.[128]-149.

Ambasz, Emilio (ed.) (1972): *Italy: The New Domestic Landscape — Achievements and Problems of Italian Design.* New York: Museum of Modern Art.

Argan, Giulio Carlo (1963): "On the Typology of Architecture." *Architectural Design.* Trans. Joseph Rykwert. Vol.33; No.12. (December) p.564-565.

Bachelard, Gaston (1964): *The Poetics of Space.* Trans. Maria Jolass New York: Orion Press. Originally published as Gaston Bachelard. (1958): *La poètique de l'espace.* Paris: Presses Universitaires de France.

Ballard, J.G. (1974): *Concrete Island.* New York: Farrar, Straus and Giroux.

Ballard, J.G. (1975): *High-Rise.* London: J. Cape.

Baudrillard, Jean (1993): "Game with Vestiges." *Baudrillard Live: Selected Interviews.* Ed. Mike Gain. London: Routledge. p.81-95.

Baudrillard, Jean (1983): *In the Shadow of the Silent Majorities.* New York: Semiotext(e).

Beeby, Thomas H. (1977): "The Grammar of Ornament — Ornament as Grammar." *Via.* Ed. Stephen Kieran. Vol.3; "Ornament." Philadelphia: University of Pennsylvania, Graduate School of Fine Art. p.[10]-29.

Benevolo, Leonardo (1980): *The History of the City.* Trans. Geoffrey Culverwell. London: Scolar Press; Cambridge: MIT Press. Originally published as Leonardo Benevolo (1975): *Storia della citta.* Rome: Editori Laterza.

Benevolo, Leonardo (1971a): *History of Modern Architecture.* Trans. Judith Landry. Vols.1 & 2. Cambridge: MIT Press. Originally published as Leonardo Benevolo (1960): *Storia dell'architettura moderna.* Rome: Giuseppe Laterza & Figli.

Benevolo, Leonardo (1971b): *The Origins of Modern Town Planning.* Trans. Judith Landry. Cambridge: MIT Press. Originally published as Leonardo Benevolo (1963): *Le Origini dell'urbanistica moderna.* Rome: Editori Laterza.

Berman, Marshall (1982): *All That is Solid Melts Into Air: The Experience of Modernity*. New York: Simon and Schuster.

Bird, Jon, et al. (eds.) (1993): *Mapping the Futures: Local Cultures, Global Change*. London: Routledge.

Blake, Peter (1964): *God's Own Junkyard: The Planned Deterioration of America's Landscape*. New York: Holt, Rinehart and Winston.

Boyer, Christine (1990): "The Return of Aesthetics to City Planning." *Philosophical Streets: New Approaches to Urbanism*. Ed. Dennis Crow. Washington: Maisonneuve Press. p.93-[112].

Choay, Francoise (1969): *The Modern City: Planning in the 19th Century*. Trans. Marguerite Hugo and George R. Collins. New York: G. Braziller.

Collins, George R. (1959a): "Linear Planning Throughout the World." *Journal of the Society of Architectural Historians*. Vol.18; No.3. (October) p.74-93.

Collins, George R. (1959b): "The Ciudad Lineal of Madrid." *Journal of the Society of Architectural Historians*. Vol.18; No.2. (May) p.38-53.

Colquhoun, Alan (1981): "The Superblock." *Essays in Architectural Criticism: Modern Architecture and Historical Change*. Cambridge: MIT Press. p.83-[103].

Cronon, William (1991): *Nature's Metropolis: Chicago and the Great West*. New York: W. W. Norton.

Davis, Mike (1993): "Who Killed LA? A Political Autopsy." *New Left Review*. No.197. (January/February) p.3-28.

Davis, Mike (1990): *City of Quartz: Excavating the Future in Los Angeles*. New York: Verso Press.

Debord, Guy (1994): *The Culture of Spectacle*. Trans. Donald Nicholson-Smith. New York: Zone Books.

Deleuze, Gilles (1989): *Cinema 2: The Time Image*. Trans. Hugh Tomlinson and Robert Galeta. Minneapolis: University of Minnesota Press. Originally published as Gilles Deleuze (1985): *L'Image-temps*. Paris: Les Editions de Minuit.

Dennis, Michael (1986): *Court and Garden: From the French Hotel to the City of Modern Architecture*. Cambridge: MIT Press.

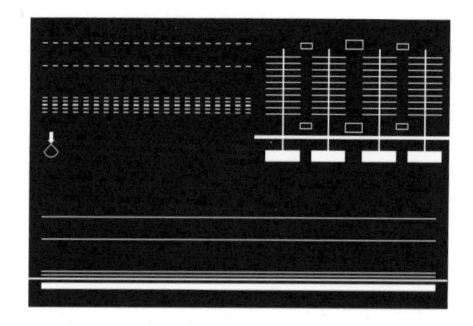

6.2 Ludwig Hilberseimer, "The Elements of City Planning."
From: *Armour Engineer and Alumnus 6.*

Eagleton, Terry (1990): *The Ideology of the Aesthetic*. Oxford; Cambridge: Blackwell.

Eliade, Mircea (1959): *The Sacred and the Profane: The Nature of Religion*. Trans. Willard R. Trask. New York: Harcourt Brace and Jovanovich..

Fishman, Robert (1994): "Space, Time and Sprawl." *Architectural Design*. Vol.64; No.3/4. (March/April) p.[44]-47.

Fishman, Robert (1987): *Bourgeois Utopias: The Rise and Fall of Suburbia*. New York: Basic Books.

Fishman, Robert (1977): *Urban Utopias in the Twentieth Century: Ebenezer Howard, Frank Lloyd Wright, and Le Corbusier*. New York: Basic Books.

Focillon, Henri (1948): *The Life of Forms in Art*. New York: Wittenborn. Originally published as Henri Focillon (1934): *Vie des Formes*. Paris: Presses Universitaires de France.

Foucault, Michel (1993): "Of Other Spaces, Utopias and Heterotopias." *Architecture / Culture, 1943-1968*. Ed. Joan Ockman. New York: Columbia Books of Architecture / Rizzoli International Publications. p.420-426. Originally published as Michel Foucault (1986): "Of Other Spaces" *Diacritics*, 16:1, (Spring), p. 22-27.

Foucault, Michel (1980): *Power/Knowledge: Selected Interviews and Other Writings*. Ed. Colin Gordon; Trans. Colin Gordon. Brighton: Harvester Press.

Foucault, Michel (1977): *Language, Counter-memory, Practice: Selected Essays and Interviews*. Ed. Donald F. Bouchard; Trans. Donald F. Bouchard and Sherry Simon. Ithaca: Cornell University Press.

Fox, Stephen (1990): *Houston Architectural Guide*. Houston: The American Institute of Architects / Herring Press.

Frampton, Kenneth (1980): *Modern Architecture: A Critical History*. New York: Oxford University Press.

Friedman, Mildred (ed.) (1985): *Design Quarterly 129: Skyways*. Minneapolis: Walker Art Center; Cambridge: MIT Press.

Gandelsonas, Mario (1991): *The Urban Text*. Cambridge: MIT Press.

Garreau, Joel (1991): *Edge City: Life on the New Frontier*. New York: Doubleday.

Gottmann, Jean (1961): *Megalopolis: The Urbanized Northeastern Seaboard of the United States*. New York: Twentieth Century Fund.

Hall, Peter (1988): *Cities of Tomorrow*. Oxford; Cambridge: Blackwell.

Harvey, David (1989): *The Condition of Postmodernity: An Enquiry into the Origins of Cultural Change*. Oxford; Cambridge: Blackwell.

Hays, Michael (1992): *Modernism and the Posthumanist Subject: The Architecture of Hannes Meyer and Ludwig Hilberseimer.* Cambridge: MIT Press.

Hejduk, John (1992): *The Lancaster/Hannover Masque*. London: Architectural Association; New York: Princeton Architectural Press.

Hilberseimer, Ludwig (1955): *The Nature of Cities: Origin, Growth, and Decline; Pattern and Form; Planning Problems*. Chicago: Paul Theobald.

Hilberseimer, Ludwig (1949): *The New Regional Pattern: Industries and Gardens, Workshops and Farms*. Chicago: Paul Theobald.

Hilberseimer, Ludwig (1944): *The New City: Principles of Planning*. Chicago: Paul Theobald.

Holl, Steven (1980): "The Alphabetical City." *Pamphlet Architecture*. No.5. New York: Princeton Architectural Press.

Howard, Ebenezer (1902): *Garden Cities of Tomorrow*. London: S. Sonnenschein & Co., Ltd.

Howard, Ebenezer (1898): *To-morrow: A Peaceful Path To Real Reform*. London: Routledge and Kegan Paul.

Hurtt, Steven (1983): "The American Continental Grid: Form and Meaning." *Threshold*. Ed. Darryl J. Strouse. Vol.2. Chicago: University of Illinois, School of Architecture; New York: Rizzoli International Publications. (Fall) p.32-40.

Isozaki, Arata (1993): "Theme Park." *The South Atlantic Quarterly*. Vol.92; No.1; "The World According to Disney." (Winter) p.175-182.

Ingersoll, Richard (1994): "Utopia Limited: Houston's Ring Around the Beltway." *Cite*. Eds. Drexel Turner and Bruce Webb. Vol.31. (Winter-Spring) p.10-17.

Jackson, Kenneth T. (1985): *Crabgrass Frontier: The Suburbanization of the United States*. New York: Oxford University Press.

Jacobs, Jane (1961): *The Death and Life of Great American Cities*. New York: Vintage.

Jameson, Fredric (1995): "Is Space Political?" *Anyplace*. Ed. Cynthia Davidson. Cambridge: MIT Press. p.192-205.

Jameson, Fredric (1994): *The Seeds of Time*. New York: Columbia University Press.

Jameson, Fredric (1991): *Postmodernism, or, The Cultural Logic of Late Capitalism*. Durham: Duke University Press.

Kahn, Louis I. (1991): "Form and Design." *Louis I. Kahn: Writings, Lectures, Interviews*. Ed. Alessandra Latour. New York: Rizzoli International Publications. p.112-120. Originally published as Vincent Scully, Jr. (ed.) (1962): *Louis I. Kahn*. New York: Braziller. p.114-121.

Kahn, Louis I. (1953): "Toward a Plan for Midtown Philadelphia." *Perspecta 2: The Yale Architectural Journal*. New Haven: Yale University, Department of Architecture. p.[10]-27. Reprinted in Alessandra Latour (ed.) (1991): *Louis I. Kahn: Writings, Lectures, Interviews*. New York: Rizzoli International Publications. p.28-52.

Khan-Magomedov, Selim O. (1983): *Pioneers of Soviet Architecture: The Search for New Solutions in the 1920s and 1930s*. Ed. Catherine Cooke; Trans. Alexander Lieven. London: Thames and Hudson Ltd.; New York: Rizzoli International Publications. Originally published as Selim O. Khan-Magomedov (1983): *Pionierre der Sowjetischen Architektur*. Dresden: VEB Verlag der Kunst.

Koolhaas, Rem, Bruce Mau and the Office for Metropolitan Architecture. (1995): *Small, Medium, Large, Extra-Large*. New York: Monacelli Press, Inc.

Koolhaas, Rem. (1978): *Delirious New York: A Retroactive Manifesto for Manhattan*. New York: Oxford University Press.

Krauss, Rosalind (1979): "Grids." *October 9*. Eds. Rosalind Krauss and Annette Michelson. Cambridge: MIT Press. (Summer) p.[50]-64.

Kunstler, James Howard (1993): *The Geography of Nowhere: The Rise and Decline of America's Man-made Landscape*. New York: Simon & Schuster.

Laclau, Ernesto, and Chantal Mouffe (1985): *Hegemony and Socialist Strategy: Towards a Radical Democratic Politics*. New York: Verso Press.

Le Corbusier (1971): *The City of Tomorrow*. Trans. Frederick Etchells. Cambridge: MIT Press. Originally published as Le Corbusier. (1924): *Urbanisme*. Paris: G.Cres and Cie.

Lefebvre, Henri (1996): *Writings on Cities*. Eds. Eleonore Kofman and Elizabeth Lebas; Trans. Eleonore Kofman and Elizabeth Lebas. Oxford; Cambridge: Blackwell.

Lefebvre, Henri (1993): "The Right to the City." *Architecture Culture, 1943-1968*. Ed. Joan Ockman. New York: Columbia Books of Architecture / Rizzoli International Publications. p.428-436. Originally published as Henri Lefebvre (1968): *Le droit a la ville*. Paris: Anthropos. p.115-133.

Lefebvre, Henri (1991): *The Production of Space*. Trans. Donald Nicholson-Smith. Cambridge: Blackwell. Originally published as Henri Lefebvre (1974): *La production de l'espace*. Paris: Anthropos.

Lind, Michael (1995): *The Next American Nation: The New Nationalism and the Fourth American Revolution*. New York: The Free Press.

Malevich, Kasimir (1959): *The Non-Objective World*. Trans. Howard Dearstyne. Chicago: Paul Theobald. Originally published as Kasimir Malevich (1927): *Die Gegenstandslose Welt*. Munich: Albert Langen.

Marcuse, Peter (1987): "The Grid as City Plan: New York City and *Laissez-faire* Planning in the Nineteeth Century." *Planning Perspectives*. Vol. 2; No.3. (September) p. 287-310.

Massey, Doreen (1992): "Politics and Space/Time." *New Left Review*. No.196. (November/December) p.65-84.

McKenzie, Evan (1994): *Privatopia: Homeowner Associations and the Rise of Residential Private Government*. New Haven: Yale University Press.

Miliutin, N.A. (1974): *Sotsgorod: The Problem of Building Socialist Cities*. Trans. Arthur Sprague. Cambridge: MIT Press. Originally published as N.A. Miliutin (1930): *Sotsgorod*. The State Publishing House RSFSR.

Moholy-Nagy, Sibyl (1968): *The Matrix of Man: An Illustrated History of Urban Environment*. New York; London: Praeger.

Mumford, Lewis (1961): *The City in History*. New York: Harcourt, Brace and Company.

Mumford, Lewis (1938): *The Culture of Cities*. New York: Harcourt, Brace and Company.

Pawley, Martin (1990): *Buckminster Fuller*. London: Trefoil Publications.

Plunz, Richard (1990): *A History of Housing in New York City: Dwelling Type and Social Change in the American Metropolis*. New York: Columbia University Press.

Pommer, Richard, David Spaeth and Kevin Harrington. (1988): *In the Shadow of Mies: Ludwig Hilberseimer — Architect, Educator, and Urban Planner*. Chicago: The Art Institute of Chicago; New York: Rizzoli International Publications.

Popper, Karl (1950): *The Open Society and Its Enemies*. Princeton: Princeton University Press.

Pynchon, Thomas (1984): "Entropy." *Slow Learner: Early Stories*. Boston: Little, Brown & Co. p.79-98.

Pynchon, Thomas (1973): *Gravity's Rainbow*. New York: Viking Press.

Pynchon, Thomas (1966): *The Crying of Lot 49*. Philadelphia: Lippincott.

Reich, Robert (1991): "Secession of the Successful." *The New York Times Magazine*. (January 20) p.16.

Reps, John W. (1965): *The Making of Urban America*. Princeton: Princeton University Press.

Riani, Paolo (1990): *John Portman*. Washington D.C.: The AIA Press.

Robertson, Jaquelin T. (1983): "In Search of an American Urban Order, Part 1: The Nagasaki Syndrome." *Modulus 16*. Ed. Robert Claiborne. Charlottesville: The University of Virginia School of Architecture. p.[2]-15.

Rossi, Aldo (1982): *The Architecture of the City*. Trans. Diane Ghirardo and Joan Ockman. Cambridge: MIT Press. Originally published as Aldo Rossi (1966): *L'architettura dell citta*. Padova: Marsilio.

Rossi, Aldo (1981): *A Scientific Autobiography*. Trans. Lawrence Venuti. Cambridge: MIT Press.

Rowe, Colin and Fred Koetter (1978): *Collage City*. Cambridge: MIT Press.

Rowe, Peter (1991): *Making a Middle Landscape*. Cambridge: MIT Press.

Ruscha, Edward (1965): *Some Los Angeles Apartments*. Los Angeles: Ritchie & Simon.

Ruscha, Edward (1967): *Thirty-Four Parking Lots in Los Angeles*. N.p.

Rykwert, Joseph (1988): *The Idea of Town: The Anthropology of Urban Form in Rome, Italy and the Anchient World*. Cambridge: MIT Press.

Saarinen, Eliel (1943): *The City: Its Growth, Its Decay, Its Future*. New York: Reinhold.

Schumacher, Thomas L. (1991): *Surface & Symbol: Guiseppe Terragni and the Architecture of Italian Rationalism*. New York: Princeton Architectural Press.

Sennet, Richard (1970): *The Uses of Disorder: Personal Identity and City Life*. New York: Knopf.

Shapiro, Gary (1995): *Earthwards: Robert Smithson and Art after Babel*. Berkeley; Los Angeles: University of California Press.

Sitte, Camillo (1965): *City Planning According to Artistic Principles*. Trans. George R. Collins and Christiane Crasemann Collins. New York: Random House. Originally published as Camillo Sitte (1889): *Der Städte-Bau nach seinen künsterischen Grundsätzen*. Vienna: Verlag von Carl Graeser.

Smith, Neil (1984): *Uneven Development: Nature, Capital and the Production of Space*. Oxford; Cambridge: Blackwell.

Smithson, Alison (ed.) (1968): *The Team 10 Primer*. Cambridge: MIT Press.

Smithson, Robert (1979a): "The Earth, Subject to Cataclysms, is a Cruel Master." *The Writings of Robert Smithson*. Ed. Nancy Holt. New York: New York University Press. p.179-185.

Smithson, Robert (1979b) "A Museum of Language in the Vicinity of Art." *The Writings of Robert Smithson*. Ed. Nancy Holt. New York: New York University Press. p.67-78.

Smithson, Robert (1979c): "A Tour of the Monuments of Passaic, New Jersey." *The Writings of Robert Smithson*. Ed. Nancy Holt. New York: New York University Press. p.52-57.

Soja, Edward (1989): "Taking Los Angeles Apart: Towards a Postmodern Geography." *Postmodern Geographies: The Reassertion of Space in Critical Social Theory*. London; New York: Verso Press. p.222-248.

Solà-Morales Rubió, Ignasi de (1995): *"Terrain Vague." Anyplace*. Ed. Cynthia Davidson. Cambridge: MIT Press. p.118-123.

Solà-Morales Rubió, Ignasi de (1989): *"Architecture debole." Ottagono*. No.92. (September) p.87-[129].

Tafuri, Manfredo (1976): *Architecture and Utopia: Design and Capitalist Development*. Trans. Barbara Luigia La Penta. Cambridge: MIT Press.

Thompson, D'Arcy Wentworth (1992): *On Growth and Form*. Ed. John T. Bonner. Cambridge: Cambridge University Press.

Venturi, Robert, Denise Scott Brown and Steve Izenour (1972): *Learning from Las Vegas*. Cambridge: MIT Press.

Virilio, Paul (1991): *Lost Dimension*. New York: Semiotext(e). Originally published as Paul Virilio. (1984): *L'espace critique*. Paris: Christian Bourgois.

Warner, Sam Bass (1962): *Streetcar Suburbs: Process of Growth in Boston, 1870-1900.* Cambridge: Harvard University Press.

Webber, Melvin (1963): "Order in Diversity: Community without Propinquity." *Cities and Space: The Future Use of Urban Land; Essays from the Fourth RFF Forum.* Ed. Lowdon Wingo, Jr. Baltimore: Johns Hopkins Press. p.[22]-54.

Webber, Melvin (1964): "The Urban Place and The Nonplace Urban Realm." *Explorations into Urban Structure.* Philadelphia: University of Pennsylvania Press. p.79-153.

Wiener, Norbert (1954): *The Human Use of Human Beings: Cybernetics and Society.* Boston: Houghton Mifflin.

Wright, Frank Lloyd (1969): *The Industrial Revolution Runs Away.* New York: Horizon Press. Facsimile reprint of Frank Lloyd Wright (1932): *The Disappearing City.* New York: W.F. Payson.

INDEX

Abercrombie, Patrick, 36, 41, 87, 111, 167
absence, 186, 194, 201, 232. *See* mass absence; *See* Smithson, Robert. and the inner city, 121; as architectural "Void," 6; as entropic counterforce, 152; as native urban space, 146; as *tabula rasa*, 238; of hierarchy, 67; of meaning, 235; of nature, 140; presence *polarity*, 6, 58, 203; unconstructed, 6
absences, 5, 232. *See* ellipsis; *See* gaps; *See* hiatuses; *See* lacunae
abstract: form of the city, 11; historical *polarity*, 152; space and capitalism, 102; system, 141; without being ideal, 238
aesthetic, 91, 140; coercion, 89; evasion, 235; language, 135; position, 206, 215; prejudice, 174; resistance, 174
agoraphobia, 37, 41
Alexander, Christopher, 87, 177; "A City is Not a Tree," 86
Alphabetical City, 124. *See* Holl, Steven; *See* New York City
apparatus: icon *polarity*, 22, 152; Manhattan grid, 35; of inclusion, 18
architectural: form, 9, 29, 49, 88, 91, 177; intervention, 7; language, 181; strategy, 91; will, 89
Argan, Guilio Carlo, 12
artificial: natural *polarity*, 51, 211
artificial cities: of Brasilia, Levittown, Changigarh, 86
astral space, 198
Atlanta, Georgia, 126-127. *See* Portman, John (Peachtree Plaza)
atrium, 113, 120, 137-141. *See* Jameson, Fredric (Bonaventure Hotel); *See* Portman, John. and inner city, 101, 125-126, 129; and Las Vegas casinos, 198; and transformation of urban morpohology, 126; as control point of centripetal development, 126; as imploded node, 129, 131; as ladder system, 143; as link to skybridge/tunnel systems, 129; as manipulative space, 129; as miniature city, 137; as panoptic eye of corporate enclosure, 126

automobile, 120, 123, 162
autonomous: discourse of modern architecture, 229-230; form and historical contingency, 229; logic of centripetal development, 79, 224; logic of the city, 7, 11-12; nuclei, 79, 157-158, 165, 175; process, 12, 33, 39, 101; production, 211; reproduction of urban grid, 32; spinal configurations, 69; urban forces, 225
autonomy: and abstraction of modernism, 234; architectural, 228; of closed systems, 224; of local configurations, 75; of urban form, 12, 103
avant-garde, 57; and totalitarian state, 232; and utopia, 234

Bachelard, Gaston, 174
Balkanization, 175, 178, 211, 221
Ballard, J.G., 145, 199
Barcelona, Spain, 31
Baudrillard, Jean, 236
Bauhaus, 72, 88
Benevolo, Leonardo, 25-28
Berlin, Germany, 36, 39, 41; and centrifugal explosion, 111; postwar, 47
Berman, Marshall, 111-113
binary, 143. *See* dialectic; *See* polarity. field, 124, 151, 154, 155, 178, 217 — *See* polynuclear (field); structure, 152, 211, 214
biology, 12
Biosphere 2, Arizona, 145
Birmingham, England, 27
Blake, Peter, 195
Brasilia, Brazil, 86, 87
Broadacre City, 9, 171, 173. *See* Wright, Frank Lloyd.; individual home as true center, 189; or Usonia, 191

Cabrini Green: Chicago, Illinois, 85
capital, 143, 146, 174, 222. *See* late capital. global, 102, 134, 178, 222; industrial, 35; multinational infrastructure, 103; organization of, 140; transformation of, 103
casino as autonomous space, 196
center, 139. *See* inner city; See urban (center). and field, 168, 175; business, 103; collapse of, 167; decline of, 93; displacement of, 189, 218; dominant, 79, 175; empty, 232; endurance of, 159, 174-175; expansion of, 79; hierarchical, 158, 165, 174; historical, 103, 111, 119; periphery

polarity, 152, 158-159, 177, 202-203, 221 — *See* Centralized Polynuclear Expansion; rehabilitation of, 189; reorganization of, 167; resilience of, 174; sub-, 167; symbolic, 174; vestigial, 171, 174

centralization, 9, 167-168

Centralized Polynuclear Expansion, 78-79, 159, 167, 171, 175-177. *See* Howard, Ebenezer. and metropolitan identity, 165; and psychological space, 174; and sprawl, 165; and urban core, 157, 173; and urban growth, 93, 176; as center/peripheral structure, 93, 152, 162; as metropolitan model, 78, 151, 157-158, 168, 177; collapse of, 151; *definition of*, 157, 165; *versus* centrifugal extension, 163

centric: development, 105; linear *polarity*, 152

centrifugal, 114, 141. *See* Krauss, Rosalind. centripetal *polarity*, 23, 59, 152; construction, 123; continuity, 88; core, 79, 93, 95, 115; *definition of*, 22; development, 35, 40, 44-47, 61, 78, 82, 93-97, 107, 123, 127; economics, 162; expansion, 22, 36, 49, 78-81, 88, 118, 186; explosion, 23, 51; extension, 33, 163; field, 29, 36, 65, 86, 119, 123; form, 22; grid, 22-23, 27, 31, 36, 41-43, 47-49, 53, 61, 71, 93, 115, 124, 137, 159, 161 — *See* field; grid *versus* ladder, 63; growth, 35, 52, 79; open development, 40-41, 59, 93, 95, 104, 124, 169; open organization, 23-24, 31-33, 36, 58, 61; open system, 17; order, 47, 107, 124; production, 43; space, 24; suburb, 161-162, 169; urbanism, 61

centrifugal city, 25, 31, 40, 43, 53, 81, 97, 117, 123, 179

centripetal, 139, 190, 199, 217. *See* Krauss, Rosalind. centrifugal *polarity*, 23, 59, 152; closed development, 47, 86-87, 96-97, 105, 153, 169; closed organization, 23-24, 41, 45, 53, 58-61, 65, 81-85, 92, 112, 125-126, 143-145, 156, 161, 177; closed system, 17; construction, 93, 107; *definition of*, 23; development, 43-45, 82, 92-93, 104, 115-118, 123-125, 139, 165, 178-179, 190, 224; development and corporate interior, 143; enclaves, 95; expansion, 45, 151-153, 161, 177, 186-187; figure, 23, 72, 83, 92-93, 101, 107, 113, 118, 125, 151, 155-157, 163, 167-169 — *See* ladder; form, 24, 59, 101, 111, 119, 126, 154, 177, 191, 221, 224; grid, 23, 45-47, 53, 72, 81, 124; growth, 93; implosion, 43, 111, 169; infrastructure, 105; ladder, 92-93, 119; metropolis, 75; order, 47, 107-109, 115, 125; planning, 44; production, 105, 119, 151-154, 168, 176, 191, 195, 209, 239; reconstruction, 53; reorganization, 111, 115-119, 124-127, 137, 140, 143, 177, 207, 225; space, 24; spine, 109, 169; suburb, 162

centripetal city, 13, 45, 114, 129-131, 155-156, 178

Cerda, Ildefonso, 31

Chandigarh, India, 86-87, 171

chaos, 196, 202, 208, 223. *See* entropy; *See* Pynchon, Thomas. and uniformity, 203; of industrial city, 27; of Las Vegas strip, 197, 199; of sameness, 201, 202, 203; or absence, 6; order *polarity*, 156; planned, 27

Chicago, Illinois, 73, 82, 85

Choay, Francoise, 35-36, 39

cinema, 238

city. *See* centrifugal city; *See* centripetal city; *See* contemporary city; *See* inner city; *See* linear (city). 19th-century, 29-33, 37, 40, 43-44, 49, 61, 67, 77-79, 96, 104, 123, 153-155; 20th-century, 25, 29, 37, 44, 49, 234; and continent, 52; and electronic media, 222; and entropic disorganization, 224; and grid, 18, 25, 35, 37, 41, 53; and landscape, 51, 91; and spatial/cultural dominant, 139; anti-city, 121, 137; as absolute, 222; as designed entity, 5; autonomous, 12; center, 89, 112, 115, 121; centerless, 173-174; centralized, 171; closed, 24, 37, 41-45, 49, 57, 101, 117, 177-178; construction of, 59, 105; conventional, 143; defined by center and periphery, 158; disappearance of, 18; displacement of, 218; dissolution of, 9-10, 58; expansion of, 52, 81, 104, 187; extension of, 66, 163, 186; fragmentation of, 222; hierarchical, 168; historical, 59, 97, 103, 133, 199, 206; hsitorical, 59; implosion of, 193; industrial, 25-27, 36, 39, 51, 79, 173, 187, 193; limits, 165; natural, 87; of absence and presence, 58; of *laissez-faire* capitalism, 32, 37; of mature capitalism, 32; of precapitalism, 32, 37; of skybridges and tunnels, 119; of space, 7, 10, 13, 17, 27, 88-91, 119-120, 125, 135, 141, 217-219, 224; of unknowable form, 190; open, 17, 24-33, 37-44, 49, 52-53, 57, 66, 81, 85-86, 89, 95-97, 123-124, 179-181, 185-187, 191-193; organization of, 183; parasitic, 3, 95; postwar, 12, 24-25, 28-29, 41,

265

53, 85, 89, 102, 105-107, 120, 155-156, 163, 199, 233; prewar, 13, 24-25, 82, 89, 93, 104-105, 119, 181, 186-187, 195, 199; -prime, 93; reconstruction, 25; reorganization of, 115, 125, 143, 177, 207, 225; traditional, 89, 162, 235; -sub, 93

City Beautiful, 40

closed, 85, 119; development, 174, 179-181, 185, 191-193, 239; diagram, 139; environment, 197, 213; open *polarity*, 59, 95, 152, 177; plan, 39; society, 29; space, 137; system, 13, 44, 63, 65, 87, 95-96, 146, 151-155, 162-165, 189, 194, 197-203, 206-211, 214-217, 223

closure, 31, 39, 44-47, 117, 125, 147, 190, 205, 209. *See* urban (closure). absolute, 120, 145, 152, 178, 190, 206, 214, 223-224; alternative to, 146, 206, 215; and interiorization, 126; and polarization, 154; degree of, 151, 195, 198; diagram, 165; economic or political, 33, 53; of centrifugal form, 109; of centripetal form, 101, 140, 145; of industrial city, 27; postwar, 208; power of, 45; strategy of, 57

collective, 13; neglect, 2, 175; urban subject, 230-232, 235

Commissioner's Plan of 1811, Manhattan, 27, 35. *See* New York City

Common Interest Development (CID), 183-185

community, 73, 83, 185; fragmentation of, 85; planned, 194

Como, Italy, 229, 232

complexity, 3, 86, 169, 171; of grid, 21; of urban environment, 21; order *polarity*, 22, 152

construction, 2, 37, 111, 195; industry, 163; of built form, 11; of high-rise, 123; of interstate freeways, 163, 168; of nature, 213; residential, 163

contemporary city, 7-8, 24, 59-61, 89, 119, 131, 135, 143, 163, 201, 231, 237-238; and centripetal organization, 156; and closure, 24; and grid transformation, 18; and inscription of subject, 190; and John Portman, 126; and polynuclear order, 151; as closed environment, 154; as entropic landscape, 214; as imploded, 85; as parasitic form, 3; construction of, 2-3, 53; design of, 5-6; form of, 173; imploded spaces of, 118; organization of, 93; spaces of, 5, 233; spatial field of, 49

contemporary urban form, 5, 8, 12-13, 17, 41, 44, 71, 118, 152, 155, 168

contemporary urban space, 6-8, 12-13, 17, 53, 85, 91-92, 101, 107, 111, 118-121, 126, 131, 135-137, 140-141, 145-146, 152, 194, 206, 214, 223-225, 232-234, 239

contemporary urbanism, 2, 6, 41, 231

Coop Himmelblau, 133

core, 44, 103. *See* urban (core). and plate organization of high-rise, 123-125; as imploded, 115, 129; collapse of, 105; consolidation of, 125; decline of, 109; dominance of, 139; hierarchical, 78-79, 95, 104, 156-157, 165; historical, 105, 157, 176; of laddered high-rise, 125; primacy of, 93; representational, 118, 173; transformation of, 107, 109

corporate: campus, 199, 203, 213; chaos of war and peace, 208; citizen, 189-191, 194; closed systems, 145; closure, 153, 209; development, 111, 140, 144, 181, 185, 191-193, 213; distribution, 198; enclave — *See* enclave (corporate); environment, 144, 155; franchises, 178-179, 206; *gesamtkunstwerk*, 101, 120, 125, 145; ghetto under construction, 120; hometowns, 179; infrastructure, 141; initiative, 185; interior, 101, 114, 139; investment, 198; landscape, 134; management, 194, 215; map, 239; native *polarity*, 152; nature, 213; nuclei, 179, 183, 199, 209; order, 208; power, 11, 146; practice, 217; production, 218; subdivision, 52; systems, 207, 214

Costa, Lucio, 87

countersite, 179-181, 201, 205, 209, 224-225

cul-de-sac, 58, 78, 169, 190, 222

cultural dominant. *See* Jameson, Fredric

cybernetics, science of, 202, 207. *See* Weiner, Norbert

Davis, Mike, 121, 130, 221

decentered communicational network, 139. *See* Jameson, Fredric

Deleuze, Gilles 235, 238; Smooth Space, 145

dematerialization: of form, 28, 88, 91

design: and total control, 197; as conscious act, 117; discourse, 3, 6; intervention, 6, 146; of absence or presence, 146; strategy, 13

Detroit, Michigan, 126, 127

deurbanization, 9

diagram, 78, 93, 105, 163, 164

dialectic, 8, 217; absence of, 96, 133, 144, 201;

between autonomy and representation, 230, 233-234; between centrifugal and centripetal, 93; between closed and open systems, 96, 152; between enclave and residuum, 152; between form and space, 7-13, 118, 201, 217-218, 224; between inside and outside, 23, 121, 124, 141-143, 146, 153 151; between modern and premodern, 133-134, 140, 176, 205, 232; between prewar and postwar, 205; between space and time, 133; between urban core and suburban periphery, 176

Dickens, Charles, 25

digital revolution, 11

disappearance, 72; of city, 9-10, 18, 43, 58-59, 91; of form, 11; of metropolitan mass, 187; of urban citizen, 232; strategy of, 237

discourse: of autonomy and representation, 233; of contemporary city, 5; of contemporary city, 3; public, 236

disorganization, 140, 201, 205, 208-209. *See* entropy

dispersion, 3, 9, 72, 91, 222; of urban mass, 91, 191; regional, 49

displacement, 47, 173-174, 181, 189; *versus* emplacement, 10

division, 151, 205, 217, 222; of labor, 49; of class and race, 221

dystopia, 145

eclecticism, 131

economic transformation, 11

Edge Cities, 158, 178-179

ego, 187-191; and disappearance of the subject, 193

ego-centric, 189-191, 230-232; city, 194

Eliade, Mircea, 174

ellipsis, 5, 119, 145, 233. *See* absences; *See* exurban ellipsis. and ladder, 119-121, 146, 152; and nature, 203; as countersite, 205; as imploded space, 118, 124, 143; as unmappable gap, 143; *definition of*, 119; emergence of, 141; inner city, 101, 140, 205, 232-234, 237; inner-urban, 143, 205; temporal dimension of, 201; urban, 232-233, 238

enclave, 144, 159, 161, 183, 217; as centripetal figure, 156, 157; as discontinuous, 162; closed, 53, 156, 162, 179, 181; corporate, 29, 92, 95, 151, 152, 155, 156, 178, 213; *definition of*, 95; exurban, 95, 205; historical, 95, 96, 181; organization of, 201; prewar, 181; residuum *polarity*, 201

Engels, Friedrich, 25

entropy, 206-208, 211-213. *See* residuum; and chaos, 203; and disorganization, 202, 211, 224; and disorganization, 202, 224; and heat-death, 208; as an aesthetic position, 215; as closed system, 203; as cultural metaphor, 206, 208; collaborating with, 214; *definition of*, 202; second law of thermodynamics, 202

environment, 51, 75, 89, 120, 196, 211, 223, 234; and body separation, 135; heterogeneous, 21

eradication, 91, 102, 105, 218

european city, 43, 82

evanescence, 9, 152, 167

evolution, 21, 37; of form, 181, 224

exclusion, 88, 120-121, 126, 129, 191, 217, 223; and seclusion, 186; by class and race, 121; degree of, 151; increasing pattern of, 190

expansion, 22-23, 45, 52, 79, 104, 161; and annexation, 33; demographic, 186; economic, 32, 36; of autonomous nuclei, 107

explosion: demographic, 32, 35, 134; implosion *polarity*, 152; of spatial field, 33, 39, 120, 145

extension, 2-3, 28, 67, 92, 113, 157; of urban core, 3

exterior, 61, 141, 194; exclusive, 49; of Las Vegas strip, 196, 197

exurban: centers, 158; disorganization and entropy, 152; ellipsis, 199-201, 205, 215, 232, 237; nuclei, 159, 165, 175, 178, 186, 199, 215; residuum, 195, 199, 213-215; space, 199-206

fascist, 130, 228-229

Federal Housing Act of 1949, 109

Federal-Aid Highway Act of 1938, 163

field, 49, 167, 215, 236. *See* centrifugal (grid); *See* polynuclear (field); *See* spatial (field); *See* urban (field). amorphous, 176; closed, 37, 45, 49, 57, 117; continuous, 65, 85; dialectical, 153; figure *polarity*, 23, 152; model, 171; of complexity, 19; of expansion, 79-81, 93, 104, 153; of Jeffersonian Grid, 51; of new construction, 198; open, 29, 37, 49, 53, 63, 83, 115, 118; pluralist, 132; polarized, 218, 221; unbounded or unlimited, 22, 31-32, 36

figure, 177, 232; closed, 23, 82, 101, 107, 118, 151-

153, 156, 163, 190, 209; field *polarity*, 152, 175; residuum *polarity*, 152
Fishman, Robert, 9
Forest Hills Garden, New York, 41, 43-44
form, 6, 23, 65, 133, 154, 225. *See* primacy of form. abdication of, 10; analysis of, 87, 201; and counterform, 235; as strong or weak, 168; as subordinate to space, 8, 11; as weak or vestigial, 163, 171; claustrophobic, 25; closed, 17, 24-25, 29, 41, 88-89, 119, 123, 146, 190, 217-218; conventional, 59; *definition of*, 205; dehumanizing, 39; dissolution of, 10; elimination of, 85; idealized, 157; irrelevance of, 10-11; liquidation of, 58; mutation of, 75; of closure, 191; of government, 185; of inscription, 191; of organization, 104, 119; of settlement unit, 72, 75; of sprawl, 176; open, 91, 101, 124; organization of, 201; privilege of, 10; reorganization of, 103; space *polarity*, 7-10, 83, 88-89, 152, 201, 217; transformation of, 224; transparency of, 10; unity of, 223
Foucault, Michel, 179, 235, 236; "heterotopia," 179
Fox, Stephen, 183
Frampton, Kenneth, 173
free space, 89, 119, 123, 153, 199, 238
freeway, 9, 28, 91, 109-115, 120, 123, 127, 139, 162, 189, 199, 205; as centripetal form, 111, 115, 125, 223; as spine or ladder, 113, 125; extension of order, 117; Houston, Texas Loop, 93; interurban, 101, 107-109, 112, 168
Fuller, Buckminster, 145, 214-215
future, 18, 33

gaps, 5, 43, 137, 143, 233. *See* absences
Garden City, 41, 75, 77-79; advocates, 40, 104, 162-164, 168; and linear city by Soria y Matta, 66; as autonomous communities, 78; as centralized polynuclear model, 77; as centripetal expansion, 177; as closed city, 17; as new towns, 66; centric expansion of, 104; legacy of, 163; morphology, 66; movement, 57, 77; planning strategy, 44, 57, 105; Queens, New York City, 43
Garreau, Joel, 185
Geddes, Patrick, 40, 79
Gibbs, Willard, 202, 208
Gideon, Sigfried, 28

global, 135, 139; economy, 11, 75, 102, 137, 222; franchises, 178, 224; local *polarity*, 153
greenbelt, 32, 67, 73, 79, 162
grid, 17, 22-24, 29, 33-39, 45, 51, 63, 67, 111, 115, 123, 137, 156, 171. *See* Krauss, Rosalind; *See* urban (grid). and ladder, 59-63; anonymity of, 190; as agent of diversity, 19; as apparatus of inclusion, 19; as bureaucratic matrix, 19; as form of social organization, 21; as icon of order, 19, 23; as infrastructure, 82-83, 87, 159-162, 217; as matrix of clarity, 58; as predictable yet indeterminate, 21; as prescriptive yet ambigous, 21; as reductive order, 19; closed, 23, 32-33, 45-47, 81, 124, 161; closure, 49, 117; complexity of, 19; construction of, 13, 57; continuity of, 13, 61, 92, 112, 153, 159-162, 190; dematerialization of, 91; design of, 11; destruction of, 111; development of, 161; disappearance of, 18-21, 58-59; erosion of, 12-13, 58-59, 85, 92, 97, 107, 115, 127, 139; evolution of, 13; expansion of, 161; extension of, 33, 36, 161-163; form, 37, 47, 61; formation and capitalism, 11, 32; fragment, 58, 61, 65, 81, 87, 91, 117; hierarchical, 63, 87, 169; historical, 117; implosion of, 13, 41-43, 52, 86-88, 121, 124, 127, 141, 145-146; logic of, 12; manifestations, 19; morphology, 65, 115; open, 23, 27, 31, 41-43, 47-49, 58, 61-63, 71-72, 82, 87, 101, 123-124, 159-164, 169, 190, 193-194; order of, 109; organization of, 13, 23, 47, 71, 101, 130, 171; power of, 21; preservation of, 117; reassertion of, 127; reorganization of, 164; simplicity of, 19; space, 18-19, 23, 37, 53, 107; transformation, 12, 18, 32, 59, 82, 85; transition to ladder, 97; vestigial, 97; weaknesses, 21
gridded city, 81, 92-93, 105, 113, 137
gridiron, 40-41, 51-52, 164, 190, 198; buildings, 123; city, 13, 17, 31; development, 51; industrial, 17; Manhattan, 43; structure, 75
Gropius, Walter, 88

Hall, Peter, 36, 78, 162
Hays, Michael, 71
Hedjuk, John, 235
heterogeneity and complexity, 19
heterotopia, 179
hiatuses, 5, 137, 143, 232. *See* absences
hierarchical, 43, 66, 79, 109, 119, 125, 152, 173,

268

175, 177; development, 105; expansion, 78; figure, 167, 171; model, 77; organization, 86; spine, 67, 87; structure, 63

Hilberseimer, Ludwig, 27, 57, 71-77, 81-88, 91, 103-105, 113, 145, 177, 189, 217, 225. *See* ladder. and contemporaries, 28; and Garden City advocates, 77; and photo-collage, 81; and postwar urban form, 75; and production of space, 85; and transformation diagram, 81; and *zeilenbau*/urban cell proposals, 71; Berlin period, 71; centripetal strategy, 81; Degree Zero Urbanism, 177; grid transformation, 82, 85; inscription of the subject, 72; linear models, 168; Marquette Park, 82; "Metropolis as Garden City," 71; planned disappearance as camoflage, 72; settlement unit, 72-76, (as metropolitan figure, 78), 81; terminal center, 103; *The Nature of Cities*, 83; *The New City*, 72-73, 77, 81; urban polemic, 81

Hiroshima, Japan, 102

historical, 17, 24, 39, 47, 81, 104, 134, 140, 174, 177, 185-187, 199-201, 236; abstract *polarity*, 152; boundary, 32; determinism, 29; development, 28, 47; moment, 133, 229, 231; momentum, 29; narrative, 25; organization, 199; perspective, 40; preservation, 124; projection, 221; prophecy, 28; rupture, 133, 232; trajectory, 27-28, 159; transformation, 101

Hitler, Adolf, 238

Holl, Steven, 123

Hood, Raymond, 123

Houston, Texas, 95, 102; and centripetal development, 178; and grid to ladder transformation, 93; center, 114, 183; tunnel system as network of corporate interiors, 114; Woodlands, 183

Howard, Ebenezer, 77-79, 163, 217, 225; and Centralized Polynuclear Expansion, 78, 157; and Garden City, 78; and Social City, 167; *Tomorrow; A Peaceful Path Toward Real Reform*, 78

hyperspace. *See* Jameson, Fredric (postmodern hyperspace)

icon, 228; apparatus *polarity*, 22, 152

implosion, 85, 103, 111, 190, 235, 238. *See* grid (implosion of); *See* spatial (implosion). explosion *polarity*, 152; of urban core, 102, 165, 173, 176; urban, 24, 41, 47, 57, 61, 107, 115, 119, 124, 193

inertia, 41-43, 217, 238

infrastructure, 72, 117; and superstructure, 132; economic, 33, 101-103; global, 101

Ingersoll, Richard, 179

inner city, 13, 43-44, 101, 111, 120, 140, 146, 153, 206; and corporate *gesamtkunstwerk*, 125; and free space, 199; as dystopia, 145; blight, 199; disorganization, 195; implosion, 173; prewar, 93; reorganization, 126

inscription: anthropomorphic, 232; of corporate collectivity, 238; of posthumanist subject, 71; of urban mass, 230-231, 237

inside, 35, 125. outside *polarity*, 127, 144, 147, 152-154, 219 — *See* dialectic (between inside and outside); without an outside, 141-143, 206, 215

interior, 22-23, 65, 113, 146; of city, 43; of Las Vegas casino, 196-197

interregnum, 151-152, 168

interurban, 109; space, 86, 232

interurban spine. *See* freeway

inundation of space, 13, 17, 101, 111, 120

irony, 7, 153

Jackson, Kenneth, 161, 164

Jacobs, Jane, 193

Jameson, Fredric, 131-145, 176-178; "Blade Runner syndrome", 141; "Postmodernism, or, the Cultural Logic of Late Capitalism", 131; Bonaventure Hotel, Los Angeles, 137; cultural dominant, 121, 131-132, 137, 140; and postmodernism, (*definition of*, 120), 132, 135, 139;; late capital, 101, 131, 137, 141, 144; postmodern architecture, 131; postmodern hyperspace, 135, (as urban "black hole", 137), 139-140, 143, 145, 199; postmodern sublime, 135, 139-140; postmodern urban space, 101, 131, 135, 137, 140; space/time *polarity*, 133-134; spatial dominant, 132, 139, 141; urban representation, 101, 103

Jeffersonian Grid, 51

Kahn, Louis I., 115-117, 127

Koolhaas, Rem, 35, 89, 178; Post Architectural Void, 145, 199

Kraus, Karl, 235

Krauss, Rosalind, 22-24, 65

Kunstler, James Howard, 185

Kyoto, Japan, 87

lacunae, 5, 43, 233. *See* absences
ladder, 13, 53, 120, 156, 222. See centipetal (figure); *See* Hilberseimer, Ludwig; and centripetal organization, 61-65, 92, 101, 119, 125, 145; and ellipsis, 119-121, 141, 146, 152; and grid transformation, 59, 63, 97, 101; and linear development, 69; and residual space, 83; and strong form, 176; and urban infrastructure, 61; as agent of division or classification, 63; as grid fragment, 61-63; centripetal, 93; closed, 63, 85, 151; extension into corporate interior, 139, 141; morphology, 65, 115; of core and plates in high-rise construction, 125
laddered city, 105, 161; as anti-city, 121
Land Ordinance Act of 1785, 51
landscape, 51, 67, 88, 92, 120, 127, 134, 153, 169, 195, 209, 211, 214, 218, 223, 232; natural, 72, 91
Las Vegas, Nevada, 3, 195-198
late capital, 143, 144. *See* Jameson, Fredric. and closure, 139, 144; and economic infrastructure, 101, 140; and production of space, 141; and sublime space, 178; global network of, 139; multinational, 135
late capitalism. *See* Mandell, Ernst. and postmodernsim, 131; as unmappable system, 141; multinational, 102; space of, 137
late capitalist state, 144
lattice, 19, 87, 103, 152
Le Corbusier (Charles-Edouard Jeanneret), 9, 67, 87-89, 173, 189, 217
Leeds, England, 27
Lefebvre, Henri, 102-103
Leonidov, Ivan, 67
Levittown, New Jersey, 86
Lind, Michael, 185, 221
linear, 71-73, 76, 171, 198; centric *polarity*, 152; city, 65-69, 75, 79, 168, 173, 198; development, 67-69, 168; metropolis, 77, 105; model, 69, 76, 168-171; organization, 171; spine, 69
Liverpool, England, 87
local, 102, 175-176, 183, 203, 207, 223; condition, 31, 51, 73, 112; coordinates, 88; development, 169; global *polarity*, 153; nuclei, 151, 222; order, 156, 176; organization, 76, 155-156, 169, 178; scale, 109, 155, 169
London, England, 31, 39, 73, 87, 167
Loos, Adolf, 235

Los Angeles, California, 52; and Bonaventure Hotel, 126, 131, 135; as centrifugal suburb, 161, 169; as sprawl, 162; downtown, 137, 174

Magnitogorsk, Russia, 67
Malevich, Kasimir, 239
mall, 5, 161, 198; commercial, 156-157, 223; interior as ladder, 156; shopping, 29, 91-93, 169, 205
Manchester, England, 25-27
Mandel, Ernst, 132
Marcuse, Peter, 24, 32, 37, 45
Marquette Park: Chicago, Illinois, 82
mass absence, 232-234, 238
matrix, 25, 44, 58, 89
McKenzie, Evan, 185
Mendelsohn, Erich, 133
metropolitan, 44, 71, 77-79, 93, 104, 168, 173, 186, 215, 222; center, 77, 151, 157-159, 167, 177, 217, 221; centralization, 178; chaos, 151, 156; community, 73; condition, 83, 175, 189-191, 219; construction, 186; continuum, 117; core, 78-79, 95, 104-105, 115-117, 165, 175; decline, 95, 209; development, 78, 179; disorganization, 151, 176; displacement, 190; evolution, 167; expansion, 78, 105; field, 44, 96, 161, 165, 189, 219; figure, 73-78, 165; form, 177-178, 186; form as strong or weak, 151, 156-159, 171, 176-178, 222 — *See* sprawl; grid, 112, 169, 193; growth, 78, 151, 159, 186; hierarchy, 77-78, 217; identity, 155-156, 165, 174-175; implosion, 104; mass, 186-190; model, 77-78, 105, 151, 159, 163, 168; order, 78, 95, 151, 155, 171, 217, 222; organization, 77, 155-157, 168, 169; periphery, 177, 221; reconstruction, 158; region, 43; representation, 175-176, 186-187, 225; scale, 66, 155, 169; space, 152; spine, 73; sprawl, 156, 168, 171, 176; strong figure, 165
Mies van der Rohe, Ludwig, 81, 88, 133-134; Seagram Building, 133-134, 140, 176
Milton Keynes, England, 171
Milutin, N.A., 67, 71, 75, 168; linear industrial city on the Volga River, 66-67,
modern: architecture, 28-29, 65, 87-91, 126, 145, 168, 173, 187, 191, 228-231, 234; future, 133; ideology, 88; painting, 17; planning, 58, 86-87, 104, 168, 187, 191-193; political state, 228-229; premodern *polarity*, 177; representation, 234;

space, 89, 92, 141; urbanism, 28, 57, 65, 71, 77, 85-88, 104, 193, 230; utopias, 71
Modern City, 44, 57, 65, 71, 87, 176-177, 187, 191-193, 217, 230, 233
modernism, 28, 57, 132, 144, 228-232, 239
modernist, 228; avant-garde, 177; dialectic, 140; early, 230-232, 238
modernity, 231
modernization, 113, 133-134, 176, 239; maelstrom, 113; maelstrom of, 11, 112-113
Mondrian, Piet, 23
monument, 52, 59, 186, 232, 237
monumental construction, 187, 229
Moses, Robert, 112
Mumford, Lewis, 25-28

National Housing Act of 1934, 163
native, 87, 211; corporate *polarity*, 152; or alternative urban sites, 147; urban space, 97, 127-129, 145-146
natural, 12, 41, 51, 213-214; artificial *polarity*, 211-214; cities, 87; condition, 213; disaster, 47; space, 205, 214; urban *polarity*, 202, 213
nature: culture *polarity*, 211-213; recuperation of, 213
negative entropy, 207; and disorganization, 209
neocapitalism, 102
New Town, 78, 158, 163, 167, 178
New York City, 27, 39, 43, 73, 78, 186; Bronx, 111-112, 120; Chelsea, 156; Commissioner's Plan of 1811, 35; Commissioner's Plan of 1811, 27; Harlem, 35, 156; Manhattan, 31-35, 87, 156, 186, 218; Queens, 41-43 — *See* Forest Hills Garden
Nolli, Giambattista, 198

office: building, 49, 169; park, 5, 29, 49, 58, 91-93, 115, 157, 161, 169, 223; planning, 125
Olmsted, Frederick Law, Jr., 41-44
Olmsted, Frederick Law, Sr., 39
open, 17, 43, 52, 63, 81, 105, 115, 125, 143, 186, 194, 196; closed *polarity*, 59, 95, 152, 177; development, 95, 179; landscape, 67; process, 39; society, 29; space, 13, 17, 24-28, 40, 44, 75, 83-91, 111, 119-121, 145, 187, 217; system, 13, 22, 44, 47, 53, 88, 95-96, 191
openness, 17, 27-29, 36, 39-40, 57, 85, 88, 91, 197, 209

order, 12, 22, 37, 45, 53, 65, 171, 177; absence of, 167; and entropy, 207; chaos *polarity*, 156, 208; complexity *polarity*, 22, 152; reductive, 87; superimposed, 101
outside, 23, 36, 43-45, 52, 95, 111-112, 118-121, 124, 140-141, 145-147, 174, 179, 194, 213, 223; celebration of, 197; fear of, 119; formation of, 127; inside of Embarcadero Center, 127; inside *polarity*, 114, 121, 127, 141, 144, 147, 152-154, 219; occupation of, 147; world, 145, 203, 209, 239

Paris, France, 29
past, 95, 238; present *polarity*, 202, 203
Penn, William, 37
periphery, 10, 18, 36, 168, 199-201; center *polarity*, 152, 158-159, 176-177, 202-203, 221; dispersion, 176
Perry, Clarence, 236
Pevsner, Nikolaus, 28
Philadelphia, Pennsylvania, 37-39, 115, 127
Phoenix, Arizona, 52, 191
Piranesi, Giovanni Battista, 6
planned disappearance, 43, 193
Plunz, Richard, 40-43
polarity, 152-153; as negative or positive, 154; between Las Vegas casino and strip, 197
polarization, 151-156, 178, 197, 217
polycentric, 104, 183; development, 78, 158, 167
polynuclear: *See* Centralized Polynuclear Expansion. construction, 171; development, 162; expansion, 159, 165; field, 29, 152-154, 157-163, 167-168, 173-178, 185, 197-198, 208, 213-218, 221, 224; model, 77, 157, 168-171, 176-177, 197; or binary field, 43, 151, 168; order, 151
Pommer, Richard, 71, 86
Popper, Karl, 29
Portman, John, 126-131, 135-141; Bonaventure Hotel, Los Angeles, 126, 131, 135, 137, 139, 141; Embarcadero Center, San Francisco, 127; Peachtree Plaza, Atlanta, 126, 129, 131, 139; Renaissance Center, Detroit, 126
postmodern, 134, 141.. *See* Jameson, Fredric; *See* late capital; *See* superurban. architecture, 131, 135; city, 177; *definition of*, 131, 133; development, 178; space, 101, 131, 141; sublime, 101, 135, 139-140; urbanism, 176-178

postmodern hyperspace. *See* Jameson, Fredric
posturban, 7, 85; city, 152
postwar: culture, 206-208; development, 102, 151, 155-157, 163, 191; housing, 193; organization, 202; production, 57; reconstruction, 53, 78, 156; redevelopment, 53, 134; reorganization, 101, 206; transformation, 18, 58, 101, 103; world, 202, 207-209, 231
premodern: modern *polarity*, 177; past, 133
presence: absence *polarity*, 6, 58, 203
present: past *polarity*, 202-203
prewar: development, 93, 163
primacy of form, 5-11, 28
primacy of space, 7-8, 11-13, 83, 92, 120, 129-131, 140, 218; and formlessness, 237
public: private *polarity*, 177, 202
Pynchon, Thomas, 199, 207-211, 221. *See* entropy; Zone, 145, 199

Radburn, New Jersey, 77-78, 81
reconstruction, 173-174; and demolition, 107; and urban renewal, 102
Reich, Robert, 185
representation, 10, 22-23, 33, 39, 53, 81, 125, 169, 187, 228, 239; and modern architecture, 234; collective, 189, 233; crisis of, 233-234; denial of, 234; of urban subject, 231; political, 234; refusal of, 239
Reps, John W., 51
residuum, 23, 49, 111, 144, 153-154, 176, 195, 199, 206, 209-218, 224, 232, 234. *See* exurban residuum; *See* spatial residuum. as economic, aesthetic, political site, 215; corporate, 218; disorganization of, 151-152, 178, 195, 201, 206, 213-215, 218; enclave *polarity*, 201; figure *polarity*, 152; inner city, 195; metropolitan, 43
Rietveld, Gerrit, 88
Robert Taylor Homes: Chicago, Illinois, 85
Rossi, Aldo, 12, 235
Rouse, James, 174
Rowe, Peter, 51, 161-162, 165
Rykwert, Joseph, 71

San Fernando Valley, California, 161
Sartre, Jean Paul, 31
Scully, Vincent, 137
secession, 41, 121, 183-186
Second World War, 24, 102, 157, 202, 230, 233

semi-lattice, 87
settlement unit, 82-83, 169. *See* Hilberseimer, Ludwig; and elimination of choice, 85; and suburban planning, 77; as autonomous centripetal figure, 72, 76, 81, 83, 87; as finite urban element, 72; as pedestrian pocket, 73; as urban hybrid, 76; design criteria, 72, 83; pedestrian scale of, 73; zones of, 73
sidewalk, 51, 114-115, 124, 152
silence, 27, 203, 235-237. *See* Baudrillard, Jean; *See* Foucault, Michel. alternative to, 235; and entropy, 202
Situationists, 173
skybridge, 91, 101, 107, 113-117, 120, 125-130, 198
skywalk, 58, 119, 123, 139, 223
Smithson, Alison, 235
Smithson, Robert, 207-209, 214-219, 235
Social City: and Centralized Polynuclear Expansion, 78, 167
social utopians, 40
Solà-Morales Rubió, Ignasi de, 118; Terrain Vague, 145
Soleri, Paolo, 87
Soria y Matta, Arturo, 66
space, 22, 31, 49, 71, 112-114, 125, 156, 189, 195, 199, 205-207, 213, 238; *See* contemporary urban space; *See* primacy of space; *See* urban (space). abstract, 102; abstract *versus* historical, 103; amorphous, 5; and capitalism, 102, 135-137, 144, 178; and speed, 9-10; as cultural dominant, 121, 131, 137; as imploded node, 129; as index of grid, 24; as unbounded field, 31; consequences of, 221; constructed, 118, 129; continuity of, 52; corporate, 114; *definition of*, 205-206; development of, 137; disorganization of, 201, 209; emergence of, 92; expansion of, 6; explosion of, 17, 120; extension of, 213; form *polarity*, 5-10, 17, 83, 152, 201, 217; historical, 103, 111; homogenous, 141, 144; imploded, 117-118, 143; international, 51; interstitial, 83; mappable, 141-143; mutation of, 124, 135; national, 51; neutral, 232; of contemporary city, 5, 118; oppositional, 215; persistence of, 234; phobia of, 41; political, 231-234; private, 121, 187; production of, 85-86, 91; psychological, 174; public, 123, 236; representation of, 23, 32, 120, 205; residual, 155, 169, 217; revitalization of, 194; time *polarity*, 9-

10, 152, 201, 213; universal, 13; unmappable, 137, 145

space/time continuum, 10, 124

spatial, 5-7, 92, 120, 125, 134, 139-140, 183, 199, 207; analysis, 57; apartheid, 121, 221; boundary, 49; closure, 39, 41, 58; concepts, 27; condition, 24; containment, 49; continuity, 31, 49, 57, 88-91, 117, 127, 134, 159, 162; continuum, 43, 51; dialectic, 7; discontinuity, 161-162; disorganization, 205; displacement, 61; exterior, 153; field, 22-23, 28, 31-33, 36-41, 45-52, 57-58, 61-65, 83, 87-88, 117, 123-127, 153-156, 181; implosion, 57-61, 65, 81-82, 85, 97, 101, 107, 113, 117-118, 121, 124-127, 137-139, 143-145, 156, 234; implosion, 11; inversion, 23, 101; mutation, 37; organization, 58; production, 33, 44, 107, 112, 117, 141; reservoir, 79, 163; residuum, 17, 61, 111, 118-119, 140, 152, 178, 198, 215, 223; rupture, 137; sensibility, 131; temporal polarity, 132, 133, 134, 199; transformation, 37

spatial dominant. *See* Jameson, Fredric

speed, 9-11

spine, 65, 69, 73, 113, 189, 217

spiral, 112, 115, 120, 194; closed, 190; implosion of, 189-190

sprawl, 156, 175, 179, 190, 198-203, 223; and automobiles, 162, 197; and closed urban systems, 199; and order, 167; and urban pollution, 195; as topological field, 165; characteristics of, 176; complexity of, 191; organization of, 179; perception of, 155; postwar, 165, 195; topological field, 171

sprawl city, 196

Stalingrad, Russia, 67

Stein, Clarence, 77, 87

street, 7, 19, 32, 36, 43, 49, 58, 62, 78, 82-83, 86, 91, 111, 114-115, 124-125, 127, 130, 132, 161-165, 169, 186, 189, 194, 235

strong: form, 151, 156, 176; grid, 21; order, 19, 23, 155; weak *polarity*, 21-22, 152

sub-center, 167

sub-development: as alter-development, 2

subdivisions, 5, 29, 76, 155, 159, 163-164, 181, 205, 222-223; sunbelt, 92

subject: inscription, 194; position, 141-146, 190, 194, 239

suburb: as xenophobic enclave, 96; *definition as* city below, 218; postwar, 162; prewar, 159-161, 169

suburban, 36, 127, 199, 205, 222; development, 92-93, 162; enclave, 96, 181; extension, 81, 157; growth, 2, 93; localities, 41; model, 81; nuclei, 104; periphery, 176; planning, 77, 161

suburbanization, 159, 161

Sullivan, Louis, 123

superblock, 73, 76-77, 168

supergrid, 161, 169-171. *See* Wright, Frank Lloyd

supergridded city, 168

superstructure: and infrastructure, 132; and substructure, 131

superurban, 105, 165, 181; *definition of*, 95; development, 96, 97, 178, 217

superurban city, 215

tabula rasa, 238

Tafuri, Manfredo, 193

Tange, Kenzo, 87

television, 9, 53, 124, 223

temporal: collapse of, 133, 176; coordinates, 134; dimension, 199-201; flow, 29; rupture, 134; spatial *polarity*, 132-134, 199; vectors, 9

Terragni, Giuseppe, 228-233; Casa del Fascio, 228-231

territorial domains, 9

Thompson, D'Arcy Wentworth, 12

time, 2, 45, 105, 193, 197-198, 202, 213; consequences of, 221; space *polarity*, 9-10, 152, 201, 213

traffic, 78, 83, 163, 183; and pollution, 72, 83; control, 72; flow, 72, 112

transnational urban space, 102. *See* Lefebvre, Henri

tree, 86-87, 125, 152, 213

tunnel, 91, 101, 107, 113-119, 125, 129-130, 139, 152

universal community, 236

universal space, 23, 28, 39-40, 44, 88-91

Unwin, Raymond, 77, 217

urban, 37-40, 81-85, 112, 115-121, 124-127, 134, 137-141, 146, 147, 158, 173-181, 187-193, 206, 209, 215-219, 222, 225, 232; aggregation, 9, 165; analysis, 37, 153; and architectural form, 29, 49, 117; and architectural space, 88; artifacts, 31; associations with grid, 59; blight, 195; center, 96, 107-109, 117, 145, 158, 167, 173-174, 179; centric arrangement, 72; centric models, 76; chaos, 155; circulation, 69; citizen, 189, 191; closure, 57, 176, 181, 198, 201, 215, 218; collective, 232; community, 82, 236-237; construction, 12, 47, 57, 69, 83, 102, 125, 129, 163-165, 178, 186, 213, 219; conventions, 2, 59; core, 2, 33, 39, 66, 81, 93, 101, 104-117, 126, 140, 156-157, 163-165, 175-177; designers and theorists, 29, 33, 65, 236; development, 2-3, 7-13, 17-19, 24-33, 39-47, 58, 65, 69-71, 81-82, 92, 95-97, 103-104, 113, 121-123, 141, 153-154, 168, 174-176, 195, 207-208, 214, 223, 239; dimension of time, 10; discourse, 5; edge, 78; environment, 5-9, 21, 53, 58, 81, 91-92, 96, 155, 169, 194, 231-232; evolution, 17, 36, 44, 57, 175; exclusion, 183; expansion, 11, 36, 45, 76-78, 153, 162-163; expressways, 5; exterior, 43-45, 130, 153; fabric, 13, 17, 25, 28, 35, 109, 113, 194; field, 29, 33, 39, 45-49, 57-58, 117, 124, 151, 154-156, 162, 167-173, 179-185, 189-190, 217, 223, 232; form, 2, 7-13, 17-21, 25, 29, 40-41, 47, 53, 58, 61, 75, 86, 91-92, 103-105, 109, 118-119, 123-124, 146, 152, 177, 185, 198, 201, 217-218, 221, 224 — *See* contemporary urban form, *See* primacy of form; *gesamtkunstwerk*, 28; grid, 11-12, 18, 24, 27, 31-32, 53, 57-58, 61, 73-75, 85, 91, 101-103, 111, 115, 137; grid and freeway, 109, 113; growth, 31, 36, 45, 52, 81, 186; heterogeneity, 197; history, 25; identity, 13, 18; imagination, 8, 52, 53, 175; infrastructure, 61, 103, 156; inscription of the subject, 72, 191; interior, 153; intervention, 6, 7; investigation, 71; isolation, 183; landscape, 17, 39, 209; linear and non-linear proposals, 67; linear models, 72, 76; memory, 59; metabolism, 35, 36; model, 66; models, 77; morphology, 65; narrative, 29; natural polarity, 202, 213; nuclei, 43; order, 21, 47, 58, 88, 124, 223; organization, 13, 24-25, 29, 73, 76-79, 126, 157-158, 167, 174, 178; perimeter, 157, 167; periphery, 107, 151, 153, 162-163, 177; phantom, 52; plan *versus* process, 35; practice, 69; production, 5-6, 71 113, 121, 129, 139, 156, 177; proposals, 67, 71-72; reconstruction, 163; reform, 21, 25, 44, 78; reorganization, 81, 101-107, 113-114, 117, 123, 153, 163-164, 175-176; representation, 101-103, 114, 156, 235-238; reproduction, 35-36, 44; scale, 51; settlements, 57; space, 7-8, 17, 24, 32, 39-40, 47-51, 58, 61, 65, 85-86, 91, 97, 101, 111-113, 117-119, 135-139, 143-145, 167, 194, 201-206, 213, 217, 223, 234; space and time, 9; spine, 72; sprawl, 171, 195-196; strategy, 8-9; structure, 53, 61; suburban dynamic, 2; system, 13, 17, 87, 96, 151, 155, 162-163, 189-191, 194, 199, 217; system as open or closed, 31; systems as open or closed, 17; transformation, 19, 24, 28, 31, 102, 177; transformation, 18, 47, 203; transition, 53; transportation, 66, 69; typology, 12; wall, 72; zones of decay, 5

urbanism: and architecture, 28, 65; postwar, 161; traditional, 173

urbanization, 32, 168, 181, 196; and individual subject, 189; postwar, 162

utopia, 51, 121, 193, 235

Van Doesburg, Theo, 88

Van Eyck, Aldo, 235

Venturi, Robert, Denise Scott Brown, Steven Izenour, 195; *Learning From Las Vegas*, 195-198

Vienna, Austria, 29, 235

Ville Radieuse, 17, 177

violence, 213, 223

Virilio, Paul, 9-10

vision, 71, 218; aesthetic, 89; arrested, 231; distracted, 2; with intent to see, 85

void, 109, 199, 231-232, 239

void of abstraction, 239

Warner, Sam Bass, 37-39

Washington, D.C., 73

weak, 19; centralization, 215; form, 156; metropolis, 156-157, 189; metropolitan form, 151; strong *polarity*, 21-22, 152

Webber, Melvin, 9

welfare state, 25, 40, 121

Wiener, Norbert, 202-203, 207-211. *See* entropy; *See* Pynchon, Thomas

world system, 145-146, 239

Wright, Frank Lloyd, 171-173, 217, 225; as urban polemicist, 9; individual home as true center, 189-191; Prairie Houses, 88; supergrid and superblock models, 168; *The Disappearing City*, 9; urban decentralization, 173

Wright, Henry, 77, 78

zeilenbau and urban cell, 71